UFOS

NOW AND THEN

UFOS

NOW AND THEN

UFO and alien encounters from both the present time and in the past.

Moira McGhee

Published by INUFOR – Independent Network of UFO Researchers

UFOs – NOW AND THEN

UFO and alien encounters from both the present time
and in the past.

Cover photos by Dino Reichmuth on Unsplash and
Simon Matzinger on Pexels.

For information address:
INUFOR, P.O. Box 169, Katoomba NSW 2780, AUSTRALIA.

INUFOR books may be purchased for business, educational,
or sales promotional use. For information please write:
INUFOR, P.O. Box 169, Katoomba NSW 2780, AUSTRALIA.

INUFOR web sites:

www.independentnetuforesearchers.com.au

www.facebook.com/inufor

Email:

ind.net.ufo.res@bigpond.com

FIRST INUFOR PAPERBACK EDITION PUBLISHED IN
NOVEMBER, 2019

ISBN: 978-0-9587-045-8-8

UFOS – NOW AND THEN

CONTENTS

INTRODUCTION

Why, in the early twentieth century, and even today, was the subject of UFOs always considered 'Above Top Secret'? Their technology often surpassed anything the major powers possessed, and there was a massive effort to study the hardware in order to adapt it for our own benefit.

The first country to develop a craft with the speed and manoeuvrability of a 'flying saucer' would have the technical supremacy to rule the planet. Secrecy and denial were paramount, and governments were certainly not sharing information gathered from the examination of crashed alien vehicles, or their own resultant prototypes.

Lt. General Nathan Twining was the US Chairman of Joint Chiefs of Staff from 1957 to 1961, and prior to that Air Force Chief of Staff from 1953 to 1957. In 1947 he headed the Air Material Command at the Wright-Patterson Air Force Base. That was the year when mysterious 'flying discs' were reputed to have crashed, both at Roswell and Socorro in the American desert.

Investigator Leonard Stringfield published copies of Twining's flight logs and reports, which although very informative, do not specifically indentify the unknown craft as being of earthly or alien origin.

His log books reveal that on 7th July 1947, he went to a secret meeting at Alamogordo Air Force Base to view the recovered remains of a craft which had crashed twenty miles northwest of Socorro. Over the next three days he also visited Kirtland Air Force Base and White Sands Proving Ground to inspect further debris.

On 16th July, he forwarded an Air Accident Report to Headquarters. In it he describes, in detail, the interior of a 'flying disc', and quotes his scientific and engineering experts as saying – *'It was not made by the US, Germany or Russia.'* Who then, did they think made it?

On 23rd September, he sent a detailed Status Report to Brigadier General George Schulgen, the Head of the Army Air Force. He stated that due consideration must be given to the possibility that these objects are of domestic origin – *'the product of some high security project not known to AC/AS-2 or this Command'*. He also mentions *'the possibility that some foreign nation has a*

1

form of propulsion, possibly nuclear, which is outside of our domestic knowledge'.

'MUFON UFO Journal', October 2002, reviewed a book by Nick Cook, (previous aviation editor of *Jane's Defence Weekly*). In it they mention the same letter, dated 23rd September 1947, from General Nathan Twining. It concluded that although some incidents may be caused by natural phenomena such as meteors, flying discs were *'real and not visionary or fictitious.'*

After describing the UFOs and their reported behaviour, he said that he believed it possible that *'some of the objects, which had a metallic or light reflecting surface, were circular or elliptical in shape, flat on bottom and domed on top, and were of such appreciable size to appear as large as a man-made aircraft. They lent belief to the possibility that some of the objects were controlled manually or automatically.'*

'It is possible within the present U.S. knowledge – provided extensive detailed development is undertaken – to construct a piloted aircraft which has the general description of the object in sub-paragraph (e) above which would be capable of an approximate range of 7,000 miles at subsonic speeds.'

One of Twining's British counterparts, Sir Henry Tizard, had urged the MoD's Directorate of Scientific Intelligence to set up a 'Flying Saucer Working Party'. When the completed report was sent to Tizard, the cover note said; 'I hope this will serve its purpose.' One of the airmen, who was quizzed by the convened officers, felt that the entire process was more of a cover-up than an attempt to discover the true facts.

On 10th December 1948, highly classified Air Intelligence Report No. 100-203-79 called *'Analysis of Flying Objects Incidents in the U.S.'* detailed a series of observations, and was signed by both the Office of Naval Intelligence and the USAF Directorate of Intelligence.

Despite governments consistently denying the existence of UFOs and aliens, some surprising legislation has crept into the United States' law books and government publications.

In July 1969, at the time Apollo astronauts landed on the Moon, Congress passed *'Title 14, Section 1211 of the Code of Federal Regulations'*. It provided for any citizen who had directly or indirectly been extra-terrestrially exposed or in contact with any other person, animal, property or other form of life which had been extra-terrestrially exposed, to be quarantined for an indefinite period.

Failure to comply carried draconian penalties, and ufologists claimed it was designed to silence both them and the witness/contactees. The lawmakers disagreed, and insisted that it was merely to prevent the introduction of unknown viruses or bacteria into the population. The law was withdrawn from the CFR in 1991.

Respected British researcher, Gordon Creighton, secured the complete text of an early U.S. Air Force Academy Text Book from the 1960s, (which was later hastily withdrawn and discarded!). Entitled *'Introductory Space Science, Vol.II, Department of Physics, USAF'*, it was edited by Major Donald Carpenter and Lt Colonel Edward Therkelson. Chapter XIII is devoted to 'Unidentified Flying Objects (UFOs)'. It is a very lengthy and detailed dissertation which states in one part; *'From available information, the UFO phenomenon appears to have been global in nature for almost 50,000 years....This leaves us with the unpleasant possibility of alien visitors to our planet, or at least alien controlled UFOs. However the data are not well correlated, and what questionable data there are suggest the existence of at least three, and maybe four different groups of aliens, possibly at different stages of development. This too, is difficult to accept. It implies the existence of an intelligent life on the majority of planets in our Solar System, or a surprisingly strong interest in Earth by members of other Solar Systems.'*

The text book's author is reported to have said; "The most stimulating theory for us is that UFOs are material objects, which are either manned or remotely controlled by beings who are alien to this planet. There is some evidence supporting this viewpoint."

'The Fire Officer's Guide to Disaster Control', a manual approved by FEMA - the U.S. Federal Energency Management – contains a most enlightening Chapter 13; *'Enemy Attack and UFO Potential'; 'In this chapter we will turn our attention to the very real threat posed by Unidentified Flying Objects (UFOs) whether they exist or not.'*

Its major instructions are;
Not to stand under a UFO hovering at low altitude.
Do not touch, or attempt to touch a landed UFO.
Get away from the scene quickly and inform the military.

Do not take chances with UFOs – people are known to have been burned by their rays.

The manual goes on to include references to many cases where the reported 'energized force fields' have affected auto and aircraft engines and caused widespread power failures. It warns against the possibility of people being burned by rays emanating from UFOs and also discusses the necessary steps to alleviate public panic and restore law and order.

Today, our modern technology is almost beyond comprehension. Where did it come from? In some cases, we will never know. In 1951 the United States invoked its 'Invention Secrecy Act', which has prevented the publication of thousands of patent applications over the years.

Let us go back just one hundred and fifty years. There were no microwaves, radios, CDs, televisions or DVDs. The electronic and digital revolution, with its computers, I-Pads, the internet and mobile phones, was unheard of. Most people travelled with a horse and cart or carriage. Aeroplanes, rockets, satellites, radar, lasers and nuclear energy were way in the future, and the medical profession had yet to discover antibiotics, X-Rays, stem cells, DNA and IVF.

Even in more recent years, plasma shields, particle beam weapons, and quantum computers and physics were the province of science fiction. Atomic – resolution microscopes, which can physically image and move atoms, leading to the nanotechnology revolution, is beyond the comprehension of most people. Today, these innovations are a reality.

Until recently, our modern astronomers had not even gained the knowledge our ancient ancestors possessed. Only one hundred years ago nobody would believe that, within a short few decades, we would land on the Moon and send countless probes into outer space. In fact, in August 1948, the *'Science Digest'* wrote; *'Landing and moving around on the moon offers so many serious problems for human beings that it may take science another two hundred years to lick them.'*

We have to remember that scientists often 'get it wrong', and are constrained by a very conservative peer group. Physicist Lord Kelvin, (1824-1907), who was president of the prestigious scientific Royal Society in the 1890s, was less than optimistic about mankind's scientific knowledge and progress at the beginning of the twentieth century. He declared that X-rays were a hoax, radio had no future and aircraft flight was impossible. Others, including Charles Duell of the US Patent Office considered there was nothing left to be invented! Were our most brilliant minds wearing blinders, or did the scientists who followed them have some kind of subliminal prompting and inspiration from alien intelligence?

One forward thinking genius was Nikola Tesla, who admitted to many strange experiences and visions in his childhood. Before WWI he was planning to experiment with a remote controlled and powered 'lighter-than-air' craft. In 1911 he told the *'New York Herald Tribune'*: *'My flying machine will have neither wings nor propellers, and you will never guess that it was a flying machine. It will be able to move at will through the air in any direction with perfect safety.'*

Whilst the aliens' advanced technology is the most obvious reason for secrecy, the knowledge of other intelligent beings inhabiting the universe would have a drastic effect on Earth's society and religions. Some researchers are convinced our Space Brothers are benign, and just want to help us. This may not be the case. Aliens, like us humans, can lie. What is their real intent and agenda? World governments do not want ordinary citizens interacting with visitors who may not have our best interests in mind.

I don't pretend to know the answers where UFOs and aliens are concerned. In fact there is no single 'answer' to this multi-faceted enigma. In this book I have written about many major incidents which have occurred in the distant past and over the last one hundred years or so. 'Now' – some may be our own secret prototypes, - 'and Then' – in the past – perhaps it is more likely they were alien craft and their occupants. It is up to the reader to consider the evidence and make-up their own mind.

There are many excellent investigators, both in Australia and abroad, who wrote articles for the 'INUFOR Digest', and conferences I hosted, but never received the recognition they deserved. Wonderful people such as Rosemary Decker, Margaret Fry, Glennys MacKay, Alan Craddock and Dudley Robb are only a few of them. I have included some of their research in the following chapters.

CHAPTER ONE

ANCIENT ALIENS and ARTEFACTS

In Earth's past, many civilisations openly recognised and recorded 'Gods who came from the skies.' All over the world, on nearly every continent, there are ancient ruins, inscriptions and artefacts recording these visitors and their interaction with Earth's inhabitants. It is interesting that none of Earth's first known civilisations claim to have invented their knowledge of science, law or culture by themselves.

In Asia, the Indian Vedic texts describe very warlike beings, with powerful celestial weapons, who came from the stars, and flew in Virmanas – exotic craft with the description and capabilities of the flying saucers which are reported today.

CHINA

China also has some unsolved mysteries in its past. Colonel Maurice Sheahan, the Far Eastern director of Trans World Airline, was flying over Shaanxi province when he reported seeing an enormous pyramid, and multiple burial mounds, at the foot of the isolated Tsinling Mountains.

Several newspapers mentioned the matter, but although Sheahan claimed to have taken a photograph, it never materialised, and the Chinese government denied the existence of any such 'pyramid'.

Investigator/author, Hartwig Hausdorf, later discovered much smaller, and more primitive pyramids in 1994, but not the one reported by Sheahan. Hausdorf did, however, uncover an incident from the beginning of the twentieth century.

Apparently two Australian traders came upon over one hundred much older and more primitive pyramids on the plain of Qin Chuan in Central China. The custodian of a local monastery told them that they were thousands of years old, and were the product of the 'old emperors', who did not originate on Earth. Rather they were the descendants of the *'sons of heaven, who roared down to this planet on their fiery metallic dragons.'*

This myth makes more sense when one examines the reports of the Dropa Tribe and their stone discs allegedly found in 1937-8 by an expedition led by Chi Pu

Tei, an archaeologist with the Chinese Academy of Sciences in Beijing. He and his team members were in the Kunlun-Kette mountains, and sought shelter in a cave.

They noticed inscriptions on the walls, some of which appeared to be astronomical. Further inside they found several tombs and strange looking skeletons, buried with unusual stone discs, which had spiralled grooves of closely written characters going from a hole in the middle to the outer rim. Eventually over seven hundred grooved discs, in some ways similar to a LP record, were uncovered in the same caves. It was not until the 1960s that academics were able to decipher them.

They told of the crash of an extraterrestrial spaceship 12,000 years ago. Many of the survivors were hunted down and killed by the terrified local Ham tribe. When the Hams realised the aliens meant no harm, the Dropas, who were unable to return to their own planet, remained on Earth and inhabited the cave area later discovered by Chi Pu Tei.

In 1938, at the time of the discovery, the area was still inhabited by two tribes, known as the Hams and Dropas. Anthropologists were unable to match their genes to any other known race. They were not Chinese, Mongolian or Tibetan, and had thin bodies and disproportionally large heads, similar to the skeletal remains found in the caves.

Due to a 1978 irresponsible and sensational 'Dropa' science fiction book, 'Sungods in Exile', many dismissed the research in its entirety. Other respectable investigators have found a great deal of corroborating evidence.

Soviet archaeological scholar, Vyacheslav Zaitsev, wrote an article in the 'Sputnik' magazine. He detailed the seven hundred plus discs, found in the mountains at the Tibetan-Chinese border. He claimed they were estimated at being at least fourteen thousand years old. Zaitsev also said they were covered with only partially deciphered pictographs, which tell of the Dropas, or 'sky people', who came down from the sky in their 'gliders'.

When Russian scientists noticed that a disc would vibrate when unusual musical notes were played, they tested one with an oscillograph. A surprising rhythm was recorded, as if it had once been electrically charged, or had functioned as an electrical conductor.

From the statues of Easter Island to the structures at Stonehenge, all over the world there are numerous ancient sites comprising massive blocks of stone. There are hundreds of these formations and Neolithic sites all across Western Europe. Many date back over 4,500 years and are usually comprised of either quartz or granite, which have piezoelectric qualities.

What was their purpose, and why were they built by an ancient culture of primitive people living in basic shelter and tribal type communities? It appears that these prehistoric monuments mark, and are connected to, anomalies in the Earth's magnetic field.

Our planet's magnetic field is not uniform, and can fluctuate greatly. The Earth, rotating on its axis, creates enormous energy. Several researchers have discovered this powerful force is released at various 'grid' points around the globe. These lines of force form strange patterns, often referred to as 'ley lines'. These areas possess a change in energy vibrations, and are reputed to result in distortions in space-time, providing a 'window area' to paranormal and inter-dimensional events, perhaps even the cosmos itself.

Ancient civilisations were obviously well aware of the Earth's energy flow and patterns, and utilised ley lines and magnetic vortices for sacred sites and rituals. The Chinese built their roads along 'Dragon Paths', and the Romans built their own roads along the 'old straight tracks' of the existing Ley Lines in Europe and the Middle East.

Some believe the Earth's energy and frequencies can be accumulated and enhanced by the precise positioning and structure of giant stones, possibly enabling a 'spiral of force and power'.

In Poland, the "Alles-Stones', near the villages of Odry and Wesjory, were erected almost 6,000 years ago. Many believe they contain an 'invisible force', and are connected to the Pleiades and Hyades constellations. Alexander Thom, a Professor of Engineering Science, researched six hundred ancient stone circles in Britain, and discovered that every one was aligned to the Sun, and in some cases the stars as well. In his book 'Megalithic Sites in Britain' he notes that our ancient ancestors had an incredible knowledge of both astronomy and geometry.

In Britain, many of these megalithic wonders, some 7,000 years old, were built on a grid point. The impressive 'Standing Stones' at Stonehenge and Avebury never fail to impress, especially when we know some of their Preseli bluestone was sourced from a long distance away in Wales. Another site, known as 'Long Meg and Her Daughters' comprises 67 sandstone blocks, each weighing up to 28 tonnes.

To the far north, the inhabitants of remote islands were also capable of these skillful feats. On Orkney, the stones are still upright, and on the island of Lewis, the great stone circle at Callanish was erected nearly five thousand years ago.

At Carnac in Brittany, France, one stone alone is over 150 feet high and weighs 340 tons! Probably the lesser known stone circles at Göbekli Tepe in Turkey, are even more amazing. They predate Stonehenge by 6,500 years, and exhibit impressive technical skill in their construction.

Stone circles and megaliths were built all around the world, by supposedly isolated societies and cultures. They all displayed an incredible knowledge of engineering, astronomy and geometry. Just how did primitive man manage to cut, transport and arrange these massive blocks with such precision?

In Baalbeck, Lebanon, the megalithic platform, upon which a Roman acropolis was built, has three mammoth stones, quarried from over half a mile away. Each one, measuring 64 feet in length, 12 feet wide and over 14 feet high, weighs about nine hundred tons!

Tiahuanacu, in the Bolivian Andes, has enormous stone blocks, each weighing between one to four hundred tons, which were originally quarried over two hundred miles away. Again, in Cuzco and Sacsahuaman, Peru, the Inca civilisation also built upon much older megalithic blocks, some weighing hundreds of tons. Experts have been unable to date the older foundations of some of these temples and ruins, but it was apparently very important to use the same ancient sites.

The Middle East is still a great source of controversy and speculation, especially the pyramids of Egypt. They are positioned on a major earth energy grid point, sometimes referred to as the 'naval of the world'. When were they made, by whom and why?

EGYPT

The ancient Egyptians credited the sudden rise in their culture and civilisation to their sky gods – Toth, Ptah, and Osiris. They brought wisdom, astronomy, mathematics, geometry, medicine, literacy, laws and the ability to construct magnificent buildings.

The Egyptian 'Turin Papyrus', compiled over 4,000 years ago, during the reign of Ramses II, states that Egypt was well established by 39,620 BC. During this time was ruled by pre-dynastic kings for 13,420 years, 'Horus Kings' for 23,200 years and 'demigods' for an undetermined period.

Originally, historians believed the pyramids were burial tombs for the Pharaohs from the fourth dynasty, approximately 2575 -2465 BC. This theory is no longer in favour with all Egyptologists. Many archaeologists have noted the correlation of the three pyramids of Giza to the sky pattern of Orion's Belt. Based on constellation alignments, we arrive at not only a date of 10,500 BC, favoured by some experts, but also 45,000 BC! Surely not!!

The Great Pyramid is massive, and covers thirteen acres. Comprised of over two million precision cut building blocks, and weighing approximately four million tons, it is hardly credible that it was constructed by a stone-age civilization with primitive tools. Some historians claim that each block, weighing sixteen tons, was quarried, moved and positioned by teams of workers. Some of the granite came from Aswan, six hundred miles away. Even with today's technology and equipment, we cannot replicate their effort.

The entire project was a marvel of precision engineering, including the fact that the sides have accurate dimensions, lined up with the 'NW-SE' cardinal points on the compass. The actual location, and internal structure of the Great Pyramid, has led many experts, including Philip Gardiner, Chris Dunn and others to suggest it was actually an 'energy vortex', which transformed the Earth's vibrations into energy.

I certainly don't know the answers, but have wondered that if the pyramids were some form of energy generator, perhaps they were constructed by and for the benefit of alien visitors. Anyone who travelled across the cosmos would not be able to bring building materials with them, and would have to rely on the natural resources available at their destination.

As is the case with many ancient edifices, most engineers have suggested that no contemporary apparatus could lift the massive tonnage of many of these stones and statues without collapsing. Perhaps the theories of 'levitation' or 'advanced alien technology' have some merit.

According to the oral traditions of Easter Island, their stone heads were moved by the use of 'mana', a psychic force which commanded them to move through the air. In Central America, a pyramid at Uxmal was said to be raised by one man, a 'magician', who 'whistled and heavy rocks would move into place.' Similar methods, including the 'sound of a trumpet', are common to the builder-gods of Stonehenge and other ancient Central American and Egyptian sites.

THE SUMERIANS

The ancient civilisation of Sumer (Mesopotamia) existed in 3,500 BC – some five and a half thousand years ago. In recent years, excavations carried out in the olden cities of Nineveh and Mari, unearthed hundreds of carved tablets. Many historians, over the last one hundred and fifty years, have carefully translated them from the Sumerian and often Babylonian and Assyrian texts.

Scholar Zecharia Sitchin devoted much of his life to this task, and wrote several books on the subject. Many historians have tried, not always successfully, to explain how the Sumerians suddenly rose to prominence with such a sophisticated civilisation.

Their society included cities and architecture, libraries, government and a judicial system. Sumerian culture boasted music, poetry, sculpture and jewellery. Their knowledge of medicine and science, especially astronomy, thousands of years ago, still astounds the experts today.

The Sumerians counted the planets of the Solar System from the 'outside/in', the way someone would if entering from space. They knew about Uranus, Neptune and Pluto, which we didn't discover until 1781, 1846 and 1930 respectively.

Several of the cuneiform texts closely mirror the details written in the Book of Genesis, but with some major differences. These tablets claim that mankind, as we know it today, was seeded by the 'Anunnaki',('those who descended from Heaven to Earth'). These beings, although regarded as gods, were flesh-and-blood individuals with whom humans sometimes had sex, produced offspring

11

and even married. Mention is made of one 'God' travelling in a 'sky chariot', and carrying a weapon similar to 'a bolt of fire.'

Although disputed by some historians, other scholars claim that these extra-terrestrials actually came from Mars, or the mythical planet Nibiru, before forming colonies on Earth, and altering our DNA, both artificially and by cross-breeding, whilst present on our planet. Records indicate they were a cruel and ruthless civilisation, who possessed weapons of mass destruction, which eventually caused their downfall when the various alien factions made war on each other.

THE MAYANS

The Mayan people were a great civilisation who settled in Central America in the areas now known as Guatemala, Honduras and Southern Mexico. Their culture peaked around 843 AD, and dramatically declined over the next five hundred years. Much of their science and wisdom was lost when Spanish missionaries destroyed the majority of their records. Remaining artefacts have demonstrated that the Maya possessed incredible, accurate comprehension and understanding of astronomy, mathematics and engineering.

The Mayan culture and knowledge can be traced back to their mythical 'god' Quetzalcoatl – who was also credited with many prophecies into the future. Was Quetzalcoatl a myth – or some form of ancient alien visitor? Regarded as a 'feathered-serpent' god, he is mentioned in many cultures with other alternate names including 'Kukulkan' and 'Bep Kororoti'.

The legends of the Kayapo Indians of Brazil claim that 'Bep Kororoti' arrived from the skies with a 'great thunder weapon', and having assisted in the progress of the natives' civilisation, vanished back into the skies amid fiery clouds, smoke and thunder.'

Quetzalcoatl was, according to some legends, the product of a virgin impregnated by a deity; but this is only one of many varying myths. To the Aztecs he was the 'giver of knowledge and all good things'. He was certainly credited with performing many miracles and importing great knowledge and wisdom, including astronomy, architecture and mathematics, to the natives of Central America.

He supposedly established the 'Age of the Fifth Sun' in about 3113 BC, (approximately the same period as the rise of the Sumerians). Some schools of thought equate Quetzalcoatl with an intelligent cosmic force rather than an individual.

The Mayan galactic time-keeping and calendars were amazingly complex and precise. One such calculation was a virtual periodic table of galactic figurines which divided the 25,627 year cycle of the Sun's revolution around the Pleiades into five great 'Ages' of 5,125 years. Each 'Age', which was said to be ruled by a different 'Sun', has faced cataclysmic destruction at the end of its span.

We are currently in the 'Age of the Fifth Sun', which it is calculated began in 3113 BC, and was due to culminate on December 21st, 2012 AD. At that time it was said that there would be a very rare alignment of the Solstice Sun with the centre of the galaxy, which happens approximately once in every 25,627 year cycle. Not all experts are in agreement with the actual timing, and say some researchers have got the dates wrong.

There are many ancient ruins scattered throughout Central America. In Mexico, Teotihuacán is a huge archaeological complex, with an avenue of flat top pyramids, with alignments of astronomical significance. Also in the high Andes, there is evidence of stone-age societies with advanced technologies. Bolivia and Peru boast megalithic structures, and like Cuzco and Machu Picchu, experts still ponder over the possibility of alien contact and support.

My friend and colleague, Rosemary Decker, also wrote about alien visitors in the olden days.

ANGELS PAST AND PRESENT

By Rosemary Decker

The word angel is from the Greek angelos, meaning messenger; and in the Biblical writings it designates a messenger from heaven, a member of a race of beings of greater power and intelligence than that of Earth humanity. Some of these ancient visitants were known to the ancient Sumerians, Babylonians, Egyptians and Chinese. The Chinese called them 'Sons of Heaven'. Some of these early peoples were so in awe of the messengers' powers that they called them 'Gods'.

According to the Hebrew descriptions, as recorded in the Old and New Testaments, and in the Hindu texts, these beings varied in the levels of status and authority, some being excessively advanced. Four of seven such arch- angels were named in the scriptures as Michael – Gabriel – Raphael and Uriel. (In general, the messengers were not named).

The scriptures detail how the messengers, who intervened in human affairs, had the task of instructing people regarding morality and justice. They promoted marriage between persons of the highest possible genetic characteristics, possibly to 'up-breed' humankind. They guided human leadership, and sometimes warned certain people how to avoid danger or death.

Among those who were using physical bodies, much like ours, the scriptures record associated strange 'objects', like that seen by Ezekiel. These constructions resembled some modern reports of unidentified flying objects. Ezekiel had a hard time describing the flying craft with 'wheels within wheels'. In one instance he actually coined a phrase used nowhere else in the Bible: Ruach search – whirling, windy thing. (Ez 3:1-18)

On one occasion he was 'lifted up' and carried some distance – a matter of perhaps seventy miles. He was then set down and released among some of his fellow exiles, beside the river Chebar, where he sat 'overwhelmed for seven days'. After all, he had not known any vehicle other than a chariot. We can empathise with him.

World-wide, since ancient times, angelic messengers have employed telepathic contact in certain instances. They have appeared in visions, often in dreams, and sometimes in a waking state. Both the Old and New Testaments contain accounts of visitations occurring in dreams. These were usually warning messages, as when Joseph was told to take Mary and the infant Jesus in haste to Egypt. He was to remain there until such time as he would be informed that the danger to the child's life was past.

From descriptions in the Old Testament, the messengers looked so much like us that most people did not recognise them as anything other than human! However, the highly educated and knowledgeable did recognise them as visitants. Was it some distinguishing feature, perhaps facial, or something they wore or carried?

A prime example is Abraham's meeting and interaction with three such visitors, whose nature he recognised at once. He bowed to them and invited them to stay for dinner. (Gen;18 and 19). The obvious leader of the three he spoke of as 'Lord', and the other two as 'men'.

For centuries it has been customary for artists to depict angels with large wings, often charming and beautiful. The origin of this concept is natural. Wings are the logical symbol of the ability to move freely through space, and even in our own times, our aviators and astronauts wear small wings on their shoulders as emblems of this special kind of ability.

Biblical winged beings, called 'cherubim', appeared on the Ark of the Covenant as golden sculptures. Two sculpted beings knelt facing each other, wings forward, with their tips touching. They must have been functional as well as emblematic, because the Ark was used as a communication device between the High Priest and the 'Lords'.

Biblical messengers, as well as those in distant lands, were sometimes observed whilst shifting from visibility to invisibility. Apparently, certain visitors were, and are, not in need of physical bodies, and are not observable through normal sensory perception. Others may normally reside in the 'other side' of the physical – the 'etheric' physical – and when they shift to our familiar 'side', no special abilities are required to perceive them.

An example of a modern day waking vision is found in the life of early twentieth century clairvoyant and healer, Edgar Cayce. He recorded that, sometime in his childhood, he had a waking vision of an angel. The 'lady' told him that if he remained true to the highest principles, he would one day be able to bless and heal people, as he had hoped. Indeed, he was able to achieve that goal.

Among Amerindians the kindly messengers are known as the 'Sky People' – (hence the title of Brinsley Trench's first book on extra-terrestrial visitors). Every summer the Hopi Indians of Arizona commemorate the long-ago rescue of their folk by the 'spirit people', (Kachinas). This is known as the 'Niman' ceremony, and the Kachina dancers have their chests painted dark, like the night sky, with a pair of crescent moons, separated by a dark band, placed on either side of the chest. (Part of the legend is told in J.Gibbney's article – 'The Niman Ceremony', Arizona Highways July 1959).

At some ancient time, the Hopi's prayers to the Great Spirit had been answered. Their drought suffering people were rescued by gifts of maize and water in jars at the foot of their mesa, beside the dried up stream bed. This continued every night until crops were producing again. The rescuers remained invisible, but at least one pair of scout runners found two men, wearing strange head gear, up near the San Francisco Peaks. They admitted to having been the benefactors.

The 'Kachinas' left the Hopi with their emblem of the two crescent moons, which signified 'friendship to all men'. They also left some spruce seedlings, along with advice to plant the spruce as far along the creek beds as possible. When the visitors departed, they urged the Hopi to always remain a peaceful people.

THE CRYSTAL SKULLS

About one hundred years ago, some unusual and unique human-size crystal skulls were individually found in Central America. Except for one with a detachable jaw, each was carved from a single piece of crystal, with no modern tool marks, and would be difficult to duplicate even today. Although much of the Earth is crystal, the type of quartz crystal the skulls are carved from, can only be found in Brazil, Madagascar and the USSR.

There are many legends, originating from the ancient Maya, Aztec and Native American Indian cultures regarding thirteen original, life-size crystal 'Singing Skulls', which were brought to Earth by the Sky Gods, who were 'Spiritual Beings' in human bodies, and came from the Pleiades to Atlantis.

Whilst the Skulls still remain an enigma, they are said to be of celestial origin, and a living library, containing all the information and knowledge of 'Twelve Worlds'. Each Skull is unique, with different properties of sacred light and knowledge. One is amethyst, another smoky quartz, and a third rose quartz. Experts have stated that one skull is shaped unlike any known humanoid. Another was examined by a forensic anthropologist, who formulated the face as if it had been a normal skull. The facial appearance resembled a young woman with oriental/mongoloid features.

When placed in a circle of twelve, with the thirteenth, (representing the Earth), in the middle, the powerful vibrations and piezel-electricity created can be used in many ways.

They can act as transceiver/amplifiers linking minds and telling other quadrants in the galaxy of our spiritual consciousness. They can also reveal great wisdom and show us the mysteries of the universe, as well as healing our own planet. The power of the skulls can also be misused, and actually bring about total destruction. For this reason, they have been hidden for centuries in different locations.

The acquisition and possession of the skulls has become an obsession over the years, by people and countries desiring their knowledge and power. Each genuine Skull is carved from one piece of natural quartz crystal, and is said to have a moving jaw. This type of crystal, known as 'piezo-electric silicon dioxide', is the same type of quartz crystal found in almost every piece of modern electronic technology, and is used for its information storage abilities.

Ex IBM scientist, Marcel Vogel, researched crystals for many years, and is credited with the invention of the Liquid Crystal Display and the Magnetic Bubble Memory System. He maintained that a crystal not only affects organic objects, but can also store, transmit and amplify thought forms. During one lecture he mentioned the greater number of crystal sides that were cut, the greater the power. He would not reveal why he used a thirteen sided crystal in his demonstrations, except to say that it stored knowledge as information. This is interesting in light of the legend of the power of the thirteen crystal skulls coming together.

The actual location, and authenticity of many skulls is very controversial, and they cannot be carbon-dated. Some replicas were attempted by German carvers, who used South African crystal, and left modern tool marks. Crystal skulls housed in the British Museum and also in Paris are reputed to be replicas, however some researchers state that this was said to prevent their South American countries of origin claiming they were 'looted' national treasures and demanding their return.

One, which the British Museum had since 1898, is contained in a sealed glass case. Museum cleaners refused to go near it, especially at night, and said they were frightened as they had seen it moving around, inside the case, by itself.

The famous 'Mitchell-Hedges' skull, is the only known one with a detachable jaw. It was subjected to six years of extensive testing by experts at the Hewlett-Packard Laboratories in California, and is considered to be genuine. Lab technicians stated that they were unable to create a similar skull with the technology available in 1970.

There are, however, several accounts of how F. Mitchell Hedges acquired it. The most accepted version is that his young daughter found it whilst accompanying him on an archaeological expedition to the ruins of an ancient Mayan city in Lubaantun, Belize, in 1924. Later evidence pointed to him purchasing it at a Sotheby's auction in 1943, however the seller was from his friend Burney's family, and it could have been a legal move, making him the purchaser, and thereby the true owner.

An even more intriguing possibility lies in a novel, *'The White Tiger'*, written by Mitchell-Hedges in 1931, where the hero is taken to a series of underground tunnels leading to a cave containing unimaginable Aztec riches, artefacts and crystal skulls. When he wrote his autobiography, *'Danger my Ally'*, in 1954 Mitchell-Hedges barely mentions the skull, and the couple of paragraphs that do, were deleted from the American edition.

Another apparently genuine Skull, said to be cursed, was donated to the Smithsonian Institute after the previous owner committed suicide. Six other skulls are said to have been sighted, leaving six more to be located.

There are many legends associated with the skulls being united again. The Maya claimed it would herald their civilisation coming back to life. The Native American Indians predict this will only happen after the 'cleansing of the Earth', when most of the population have perished, and the survivors have learned to live in harmony with each other and Mother Earth.

THE WINGMAKERS

In my book, *'The Alien Gene'*, contactee Leesa Donahue and her mother Linda, connected to an internet site called 'The Wingmakers'. They were captivated at first, due to their own research into genetic bloodlines, ancient aliens and the Sumerians. After a while they felt 'something was not quite right'. They realised that somehow, watching this site was dangerous. Because it had an almost inter-dimensional aspect, affecting their minds, and very 'being', they decided to stop logging on. If it weren't for their very real experience, I may not have looked into this at all.

According to the website and several articles, in 1972, some hikers in a remote part of New Mexico found some interesting artefacts which dated back to 840AD. NASA scientists thought that the artefacts were extraterrestrial, and filed everything away under the code name 'Ancient Arrow'.

In 1994 a rock slide revealed a previously hidden entry in the cliff face. It led to a system of tunnels and twenty-three chambers, carved into the solid rock. More artefacts were examined by NASA's Advanced Contact Intelligence Organisation (ACIO), which researches alien technologies with the intention of reverse engineering whatever they can. It was claimed that the artefacts were more advanced than any other alien technology they had ever studied. Due to lack of funding, the project was shelved, with only a couple of scientists continuing the study in their own time.

One of them went public, under the pseudonym of 'Dr. Anderson', however an article in *Nexus* April-May 2001 claims that 'Anderson' was in fact a Dr. Jamisson Neruda, whose father, a highly placed Bolivian engineer, had discovered a crashed disc in 1956 which subsequently gained him a place with ACIO.

'Anderson' described paintings and glyphs in every chamber, some of which he felt may be 'portals' to another time or dimension. There was also an optical disc in the last chamber, and by using it as a 'key', he was able to utilise his linguistic expertise to translate the apparently Sumerian text into philosophical and scientific papers. There was also music, poetry and an introduction to the culture and identity of its creators.

According to 'Anderson's' translations, this was created by an advanced race from our future who time travelled back to create the underground complex and leave a 'time-capsule' for us to find. They called themselves the 'Wingmakers', and claimed to have built seven such capsules around the world, which were meant to be discovered at this time in our history.

These 'Wingmakers' claimed to have seeded life on Earth, given us all our knowledge and spiritual understanding, and facilitated evolutionary leaps and biological transformations.

One article, by Rita Copeland, which can be read in its entirety in Queensland's *'UFO Encounter'*, details a lot of 'Anderson's' belief that some of this technology links into the politics of the New World Order. His comments about the composition of some items indicate possible holographic and telepathic components of the technology. One document has an interesting quotation; *'molecular-based computer systems activated by a specific human touch.'* Copeland suggested that *'reference to such a bio-computer chip being linked to human consciousness takes the technology even higher.'*

A 'Wingmakers' website was created, but after a while, Mark Hempel, the webmaster and some participants and researchers, started sounding warnings that this entire scenario was dangerous and insidious.

Mark Hempel, became worried. He had been contracted and paid by an anonymous group (Labyrinth) to host the site. Although the material being downloaded by his sponsor seemed innocent enough, he was receiving anonymous threats, which he believed came from an unknown intelligence agency.

CAUSE (Citizens Against UFO Secrecy) received information that the site may be some form of experiment in subliminal, or similar programming, affecting the subconscious mind. They had also heard of people describing unusual experiences and altered states, especially when viewing the art or listening to the music in two of the chambers.

The hidden elements in sound and music have been well known and utilised, through the centuries, from the time of the ancient Egyptians and Sumerians. They are still employed by various religions and others today, and Tibetan Lamas are reputed to be able to levitate huge boulders by the use of sound alone.

It has been stated by many scientists that everything is frequency and vibration, and when I see people glued to their computers and mobile screens, I wonder if the internet is projecting some form of addictive frequency which affects the subconscious minds of its users. Certainly the Wingmakers website makes reference to the Internet, and our digital technology becoming a 'gateway to a connected intra-galactic, digital nervous system.'

For those who may wish to look further into this, several investigators have given the warning – 'Enter at your own risk!' The interactive technology may not be as innocent as it seems.

I wondered about the other six capsules, purportedly hidden around the world. Were they essentially the same, or was each one different? I came across an interesting article written by Philip Coppens in the 2006 June/July edition of *Nexus* magazine.

In 1969 Janos Moriez claimed to have found a similar enormous subterranean tunnel system in Equador. He said it was 'guarded' by a tribe of indigenous natives. Over the next few years there was much controversy over Moriez's claim that within the complex was a cave containing a 'metal library'.

Moriez died before revealing the exact location of these mysterious artefacts, but a burial chamber, dating back to 1,500BC was located in 1976. Investigators finally met another man, Jaramillo, who said he had seen the library in 1946, when he was only seventeen. It had originally been shown to his uncle, years earlier, by members of the local tribe.

Jaramillo said there were thousands of heavy metal books, piled upon shelves. Each page was impressed, from one side, with ideographs, geometric designs and written inscriptions. There was a second library containing what appeared to be small crystal tablets, grooved with parallel, encrusted channels. There were also zoomorphic and human statues, metal bars of different shapes, and sealed 'doors', possibly tombs, covered in mixtures of coloured, semi-precious stones. In addition there was a large sarcophagus, sculpted from hard, translucent material, containing a gold-leaf skeleton of a large human being.

Although several plans were made to locate the secret entrance to the mysterious caverns and library, fate intervened and both Moriez and Jaramillo died before they came to fruition. Some intrepid explorers still plan on eventually locating these hidden tunnels and caverns. Perhaps one day. ?

The 1997/8 edition of *Exposure* magazine carried an article by Paul White, about the Burrows Cave, located in a remote part of Southern Illinois in the USA. In 1982, Russell Burrows, and some fellow speleologists, who discovered the limestone cavern system, were met with derision and scepticism when they contacted the experts for assistance with the identification and documentation of the artefacts located in the cave.

There were about four thousand rock fragments engraved with ancient drawings, hieroglyphs and script. There were maps, and pictures of gods, ships and non-indigenous animals. It was like a huge library on stone tablets, and there were also gold coins and relics, including several stone crypts containing skeletons interred with jewellery and statues.

Some of the material, which represents several cultures, has been deciphered and translated from ancient Egyptian and Hebrew, but there is also Greek and Phoenician script. Some carvings appear to be copied from ancient Greek and Mesopotamian sources. Others have an Amerindian flavour. Experts dated many of the artefacts to the early first millennium, and have hypothesised as to their origin.

One has stated; *'Although I speak with caution, as it is too early to say for sure, there are many indications that the bodies found in the crypts are the leaders of a colony of refugees from Ptolemaic Egypt, including a Jewish contingent from the Roman controlled Kingdom of Mauritania.'*

So far, there seems to be no indication of an actual alien or extraterrestrial component to these artefacts. Given the similarities to the hidden caves in New Mexico and Equador, one can but wonder.

CHAPTER TWO

HOLOGRAMS, UFOS AND PROPHECIES

Throughout the vast array of investigated UFO reports, there is often a common denominator of the 'mystical', or paranormal. Many investigators think a hologram may explain what the witness has seen, others consider there is an inter-dimensional aspect to the event. Sometimes it is hard to differentiate. In some cases a more spiritual or religious reason may be suggested. What is of significance is that basically the same message was being given to thousands of people, rather than individual contactees.

Rosemary Decker had several thoughts about the 'visitors' employing holograms when communicating with us.

'The frequent presence of holograms within the UFO scenario comprises only one component – but an important one – in the vast array of phenomena, both physical and para-physical, which have long baffled, intrigued, frightened, thrilled and sometimes educated a steadily growing segment of humanity world-wide. In an area of our experience, in which there have been countless questions and very few answers, the hologram shows promise of at least some solutions.

'Many of you will be familiar with the technical principles involved in using a laser light beam to create a holographic projection. The word 'hologram' means 'entire picture', and in our own recently invented technology it is a '3-D picture created by light-energy interference patterns'. Formed by laser light-beams, the actual object is 'photographed' on a plate, standing upon it in full three dimensions. You can walk around it and see the other side.

'Human science has been developing these images since the 1960s, but who has been producing them, for many centuries, with a technology far beyond our own? Whoever they are, they can remain out of our view, while projecting 3-D images 'as large as life and twice as natural'!

'Where have we seen these? Many ancient historical accounts are very suggestive of describing holograms. Perhaps the earliest one, familiar to us in the western world, is the 'Handwriting on the Wall' episode in Babylonian history, when King Belshazzar was giving a feast to his officers in 538BC.

Amidst the merriment, on the wall just behind the King, there appeared a hand – no body attached – writing out a cryptic message for his Royal Highness. (Daniel 5; 5-30)

'Although this incident was recorded in a religious as well as historical context, it was so long ago that we have no way of stating that it was a hologram. It bears the earmarks of one, and is certainly an intriguing possibility.

'Moving on to modern times, but still long before Earth scientists invented the hologram, there are excellent documented examples of what we now recognise as holographic projections. Some have a scientific context, some historic and others were of a religious or prophetic nature.

The Shrine of Knock

'It was the evening of 21st August, 1879, in the little village of Knock, Ireland. It was raining lightly when the local pastor's housekeeper and her friend went to lock the chapel for the night. As they passed the small, girls' school house, which was near the church, they saw a lighted group of human figures standing a few feet away from the rear wall of the chapel.

'Upon coming closer, they realised that these figures were floating about twenty inches above the ground. They were mostly white in colour, and looked like life-size statues. The central figure resembled the traditional Madonna. Her eyes were uplifted and hands open at shoulder level.

'To her left was a statue of a young man, whom they thought may be St. John. He was holding an open book in his left hand, and his right hand was raised in teaching or blessing. To her right was a grey-bearded man, understood to represent Joseph.

'The housekeeper and her friend were both excited and joyful, and ran to inform all the other villagers, who all came to look and linger. Passers-by wondered if the priest had obtained some statues for the church. They couldn't understand why they had been left out in the rain, and were puzzled at the source of illumination, which was a soft, but strong white light across the greater part of the gable wall. After about two hours, when no-one was present for a few minutes, the display disappeared.

'Within a week, healings at the site were reported. Journalists soon arrived from various newspapers as far away as Cork, and the Archbishop of Tuam set up an inquiry to ascertain the facts. To this end, depositions were obtained from fifteen of the observers of the event. Witnesses ranged in age from little John Curry, who was six, to an elderly seventy-five Bridget Trench.

'Although not everybody recalled exactly the same details, there was general agreement regarding the appearance of the life-size figures: They gave the impression of statuary familiar in Catholic churches, and were white to creamy-white with some details in colour.

'Just to the right of the three human figures was a block or altar with a lamb standing upon it. Some thought there was a cross behind the lamb, and several witnesses said there were tiny golden stars twinkling around it. Others said these were like little sparklers darting in and out, forward and back throughout the whole scene.

'Those who climbed over the stone wall, to get a better look, noticed that the figures, as a single unit, receded somewhat towards the church's gable wall when they got too close. John Curry was curious to discover whether the wide-open book in St. John's left hand, had any words printed in it. He found plenty of print, but told the others present that he couldn't read it all.

'Bridget Trench knelt at the Lady's feet, wanting to clasp them in her hands and kiss them. She was startled to feel nothing in her hands except a tingling feeling. She pushed her hands all the way back to the gable wall before feeling anything solid. She realised the ground below the figures was bone dry, even though the rain was still falling and blowing against the south gable.

'Within a few days the news had spread far, and most of those who came to the site were convinced it had been blessed from Heaven and become a 'Centre of Healing'. Consequently, healings soon took place...witness the power of faith... and the record book, kept by the local clergy, contains the statements of the healed, their physicians and other witnesses from that time on.

'The fact that the apparition was holographic in nature does not diminish its value. One of the benefits to that area of Ireland, following the occurrence, was of emotional healing. The mostly poor and oppressed folk, feeling honoured and blessed, picked up hope, improved their relations with other *people, and started to prosper. The improved economic level has continued to the present day. The little village of Knock, which is still small, benefits from the many thousands of visitors who come from overseas as well as locally.'*

Her words brought to mind many of the 'Marian Apparitions' which have occurred during the last hundred years or so, and the possible holographic features involved.

During the twentieth century there have been several well documented sightings of the Virgin Mary, often in the presence of thousands of witnesses. The Catholic Church has virtually authenticated some cases, and there have been countless miracle healings associated with the visions. Many researchers have difficulty with these occurrences, as the witness reports are also consistent with many UFO sightings and holographic images.

FATIMA

The visions of three children at the tiny village of Fatima, high in the Siera D'Aire Mountains of Portugal, are perhaps the most famous of the Marian Apparitions to occur in the twentieth century.

On 13th May 1917, Lucia, who was ten, and her cousins Francisco, eight, and Jacinta, seven, were tending the family's flock when a brilliant flash illuminated the sky and countryside. Suddenly a little bush began to glow, and a lovely maiden stood before them. She was in a bright glowing light, and identified herself as the Virgin Mary.

She told them to pray the Rosary, and to return to the same spot on the thirteenth of each month. In October she would explain the reasons for her visit and perform a miracle.

On 13th June, the apparition said God wanted the world to give devotion to the 'Immaculate Heart'. The children were shown a vision of hell, with sinners and their souls on fire. The Lady also prophesised that two of the children would die early, but she had a purpose for Lucia on Earth.

Two separate rays of light came from her hands. One surrounded Lucia, and the other Francisco and Jacinta. True to the prediction, both Francisco and Jacinta died from the Influenza Pandemic which swept Europe.

During the six months of apparitions, witnesses described globes of light in the sky, self-impelled clouds, soundless buzzing noises and flashes of light. In August, a local official kidnapped the children and tried, unsuccessfully, to intimidate them.

On 13th September thousands of witnesses reported that the sky grew dark at noon, stars could be seen, and they saw a luminous globe in the air, like a great jet of light in the sky. It came from the east and descended to tree-top level. There were disintegrating trails of 'rose petals', ('angel hair'?) falling on those below. The object then rose and travelled back across the sky to the east.

Researcher, the late David Barclay, has gone so far as to suggest that on 13th June 1917, the two youngest children were infected with the 'flu by a UFO, and spread it to the crowds. His theory is not totally improbable, given the witnesses' accounts of the visitations, especially on 13th October 1917.

The 'miracle' of 13th October, (which was also a 'solar noon'), has been described as the 'Dancing Sun of Fatima', and was seen over an area of thirty-two miles by twenty miles, although the observatories reported they saw nothing unusual with the sun that day. It was very cloudy and raining, but thousands of people congregated for the promised miracle. Many media representatives, most quite sceptical, also attended.

Suddenly the rain stopped, and *'the clouds were rent apart'*. They could see the 'sun', which looked like *'a silver disc, the colour of stainless steel'*, with a clearly defined edge. Witnesses described it as *'revolving on itself and zigzagging in a circle'*, - *'spinning and stopping, and spinning around again'*. The *'Daily News'* reported that *'The Sun appeared like a dull, silver plate, spinning around in a circular movement as if moved by electricity.'* Dr. Garrett, a University Professor, described a *'disc with a clear-cut rim, luminous and shining, but which did not hurt the eyes. It looked like a glazed circular piece cut from a mother-of-pearl shell.'*

The people all thought it was the sun, and were terrified when it appeared to be coming towards the Earth. The Catholic Church initiated an eight year inquiry in 1922, and eventually pronounced the visitations as being 'worthy of belief'.

There were three secrets imparted to the children:

1. A vivid and horrific description of 'hell'.

2. An accurate prophecy of the start of World War II.
3. A secret prophecy to be given to the Vatican by Lucia. This was to be read and revealed to the world in 1960.

Whilst the Vatican are obviously aware of the contents, in 1967 a spokesman for Pope Paul VI said it was not yet the time to reveal the secret. It was reported that when Pope John XXIII read it, he trembled with fear, and almost fainted in horror.

It was also suggested that just before his mysterious death on the night of 28/29th September 1978, Pope John Paul I was about to release the third message. It may only be coincidental, but there was major UFO activity witnessed on 14/15/16th September, when a strange object was seen hovering over Rome, and a huge UFO was reported traversing the entire length of Italy.

In 1963 a German magazine disclosed what they claimed was the third secret. The Vatican will neither confirm nor deny the following prediction: *'The peace after World War II will only be temporary, and during that time the Earth will shake because of many concussions and convulsions. We will endure many continuous wars which will finally lead to one last great war, near the end of this century. From moment to moment millions of men will perish. Only Faith, Love and Hope can bring reconciliation between people and nations, and save us from war and eternal death.'*

In a much later interview with Monsignor Corrado Balducci, from the Vatican, he is alleged to have confirmed that prediction.

BEAURAING – BELGIUM

From 29th November 1932 to 3rd January 1933, visions of the Virgin Mary were seen at a convent school near the French border. The first witnesses were five children, from two families, who saw a 'shining lady' walking over the bridge. As the sightings of the apparition continued, word spread of the phenomena, and by the time of the final vision over twenty-five thousand people were gathered around the area.

At times the figure seemed to be on a cloud, at other times over a bush. On 3rd January, a 'large ball of fire' struck the base of a tree. The messages the children received were basically to 'be good', and whilst these events were very similar to other 'Marian Apparitions', I am not aware of any predictions.

GARABANDAL

On 18th June 1961, in a small Spanish mountain village, four girls, Mari Mazon, and Conchita, Jacinta and Mari Gonzales, were playing when they heard a sound like thunder. Suddenly a dazzling 'Angel' appeared before them, but said nothing and disappeared. That night, as she was praying, Conchita heard a voice telling her not to be troubled and that 'you will see me again'.

The 'Angel' appeared several times between then and 1st July 1961, when the apparition finally spoke to them. They were to go to Our Lady of Mt Carmel at 6pm the next day, where the Blessed Virgin Mary would appear.

At the appointed time she appeared as promised. There was an angel on either side of her, and what seemed to be a 'large eye' above.

Over the next few months the girls would see hundreds of visions. After receiving 'three internal calls' they would have to return to the sunken lane where the visions began. They would fall to their knees and enter a 'rapture-like trance'. They were insensitive to external simulation, and their body weight seemed to increase during their altered state. Sometimes they would rise up and move, (often over difficult terrain), either collectively or individually, in an apparent state of ecstasy.

The girls also seemed to develop heightened psychic awareness, especially in the art of psychometrics. They were examined by psychologists, who found the children to be quite sane, with no mental aberrations.

Generally the visions were only seen by the young girls, however on one occasion, a young Jesuit priest, Father Luis Maria Andrew, also saw the Blessed Virgin during the girls' ecstasy. He cried out "Miracle!" several times. The next morning he died of unknown causes, which was officially documented as being due to *'an excess of joy'*!

Conchita started receiving messages over a four year period, the last vision occurring on 13th November 1965. The Virgin encouraged mankind to lead much better lives: Dependent upon our response to warnings and miracles, a 'Great Chastisement' will fall upon us, in which two-thirds of the world's population may die. She said we must make atonement and sacrifices – ask for forgiveness – and most of all, mend our ways and do good. Failure to change will bring about great punishment.

There will be both warnings and miracles. In 1961, she foretold a great miracle of hope for all to see. The warning, which will be something seen in the air by everybody, everywhere in the world, will terrify both good and evil people alike. It will only last a short time, but will immediately be transmitted to our souls, with long lasting effects.

In June 1962, the girls received a horrendous vision of the chastisement. Witnesses described the distress and screams of the girls during the experience. Conchita said many of those things would come to pass during her lifetime. She had another message which she could not divulge until eight days before the actual event.

CROSIA - ITALY

On 2nd June 1987, hundreds of people were gathered, and praying, at the local church, following the miraculous weeping of a statue of the Virgin Mary. Two children, a boy and a girl in the congregation, claimed they heard 'voices' and 'messages' in their head to go outside as 'the Virgin was going to show a great sign in the sky'.

Some minutes later everybody saw a UFO in the sky, and it was observed over Crosia for fifteen minutes. The local barber, Pasquale Campana, captured six minutes on his video camera. It shows a circular, luminous shape zig-zagging, and making 'aerodynamically impossible evolutions'.

ZEITOUN APPARITIONS

Zeitoun, a suburb north of Cairo, in Egypt, was host to many sightings of the 'Holy Family' during 1968. On 2nd April, two mechanics, working opposite the Church of St. Mary, noticed a white robed 'nun' on the church's central dome. For the next few months, hundreds of apparitions of Mary, Joseph and Jesus were witnessed by thousands of people of all religious beliefs. The sightings varied from short periods of time to over seven and a half hours on the night of 8th June.

The figures themselves seemed to be composed of light, and many photographs were taken of these occurrences. Their arrival was often accompanied by mysterious lights and glowing clouds in the sky. Also, luminous 'birds' with rigid wings, like 'gliders' would move across the sky, often in formation, then suddenly 'disappear' as if the light had been 'turned off'.

Many worshippers reported that serious medical conditions were instantly cured, and some of these cases were verified by Dr. Shafik Abd El Malik of Ain Shams University.

Plain human greed curtailed what might have been one of the most important paranormal events of the century. Local government officials cleared an area around the site, and started charging admission. The appearances scaled down and ceased in 1971– although miraculous healings are still reported from the Church of St. Mary.

The apparitions were seen by Christians, Moslems and Jews, and all were deeply affected by the 'miracles' to the extent that smouldering hostilities were diffused and possible violent confrontations avoided – a second collateral 'miracle'.

The visions, initially approved by the Coptic Church, were submitted by Roman Catholic Cardinal Stephanos to Pope Paul VI in May 1968. He approved them as a visitation of the 'Mother of God'.

BETHLEHEM

The Marian apparitions have continued. At the end of August 1983, hundreds of Palestinians saw the Virgin Mary, surrounded by light, walking back and forth near a church. This report is most interesting, as it is in the general area where the Dead Sea Scrolls were found, and where Edgar Cayce claimed the Essene Temple, the original 'School of Prophets', was located at the time of Jesus. Nearby are the ruins of the first monastery of Elijah.

Is it merely coincidental that, in latter years, the sightings of the Virgin Mary have moved from traditionally Catholic countries to the multicultural Middle East, where religious differences are so pronounced, and prophesised to trigger the predicted Third World War or Battle of Armageddon?

———————————

Holograms have not only been utilised to promote religious phenomena. They have also appeared during many wars. The following case certainly defies conventional explanation.

Researcher John Schuessler unearthed a letter, held by the Historical Society of Pearisburg, Virginia, which was written by soldier James Peck to his uncle and aunt in 1863, during the height of the American Civil War. Apparently there was something mysterious seen near Lewisburg and at different places in the County. A gentleman and his neighbours all saw a body of mysterious rectangular objects moving vertically through the air, just above the trees, in an adjacent Sugar Orchard.

'The objects were apparently eight foot long, two and a half in width, and one inch thick. They were white, tinged with a little green. They moved directly north in a column of about fifty yards wide, with the order and regularity of soldiers. The rear was nearer the ground than the front, and consequently had to pass through the orchard. In emerging from the trees they resumed their original order and so remained until out of sight.

'Immediately following, but a little further west was seen a vast army of men dressed in white and moving in quick time and in as good order as soldiers on dress parade. After passing any obstacle they would resume their places in ranks. Thus passed the entire column occupying more than an hour, and presenting a scene of awful grandeur and sublimity to all who beheld it.'

James believed in the reliability and sobriety of all the witnesses, and speculated on an optical illusion or vision from God, which seems improbable. However, given the UFOs, which were not compatible with any known technology at the time, I wonder if some form of hologram was utilised?

Rosemary's article continued with further examples of cases containing some unusual phenomena;

'Moving forward in time, the next outstanding case we shall examine is in a scientific rather than religious setting. It brings us to the autumn of 1923. Raymond F. Fowler, (the father of Raymond E. Fowler, noted UFO investigator and author), was working as a Naval Radio Station Operator on the Maine coast. When he arrived for the late shift, a violent storm was raging, and ships were constantly calling in for bearings.

'At about 11pm, a lightning bolt hit the outside cable, grounded through the transmitting key, jumped the air space and landed right inside Raymond's abdomen. Lodging behind the solar plexus, it remained, spinning like a fiery sun.

'In his own words; "I sat in the operator's chair, transfixed. I thought I should be dead. It was pulsating resonantly with my heartbeat in a slow and steady rhythm. When I looked up, there was a soft light that went through the compass station roof, up to what appeared to be a radiant star. I tried to move, but could not move even an eyelid.

"I looked down and saw that the ray went through the floor, deep into the rocks. The peace was beyond description. It seemed neither time nor space existed."

'Suddenly, the light rays expanded about seven feet in all directions. Three flashes of light revealed three majestic looking, smiling men in robes of light. Each wore a three-tiered turban, matching the blue of their robes. The colour of their eyes and hair were difficult to determine due to the brilliant aura around them.

'They did not speak, but Raymond felt their thoughts and his were perfectly attuned, making verbal speech unnecessary, although they did not answer his mental questions.

'At this point the strangest part of the whole experience began; - a ball game, like none other. The figure to the left pointed a finger at the fiery ball in Raymond's interior. With a flash it leapt into his open hand. He held it briefly, and it reduced in size to six inches in diameter. He then tossed it into the open hand of the being in front of Raymond, who reduced it to about four inches. Next it went to the being on Ray's right, who shrank it to two inches. He returned it to the first being on Ray's left, who chucked it right into the copper mesh screening of the station, where it disappeared in a shower of sparks.

'All three then smiled, bowed and disappeared in three flashes of light. Ray found himself quite unharmed, and was feeling privileged as he checked the burned-out transformers and melted insulation that remained all over the operating table.

'Although there were no fellow witnesses to this event, Raymond F. Fowler's personal integrity, evidenced throughout his long life, as well as other factors, point to its reality. It is significant that he was involved in radio at the time, and it was still an infant science, an electrical science. Was the control exercised over the lightning strike a demonstration of the future potential for the conversion of violent raw electrical energy to a harnessed condition?

'Another fascinating element in the occurrence was the great amount of interaction between the three beings and Fowler. They were handling a real lightning ball in real time – they smiled at him twice, were telepathically attuned to his thinking, and bowed him a farewell.'

'Clearly, this event went beyond the typical hologram. The beings responsible were pouring a tremendous amount of their personal, dynamic energy into it. No wonder Fowler felt blessed and privileged. His life had literally been saved by this intervention.'

'Moving on to our next case, the classic encounter of 'Peter and Frances', which was detailed by Cynthia Hind in 'African Encounters'. On 31 May 1974, the couple were making a long late-night dive from Salisbury, Rhodesia, to Durban, South Africa. They soon realised they were being closely followed by a UFO which took control of their car, so that Peter was no longer steering or driving. When they entered Fort Victoria the UFO sped away and Peter, regaining control, stopped for gas at 4.30am.

'After a brief rest they resumed their journey. Not far beyond the city the UFO, with a smaller object, rejoined them. Their vehicle was again engulfed in a light-beam and controlled by the craft above. This time the wheels of their car lifted a bit off the road. Their speed increased to well over one hundred miles per hour, and the surrounding scenery looked strange. They were crossing desert terrain, but what they saw was lush, green wetlands! (Enter their first evidence of a holographic element in the journey.)

'No crickets of locusts could be heard. "It was as though someone had switched the sound off." Peter commented later.

'About 7am, approaching the South African border, the craft departed, and Peter was able to resume driving. Their arrival in Durban was an hour early, and the gas used was proportionately less than expected. Although the car developed some electrical problems, which had to be repaired, there were some compensations.

'Frances began having prophetic dreams, which came true. This sudden development of ESP, or a marked increase if it is already present, occurs to close-encountered people with such frequency that has become accepted as the norm. In Frances, case it was precognition. In time, she may have made other gains. Many experiencers do.

'On the strange journey, Peter had considerable mental communication with the entities operating the UFO. One of them told Peter that he could project an image, appropriate in appearance to Peter's acceptance, and he did just that. Shortly after a humanoid male was suddenly sitting on the car's back seat, and remained there for some time.

'This is an example, among many which could be cited, in which the visiting beings explain to the percipients that certain specific images in the experience are indeed beamed projections. (Is this part of a deliberate educational process?)

'Our final example brings us up to the UFO 'wave' around Fyffe, Alabama, which began in early 1989 and continued through 1990. Events were so varied and unusual – even for UFO activity – that samplings will be touched on, to indicate the background tone and context of the over-all 'wave'.

'In early 1989 the 'wave' had become unmistakable, and initially it was given nation-wide publicity by press, radio and television. Then coverage subsided quite abruptly, and local newspaper editor, Carey Baker, explained why when he spoke at the 1990 Ozark UFO Conference at Eureka Springs, Arkansas: "Witnesses to the strange events were so ridiculed by the media – and worst of all on TV – they learned to keep the continuous sightings and events largely to themselves."

'Carey, who was sympathetic with the feelings of the experiencers, used pseudonyms when speaking of all those who wanted their identities protected. Some key points in his talk are as follows:

'The type of craft most often reported was very large – well over three hundred feet long, silent, somewhat triangular shaped and well lighted. Usually there were red and green lights around the periphery, and two enormous red lights, 'as big as small houses', on the underside. They usually showed up on Friday nights, so gatherings of crowds matched that trend.

'One such bonfire vigil, which Carey attended, was held on 3rd March 1990. Among the crowd of about fifty people, including locals, news reporters and TV crews, were three pairs of eyes looking at the crowd – not the sky! Two of the fellows, known locally, were there just to poke fun at the others. One of them, wearing an ET mask, kept trying to get televised. The third man, 'Phil', was quietly watching the crowd, explaining that he wanted to learn their reaction to the UFO 'wave'.

'Carey, his wife Terri, and their reporter, Susan, became intensely interested in 'Phil's' apparent knowledge, and got acquainted with him on the spot. On later occasions he showed an uncanny ability to predict accurately many events that soon followed. Although no UFO showed up that Friday night, much to the disappointment of about three and a half thousand hopefuls, (three times Fyffe's population), it became a date to remember.

'Among the odd happenings that soon occurred were newspaper personnel becoming invisible in the office, then reappearing within the hour. There were apparent holograms, and an automobile was seemingly run clean through by another car – without harm! A teenage boy began to display precognitive abilities, and a commercial, showing 'greys', was aired, but only once, in one home.

'One evening, in March 1990, a Nashville TV crew and some other people went over to 'Fred Nettle's' house. The locale was a 'hot spot' for UFO sightings. In Carey's own words:

"Nothing happened for a couple of hours, then as they were leaving, out of the south-west sky came a transfer truck – flying! It came in and seemed to land in the woods near 'Fred's' house. They went to investigate. There was no truck and no road! That was rather interesting in itself, but on the same night, over in Louisiana, a couple of ladies reported a transfer truck passing them on the road, and then taking off into the sky."

'At the start of this article I stated that there could well be some answers to at least the holographic content in the UFO scenario. The reason, of course, is that our own science has recently grasped and used the basic principle involved in the creation of holograms. This reveals something of the basic how, but why do visitants employ holograms so often?

'One likely answer is that it enables them to inform us, without risking possible harm to their own persons and craft. Another is that it may have become one small element in a millennia-old program aimed at assisting Earth to climb the 'long ladder of liberation'. Understanding how the Universe works is part of being set free.

'This brings us to a new and broader definition of hologram. According to some pioneering physicists, the whole universe is holographic. One of the amazing characteristics of holograms, as we know them, is that each one, when the plate is cut to pieces, results in each piece being a small replica of the whole. (Although some detail is lost).

'If this new hypothesis is valid, and the whole universe functions holographically, it becomes easier to grasp the truth that everything is interconnected with everything else; and not only space-wise. There are resonances between the non-physical universe and the physical; 'As Above, so Below.'

'This could be the most important answer to why holograms, and the whole UFO presence, are so increasingly prevalent as our world crisis deepens. Psychologist Leo Sprinkle Ph.D., well known for his work with several hundred contacted and abducted persons, over many years, stated this view in a recent paper;

"In my opinion, UFO activity is one aspect of a huge educational program (which) can be called 'Cosmic Consciousness Conditioning'. This program is apparently conducted by representatives of extra-terrestrial and ultra-terrestrial civilisations. These...seem to be highly sophisticated. They can remain invisible to the human eye, and to the dominant Earth culture, except when they choose to arrange an encounter. The purpose seems to be an initiation for the individual, and a stimulus to society, so that human development moves from Planetary persons to Cosmic citizens...

"We can anticipate further UFO reports which confound our view of science and reality... The eventual goal seems to be an integration of planetary forces, and achieving twin tasks: Sufficient knowledge for space/time travel, and sufficient spiritual growth for compassionate interaction with other levels of consciousness."

CHAPTER THREE

FLYING SAUCERS OUR OWN PROTOTYPES?

Any responsible investigator must give serious consideration as to whether the object a witness has reported is, in fact, of earthly origin. In the 21st century, it is near impossible to decipher if an unidentified aerial object is other-worldly, or one of our own clandestine experimental test-flights.

Even if most witnesses have just been seeing our own secret technology, remember it only takes one, just ONE, out of the millions of reports, to be of extra-terrestrial origin, and we are entering a new ball-game which requires our undivided attention!

In 2007, a US Pentagon project called the *'Advanced Aviation Threat Identification Program'* was reportedly established. It was said to be aimed at investigating unexplained aerial phenomena that appeared to be using novel propulsive, hovering or otherwise advanced technologies. Some enthusiasts immediately claimed it was a clandestine UFO investigation, however I think it was merely a new endeavour to determine what new military prototypes less than friendly nations had hidden away in their arsenals.

Following World War II, a lot of the unidentified craft reported were 'cigar' shaped. They may well have been missiles, tested by the emerging world powers in light of the Cold War.

It also cannot be forgotten that by the 1950s we were launching satellites, and a relatively few years later had landed on the Moon. Some say it stands to reason that by then we had the technology to develop more exotic craft, including flying discs. If that were true, why would we bother with the more primitive Space Shuttle and rockets?

In the early days, scientist T. Townsend Brown had been experimenting with anti-gravity, and after the war, the DOD contractors, including Bell Aircraft, General Electric, Glen L. Martin, Sperry Rand and others were working to achieve this. Later, through a series of mergers, Glen L. Martin became the more prominent Martin-Lockheed Company.

How successful were they? We don't know, but in the early 2000s, according to *Jane's Defense Weekly*, Boeing's 'Gravity Research for Advanced Space Propulsion' was still investigating various theories and technologies.

The military and their design and development corporations are very guarded about their latest developments in aerial technology. Private corporations do not have to account to the public or inquisitive politicians. It can be a couple of decades before we discover that what we thought was a UFO was in fact secretive new technology.

Today we know there is a multitude of exotic craft, mostly of earthly origin, in our skies. The military possess all kinds of 'goodies', including the most sophisticated Stealth bombers and fighter planes, Black Hawke Helicopters, Eurofighter Typhoons, and all manner of circular disc-shaped craft. They boast the latest electronics, and formidable weaponry. Given our accelerated scientific advancement, who knows what the 'US Space Force' and other world powers have up their sleeves?

While I do not dispute what witnesses report or have experienced, one has to ask how much was alien, and how much of very human origin? I suspect that many, (certainly not all), of the strange craft, seen over the last century, were in fact experimental prototypes being tested by one or more of our own foremost nations. Often, years later, when reviewing earlier sightings, they can be explained as products of our own secret research and development.

Sometimes, without being really sure, we can assume that perhaps what was observed were our own prototypes. In October 1968, several witnesses in Lakeland, Florida, saw a strange disc, thirteen feet wide and eight feet high, hovering above a palm tree near the house. A few days later, on the 1st November three farmers and the staff of the Philippines Communication Satellite ground station near Manila, reported seeing a white, low-slung saucer-shaped vehicle landing and taking off nearby.

In both the Florida and Philippines cases the occupants, seen inside the transparent dome of these craft, were described as being Caucasian in appearance and wearing white, tight fitting 'flying suits' with glass-like or plastic headgear – more like human engineers of the day than alien visitors!

Ben Rich, who was aerospace Skunk Works director from 1975 to 1991 was once reputed to have said; "Some are ours, some are 'theirs', and some are hand-me-downs!" In 1993, during a lecture to his peers, he stated; "Anything you can imagine, we already know how to do."

He had worked on some of the most exotic and technologically advanced covert new craft, but was unable to say much due to secrecy obligations. During his lecture he commented that we have the capability to travel to the stars and 'take ET home'. The technologies are locked up in black projects, and 'it would take an act of God to ever get them out to benefit humanity'.

Ben Rich pointed out that to travel faster than the speed of light would require something other than chemical propulsion. He admitted that then, in 1993, theoretical physicists were devising new propulsion technologies. Author Tom Keller, who attended the lecture, got the impression they did not fully agree with Einstein's equations. When asked about this, Rich said; "Let me ask you, how does ESP work?"

"All points in time and space are connected?"

"That's how it works!" Rich replied, and promptly left the room.

He died of cancer, approximately three years later. A week before his passing, he made the following comment to Jim Goodall, during a telephone call: "Jim, we have things out in the desert that are fifty years beyond what you could possibly comprehend. If you have seen it on Star Wars or Star Trek, we've been there, done that, or decided it was not worth the effort."

By the late nineteenth century, we had an influx of 'airships' and Count von Zeppelin's airborne devices. After the Hindenberg tragedy, enthusiasm diminished somewhat, but this didn't prevent innovations and improvements to the original concept.

In 1925, the Soviets developed a glider, with a semicircular wing, known as Tscharanowsky's 'Parabola' glider. During the 1930s Swedish skies were haunted with 'ghostfliers' which 'skimmed over the hills' and were piloted by strange figures in hoods and goggles. Was the 'Parabola' responsible? 'Hoods and goggles' are not the usual alien attire!

Russian scientists continued to improve their designs, and in 1992 unveiled the 'Rossiya' – a massive oval-shaped dirigible, a product of 'Project Thermoplane'. In the following years they planned to build a fleet of more than one hundred, all in the shape of a 'flying saucer'! The VTOL craft, often with a rotating axis, are very efficient and cost effective when used to lift and transport large loads, especially to inaccessible locations.

These craft incorporate all the latest technology, and can cover a distance of over five thousand kilometres without refuelling. Many other 'First World' countries have also been developing and patenting new and better hybrid dirigibles, with a variety of incredible shapes. (Some models even have metal covered elliptical hulls.) Many of these could be mistaken for some UFOs, however they cannot account for the speed, aerobatics and other distinguishing features mentioned in many sighting reports.

There is no absolute evidence that these vehicles were actually built, however, on the balance of probabilities, we can assume they probably were. The US Air Force had already acknowledged that it had used heavy-lift balloons to raise unusual air-frames for aerodynamic tests, and in fact, although it is unlikely, attributed the 1947 'Roswell Incident' as being due to a subsequent mishap.

It has been well documented in the past that German scientists, before and during World War II, had been designing 'disc' technology – often referred to as 'flying pancakes'. (I have often wondered about the source of inspiration and knowledge of these gifted scientists.) One German prototype was the Alexander Lippisch designed disc-shaped Messerschmitt AS-6. After the war, Lippisch's work was improved upon to design more advanced jet powered versions, including the circular winged F-6 Skyray jet fighter.

Many plausible claims have been made concerning the Third Reich also back-engineering crashed alien discs, including one from Northern Italy in 1933. (See 'The Alien Gene'). Some years ago, the Italian TV station, Rai Due, interviewed the editors of the magazine 'UFO Notizziario' (UFO Messenger). They claimed that in 1933 Mussolini founded a secret group, headed by G. Marconi, to examine the UFO phenomena. During their studies, from 1933 to 1940, they collected many photographs and documents, one of which mentions some kind of UFO landing near Milano. This explains a strange speech Mussolini made in 1941, suggesting that the USA should worry more about an extraterrestrial attack than the Axis forces.

His thoughts were echoed in October 1955, when the New York Times repeated a comment allegedly made by Douglas MacArthur, in which he said all countries in the world needed to unite – 'to survive and make a common front *against attack by people from other planets. The politics of the future will be cosmic or interplanetary.'*

Another, lesser known case, researched by Polish researcher Robert Lesniakiewicz, involves a UFO which crashed into a field in German occupied Czernica in 1937. The wreckage was immediately seized by SS-troops and taken to Jelenia Gora, where there were uranium deposits and ongoing nuclear research. A year later, several leading German physicists , who later worked on Nazi nuclear research, attended a top secret meeting, presumably in regards to the crashed UFO, which was delivered to an underground facility in 1943.

Besides the Vril, Hannebu and V-7 disc, one prototype, just about ready for mass production, was the Go-229 V3, a jet-powered combat aircraft with stealth capabilities. Another prototype, allegedly only flown once, was the Kugelblitz, which combined the principle of an aircraft with a round symmetrical plane. It had direct gyroscopic stabilisation, employing an ejector-gun using grisou and a gelatinous organic-metallic fuel for total-reaction turbine. It had added remote control vehicle take-off, infrared seeking equipment and static firing systems. To prevent its capture, it was destroyed when allied forces crossed the Rhine.

The Germans had already utilised various 'gases' in their new airborne weapons, and were experimenting with liquid oxygen as a component in new turbine engines. Even before World War I, they were developing the 'porous sinterization of metals' for use in certain aircraft.

Controversial author, Vladimir Terziski, claimed in his book *UFO Secrets of the Third Reich*, that the German Secret Societies had 'alien tutors' who secretly co-operated with certain German scientists in the late 1920s. Terziski suggested that they were far more advanced in anti-gravity and space travel than we realised. He mentions, among other projects, an anti-gravity circular craft, the RFZ-1, constructed in 1942/3.

At the end of the war, there was a race to capture the Nazi's advance military and aeronautical technology, and the Americans, British and Russians were not about to disclose, for good reasons, what they had grabbed.

Sir Roy Fadden, who headed the British Ministry of Aircraft technical mission to Germany in 1945 said; "I have seen enough of their designs and production plans to realise that if they had managed to prolong the war some months longer, we would have been confronted with a set of entirely new and deadly developments in air warfare."

It must be remembered that most of what was captured from Germany were advanced concepts, plans and designs. Many experts believe that very few prototypes were ever actually built, however they had many types of guided missiles in various stages of production and development, and were advancing in magnetic and jet propulsion.

On 3rd September 2003, the 'UK Telegraph' newspaper, which had come into possession of recently declassified government documents, was quite outspoken in regards to the less than admirable means used by the British to virtually force these experts to divulge the German trade secrets and intellectual assets.

They claimed an elite British Army unit, known as the T-Force, tasked with seizing anything of scientific or military value, started their mission immediately after the D-Day landings, and didn't cease this operation until 1947. They collected as much documentation and equipment as possible, first to the UK, and then, in successive phases, some was sent on to Canada and Australia.

Various specialised research teams were established. Whilst there was interest in the original 'fire-balls', some concentrated on 'advanced projects, missiles, and jet and turbine craft', and others on 'thermo-refraction'.

Although some German scientists and technicians volunteered their services, many more were rounded up and transported across the Channel to work in government ministries and private companies. Often their 'targets' were removed by armed personnel in the middle of the night.

These activities were conducted in the British controlled zone of post-war Germany, under the orders of the British Intelligence Objectives Sub-Committee (BIOS) that comprised armed forces and Whitehall representatives, answerable to the government. Also involved was the Field Information Agency (Technical) or FIAT, a joint Anglo-American military intelligence unit that 'earmarked' scientists for 'enforced evacuation' from Berlin and the US and French zones.

Deplorable as this entire government sanctioned activity was, at the end of the war, the biggest 'prize', – snared by the British, Canadians, Americans and Russians - was the advanced Nazi technology and their designers. The Western

Allies were fearful of advanced technology and 'know-how' falling into the hands of the Soviet Union or any other hostile nation, but during the final hours of WWII, the Soviet Army had already raided many of Germany's most advanced weapons research laboratories. The Russian 'Operation Osvakim', had also snared key scientists, equipment and design documents.

The victorious Allies were not just content with military and engineering secrets, they also pillaged all German industrial patents. In 1946, *Harper's Magazine* published an article by Charles Walker, which detailed just how lucrative the cache had been. The US Office of Technical Services was already releasing the commercial discoveries into the public domain, and selling them to any interested parties.

New innovations included an infrared night vision device, electric condensers and communication equipment, synthetic mica, and food and medical research. The plants and laboratories of the company 'Farbenindustrie' were raided, and a wealth of information on liquid and solid fuels, metallurgy, synthetic rubber, textiles, chemicals, plastics, drugs, and dyes was stolen.

Many German scientists willingly relocated to the United States, and enjoyed lucrative employment and conditions there. Were they also involved in producing advanced craft – perhaps reverse engineered? Most possibly.

The Nazis, like many modern super-powers, tended to compartmentalise their scientific aerospace and weapons research, and hide it in diverse, scattered locations, many of which were later occupied by the Soviets. The Allies were quite correct in the assumption that the Russians had also captured some of the advance technology and scientists.

Renato Vesco, was attached to the Italian Air Ministry, and had worked with the Germans at the Fiat Lake Garda secret installation during World War II. In August 1969, he published an article in the *'Argosy'* magazine. He was quite adamant that all the reported unidentified craft were the result of British, Canadian and Australian improvements on the original German technology.

This doesn't explain the American concern about unidentified objects invading their air space. The Air Force commissioned an *'Intelligence Report No. 100-203-79'*, which was dated 10th December 1948, and de-classified in 1985.

It is a very lengthy document, which relies on 'expert and reliable' witnesses to various sightings of unknown craft. Most 'unidentified' reports, classified as 'foreign', come from pilots and air traffic controllers during 1947/8. It is of interest that there was absolutely no mention of any incident at Roswell in 1947, Los Angeles in 1942, or any other purported crashes and retrievals.

Before one jumps to the conclusion that these events never happened, it must be remembered that the Army lost control the same day the US Air Force was founded on September 18th 1947. This happened just a few weeks after a spate of UFO sightings and shortly after 'Roswell'. One of the reasons later given was that there was an 'admin battle' within the Army for control of aviation. One wonders if the Army, miffed at being usurped, divulged any information at all?

The report mentions several suspected Nazi prototypes, plus the doubtful possibility of domestic innovations produced by Britain and a couple of US private companies. Special attention is given to Dr.Geunther Bock, who had been in charge of Germany's flying-wing program at the end of World War II. He was now working with the Soviets, and had given the Russians all the German aerospace and secret craft plans.

I received an edited copy of this report from MUFON's Walt Andrus, and as he noted, whilst there were vague references to an interplanetary origin for the saucers, the main concern was that the German scientists in the USSR had developed and perfected the technology. It was stressed that this was the most probable explanation, and all possible action must be taken to avoid the Soviets gaining technical superiority. The Department of the Air Force were so concerned that in September 1950 they ordered all copies of the report to be destroyed. This was supposedly done in the October, but luckily some copies survived.

Often, with the assistance of these German engineers, the 'Super-Powers' continued the research and development of many projects, including the curved wing craft and 'flying pancakes'. The plans and designs for the craft were classified in 1962, and remained so until 1999 when they were declassified to 'restricted distribution'. *'Popular Mechanics'* obtained copies through a Freedom of Information application.

The RAAF files contained a then 'Secret' memo, dated 28th January 1959, from the Australian Military Mission in Washington USA. Titled 'Flying Saucer

Avrocar', it detailed how the US Army had developed a 'flying saucer'. It described the 'Avrocar' and had photographs of the vehicle attached. It was a 'two man, gas turbine engine circular disc'.

Although the Canadian Minister of Defence announced that the tests of the AVRO were a failure, many people suspected that it was successfully developed in secret. In 1956, Edward Ruppelt , who was involved with 'Project Blue Book', claimed that only two Avro-type discs were in existence. They never strayed 'but a few miles' from Edwards Air Force Base, where they were housed.

It is not known if all projects led to a successful outcome. In 1956, the Aeronautical Systems Division of the US Air Force was devising a typical 'flying saucer' known as Project 1794. It was designed to land vertically, cover a range of over 1,000 nautical miles, and have a top speed of Mach 4. Officially, conventional planes reached Mach 3 in September 1956, and Mach 4 five years later in March 1961.

However, Australian researcher, Debbie Payne, unearthed a May1954 report from Woomera Rocket Range, where a disc was seen and tracked hovering over a Canberra bomber, then flying off at a speed in excess of 3,600 miles per hour, or Mach 5!

The concept of a flying, circular craft was not new. *'Scientific American'* 2000 discussed some earlier designs, one of which was patented by F.A. Jone on June 14, 1898. (No. 605,579) Other patents have been granted in the nineteenth century, but it is unknown if these craft were ever made.

On June 7th 1960, inventor Heinrich Flessner registered US 'Patent no 2,939,648' for a disc-shaped aircraft. It is also very interesting that 'Patent No. GB 1310990' was granted to British Rail in 1970/73 for a classic flying saucer, very much like the ones reported over the previous two decades. Since British Rail has never shown any inclination to expand into the aerospace industry, we can only speculate they that they were acting on behalf of some other government department or agency. (Full details in *'Contact Down Under'*.)

Of special interest is the suggestion that a prototype of a similar craft may have been tested over the Australian Outback in the 1950s. Certainly, at about that time, several reports from the NSW towns of Wilcannia and Broken Hill were of more 'primitive' type saucers, and the military were quick to confiscate all photographs. (See *'Contact Down Under'* pp112/3)

In addition to the reports from Western NSW, more reports came from across the border in South Australia. In August 1957, an employee of the Port Elliott drive-in theatre, near the Murray River, was driving home to Goolwa, when he saw an object on the ground, about half-a-mile away from the sea. It was oval in shape, and about fifteen feet long with lights shining from eight or nine portholes. It took off quite rapidly, climbed at a forty-five degree angle towards Hindmarsh Island, and soon disappeared. Many of these discs, in some ways, resembled the craft photographed by George Adamski and others of that era. I definitely suspect there was a testing range of our own, somewhere in the desert nearby.

Some unusual objects also came down much closer to major cities. During the 1950s George Brown and his mate were in Lambton, on the NSW Central Coast. It was dark. They had left the pub, and were sitting on the park bench having a chat before going home.

Suddenly a huge disc landed on the grass in front of them. Terrified they rushed to the local police station to report a 'flying saucer'. The constable just assumed they were drunk, and at that time didn't even make a report.

The incident became more serious the next morning. Other witnesses came forward and the council gardener claimed someone or something had caused malicious damage to the park. There was a forty metre diameter burnt circle in the middle of the grass. The local newspaper followed up and reported that nothing would grow on the spot for the next eighteen months.

Jacques Vallee reported one incident which could not possibly have been one of our own prototypes. In 1828, during a period of missing people and animals, a cigar-shaped object was seen to land near the NSW town of Wingen, 224 miles north of Sydney.

During the 1950s, there had been rumours that we were on the brink of overcoming gravity. Canadian engineer, Wilbert Smith, had done extensive research on gravity, including the effect of nuclear weapons upon Earth's gravity field. He was also closely involved with 'Project Magnet', and spoke of 'the boys topside', and information from other undisclosed 'channels'.

When all talk of anti-gravity ceased, many experts thought that the research had become classified and gone 'black budget'. Certainly it has been developed to a considerable extent, and by the turn of the 21st century, the Mitre Corporation was hosting an 'International High-Frequency Gravitational Waves Working Group Programme'.

In the March 1991 edition of the *'Australian UFO Bulletin'*, Paul Norman from VUFOR published a very detailed analysis of the 'Magnocraft'. Its author, Polish Dr Jan Pajak, who was attached to the New Zealand University of Otago, was convinced that all the UFO sightings over the previous twenty or more years, were due to the innovation of this amazing craft. Another saucer-shaped object, called 'Silver Bug', was being developed in the USA in 1955, and was the forerunner of more exotic prototypes. The official report on 'Project Silver Bug' was not declassified until 1995.

However, some were not so likely to have come from this planet. On 18th October 1952, Keith Hooper, and other independent witnesses, saw a 'flying saucer' near Adelaide. Astronomer, George Dodwell, who believed these objects came from outer space, calculated the craft's acceleration speed as being 72,000mph.

John Schuessler wrote of another interesting case in 1952 when two twelve meter diameter fiery discs hovered, glided and flew over a Belgian Congo uranium mine. Commander Pierre, from the Elisabethville airfield, set off in pursuit, but his plane could not match the 1,500kph of the silver 'saucers'.

Later investigations by the CIA contained a sketch and construction details of this and similar craft reported around the same time. Their report explained exactly how the objects operated, and claimed that the information came 'from pilots and materials from unnamed secret research installations.' Schuessler commented that 'the technology displayed in this report is far beyond our aerospace technology back in the year 1952.'

On 6th September 1956, a farmer, and other witnesses, in Kaponga, New Zealand, saw one of these early discs as it flew over the countryside. It was about sixty feet long, thirty feet wide, and appeared to have a turret-like glass nose, which bulged out at the front.

In *'Contact Down Under'*, I also discuss another 1956 case from Hughenden in Queensland, where a witness was taken aboard an eighty metre diameter domed saucer, and saw two men at the controls. Were we actually manning these vehicles so early after the war, or had she encountered human-looking aliens?

Following the seizure of wartime technology and scientists from Nazi Germany, much of the covert experimental work was relegated to secret bases and establishments in the remote Canadian areas of Alberta and British Columbia.

The British also had joint military ventures with the Australians, and it would be logical to assume that in any joint projects involving secret craft, they would find the vast outback of Australia an ideal area and quite useful.

The same applies to US covert prototypes and their testing grounds. It is known that several Lockheed U-2A spy-planes were based in Britain at Lakenheath in 1956, and later the Mach 3 + SR-71 Blackbird at the adjoining RAF Mildenhall.

Some scientists had totally 'hair-brained' ideas, which were fortunately not adopted. In 1958, after the Russians had launched their first satellites into space, Professor Freeman Dyson encouraged the US to build a spacecraft powered by nuclear explosions, in particular the hydrogen bomb. Public concern prevented him from ever testing his dangerous theories.

In the 1990s the *'New York Times'* published an article by William Broad. He quoted a CIA study, which noted that in the 1950s and 60s, during the Cold War, the military lied to the American public about the true nature of many UFOs in order to hide its own growing fleet of spy planes. The U-2 and SR-71 were capable of flying between 60,000 to 80,000ft, while commercial airliners only reached altitudes of 30,000ft.

During the 1980s the supersonic F-19A Specter arrived. It was a 'stingray' shape, very quiet and nearly invisible to radar. Rumours persist that the triangular TR-3A was also seen near UK air bases.

For decades the world, especially Europe, had been plagued with reports of large triangular shape planes. The TR-3A is coated in black radar absorbing paint, and certainly fits the description of the near silent craft reported by so many witnesses.

In 1989/90 a plethora of sightings of 'Black Triangles' occurred over Belgium. They were basically all the same size, and carried three strong orange searchlights which lit up the ground below. These craft were relatively soundless and capable of hovering, motionless, and travelling at unusually low speeds, much slower than conventional aircraft. While the Belgium Air Force denied that the American F-117A or B2 bomber was responsible, many sources said that official complaints had been quietly made to the U.S. for invading Belgium airspace with their new plane.

Of course the Americans denied it, and some experts pointed out that experimental craft are expensive. Not many are produced, and the sightings were too numerous for a conventional explanation.

In *'Contact Down Under'*, (Chapter One), I have described some of the new technology and 'aircraft', so I won't repeat myself here. However, information comes out in 'dribs and drabs'. In the 1980/90s, *'Aviation Week and Space Technology'* published several articles about 'secret advanced technology', including talk of a new quiet triangular shape plane, as well as very high speed aircraft.

All of the world's military keep their new toys secret for as long as they can, and often their denials can lead the average person to think they have seen something 'alien'. The US was secretive about remodelling a Boeing 767. Above the plane they attached an 86ft long cupola, with a seven foot door, and a 5.5 ton sensor assembly welded to its top.

The American F-117A plane was first displayed to the media in April 1990. The Air Force had been denying its existence until November 1988, when training requirements expanded into daylight hours. In fact, its first test flight was made in 1981, and the first plane delivered to Tactical Air Command in 1982. It achieved operational capacity by 1983.

It is known that this was followed by an even newer, larger version of the super-cruise Stealth bomber which was kept under wraps for a very long time. Some years ago journalist Bill Rose wrote about the numerous reports of British secret 'one-off' prototypes, including small manned and unmanned HALO, (High Agility, Low Observability), demonstrators to large LTA (Lighter Than Air) triangular vehicles which he thought may be undergoing trials as exotic sensor platforms.

He discussed several valid reasons for keeping the test craft secret, one of which being that the moment you unveil a new piece of military technology, every potential adversary, with the technical resources, will attempt to counteract or duplicate it. He also pointed out that the Pentagon has complete access to the airspace of all its allies, where classified aircraft are regularly deployed to assist USAF bases with test flights and operational missions.

It must be remembered that, after World War II, the Russians also commandeered many of the German scientists and technicians. They have been busy developing new technology and 'flying machines' as well.

As early as 1954, there were mutterings about new Russian technology, as well as US prototypes. In October the Yugoslav Air Force investigated reports from many areas of the country where up to seven flying saucers were seen. The Belgrade Astronomical Observatory saw four of the objects, which travelled to the south-east and returned half an hour later. The Director, Peter Djorkovic, said they were a 'mechanical contrivance , probably some secret weapon of the Americans or Russians'.

In the 1960s there were many excited Russians claiming crashes of alien craft. The Soviet authorities didn't discourage this enthusiasm. In fact they were their own illegal tests of space-to-earth nuclear warheads, which made one circuit of the globe before being diverted back to earth in Russia. These weapons, dubbed a 'fractional orbit bombardment system' by the Pentagon, were a clear breach of an international treaty banning the existence of orbiting nuclear weapons.

In 1994, Russia announced plans to build 'Ekip' an unmanned 'flying saucer'. The London 'Sunday Times', April 24th, published the news, along with a diagram, showing the proposed prototype would, at eighty-two metres long, be longer than a Boeing 747. Weighing in at five ton, it could carry a two-ton load, and reach a speed of 400mph.

NATO was very concerned when they heard about a secret Russian aircraft, known only as the Article 1.44, built by MIG. They were just as worried when the Soviets unveiled their Sukhol S-37 'Berkuf', (nicknamed 'The Golden Eagle'), at the Moscow Air Show. It was a fighter plane with incredible manoeuvrability and fantastic fire-power. It could out-pace most NATO aircraft.

Weighing twenty-five ton, and made from some 'secret' material, its wings were swept forward, and it could withstand the forces incurred during extremely quick turns. Its advanced tracking and radar system could detect an enemy in excess of a sixty mile range.

One colleague advised me of an interesting triangular ATB – the T-4MS/200 proposed in 1970 by the Russian Sukhoi team. Designed to cruise at a speed of Mach 3.5, the plans were apparently never realised – but who knows now, some fifty years further on? Certainly the Soviets and the Chinese have developed national aerospace industries and have just as many prototypes of their own. The Russians have the Sukhoi Su-27 Flanker, with advanced avionics which allow seemingly impossible aerial manoeuvres.

The Lenticular Re-entry Vehicle is another intriguing craft. *'Popular Mechanics',* (November 2000), carried a very interesting article regarding secret US plans to build a Lenticular Re-entry Vehicle which would certainly resemble the unidentified saucers reported by so many thousands of witnesses over the last fifty years. The magazine also detailed how a piece of 'honeycomb' type debris' found at a property south of Brisbane in 1975, was strikingly similar to the design of the cabin wall construction in the LRV engineering study. Laboratory tests and analysis of the debris indicated that it was most likely of earthly origin, and not alien.

In many ways, this information raises as many questions as it answers. Even if, for arguments sake, the LRV was built and flown, would it really account for **all** the reported 'saucer' sightings and encounters? (Personally, I think not! How many prototypes would there be at any one time?) Further, we do not know what percentage of the LRV design and technology was due to unaided human effort and innovation. How much, if any, was the result of alien influence, (direct or indirect), or the mooted 'reverse engineering' of captured craft?

And so the introduction of new and exotic craft continues. How is the humble ufologist, let alone the general public, able to differentiate whether something strange in the sky is alien or one of our own 'new-fangled' prototypes?

The *'Aerospace Daily'* January 23rd 1995, said that, for the past year, McDonnell Douglas engineers had been testing several versions of the 'Diamond', an unmanned craft. The prototypes were not successful, but they resulted in the development of a tailless test aircraft which was successfully trialled at Edwards Air Force Base on several occasions.

In January 1999, *'IEEE Spectrum'* considered the probable future of the aircraft and aerospace industry. While, at the time, Global Hawk and Dark Star were the best of the unmanned air vehicles, studies were already underway for 'bat wing' and 'flying saucer' type unmanned attack aircraft. Undoubtedly some of these concepts have been covertly realised, and are now quietly traversing our skies.

Over the past twenty-five years, aircraft technology has advanced beyond our wildest imagination. In 2013 the US Air Force were gleefully testing the sleek missile-shaped X-51A WaveRider off the Southern Californian coast. The unmanned supersonic aircraft, built by Boeing Phantom Works, had a scramjet engine capable of reaching a speed of Mach 5.1 (five times the speed of sound), at 60,000ft. Their recent robotic space plane, the X-37B is even more sophisticated.

Pilotless craft, from tiny drones to much larger, sophisticated machines, have come into their own for over three decades. Much longer in fact, if you consider satellites and other related technology. It often makes it nigh impossible to differentiate what is ours and what is not.

In the late nineties, the Australian Defence Force announced that, in a lead-up to Defence Exercise 'Crocodile 99', it would be testing a pilotless vertical take-off and landing craft over the Northern Territory. Their new toy, about 1.8m tall with a rotor diameter of four metres, could travel up to 200km from its ground control station. Its flight path could be pre-programmed or remote controlled.

Wing Com. Carrer said there were no other aircraft of its kind in use in Australia at that time. I wonder if that was exactly true. In October 1981, the Department of Defence wrote to investigator John Auchettl, following his questions about the Jindivik Drone.

They advised that during the mid 1970s it conducted operations at Woomera Rocket Range for both National and International projects. At the time of their correspondence, it was stationed at the NSW Jervis Bay Range Facility. It was operated by the Navy for use by the three Australian Armed Services, and was not being deployed or operated anywhere else in Australia. This information was also not entirely correct. Woomera Testing Ground was apparently using the 'Jindivik' as early as 1957.

Years before the Pentagon had unveiled a saucer-shaped pilotless reconnaissance plane, worth ten million dollars, which they claimed could 'detect a basketball on the ground from a height of 13,500 metres, even in poor weather'.

The *'Times'*, a New Zealand provincial newspaper, said that serious experimentation with drones, as electronic counter-surveillance craft, commenced in the 1960s. It has also been reported that at that time, Lockheed Skunk Works had manufactured thirty-eight D21 unmanned drones, and in 1963 they were mated with a mother-ship aircraft for the first time, although the initial flight did not occur until December 1964. This would explain the many reports of smaller objects leaving and returning to a larger craft.

However, there were earlier reports of exactly such an aerial system. In 1958, in the N.S.W. town of Goulburn, a shearer's wife looked out of her window one morning. It was just after daybreak, and was surprised to see what she described as a 'clear shaped object' in the paddock, approximately half a mile away. It was about five hundred feet above the ground, and five or six smaller, silver disc-shaped objects flew up to it and disappeared inside. The larger craft then took off at great speed and disappeared.

We have no way of knowing if this was alien, or one of our own later craft being covertly tested. In *'Contact Down Under'* I have noted several other similar incidents off the east coast of Australia.

'Jane's Weapon Systems', 1976, confirmed drone programs as being interim measures by the USAF until their advanced Multi Mission RPV, still in its planning stage, became the 1980s likely system.

'EEE Spectrum', in January 1999, discussed the military and security agencies 'wish list' being considered by DARPA and various corporations. One concept was for a micro air vehicle (MAV) carrying a miniaturized video camera. The 'powers-to-be' also sought an insect-size device, which could fly in the sky and perch on walls as an eavesdropping 'bug'.

The Sanders corporation won a contract for the fixed-wing MicroStar. It weighs 85g, and is small, with a front propeller and a 15cm wing span. It has excellent computational skill and economy, and can fly independently with a 5km range and a twenty minute flight time to a target located on a digital map.

Now we have thousands of military, commercial and privately owned 'drones', of all shapes and sizes buzzing about over our heads. They serve a multitude of purposes, from espionage, border protection, and police and emergency services surveillance. Farmers and mining companies have found them invaluable, as have movie producers and delivery services. No wonder people have been seeing 'lights in the sky'!

Another important consideration is the multitude of satellites mankind has launched. They orbit the Earth, and often come crashing down when their time is spent. Space junk is responsible for many UFO sightings.

In 1979, when forty metre long, ninety tonne Skylab landed in the Australian desert, it caused a bit of a scare amongst the general public. The *'Sun'* newspaper published an attention-grabbing article on 4th July 1979. In it, they claimed that since the space race began in earnest, 'over eleven thousand objects had been flung into space in one form or another. About six thousand had come back down to earth, usually vaporising on the way, but at least nine had landed in Australia – six in N.S.W.'

Of the remaining five thousand, it was assumed many were decaying debris – 'space junk.' The article pointed out that in the twenty-one years since Russia launched Sputnik I, more than two thousand satellites had been successfully launched into space. Most were in earth orbit, and some may remain there for hundreds of years. Another ninety were sent into space, to the Moon or beyond.

Peter Tylosley, who wrote the article, noted that neither the Americans nor Russians publicised their military satellites, which were in addition to the numbers he quoted, and finalised by quoting one Australian scientist; 'If the real number of satellites circling the earth was known, there would be a public outcry.'

That was forty years ago. Since then, many more countries have launched their own satellites. By the 1980s there were also nuclear powered satellites. Officials, who knew in advance when they were due to re-enter the earth's atmosphere, were told to avoid media interest by merely classifying them as 'probable space debris or a meteorite.' The mind boggles when considering how many artificial objects may be orbiting our planet now!

At the beginning of the last century dirigibles were making a more regular appearance, and our intrepid pilots were getting our first planes into the sky. Our progress has been phenomenal. Many theorise that we have had help, perhaps by reverse engineering crashed saucers, or maybe from the aliens themselves.

In 2008, researcher Dr. Michael Salla posted an interesting article on his website. I must stress that I cannot say whether this information is accurate or not.

He wrote about Clark McClelland, a retired NASA Spacecraft Operator, who spent thirty-four years involved with numerous NASA missions, including Mercury spaceflights, Apollo missions, and the International Space Station and Space Shuttle.

Dr. Salla claims that McClelland has made a testimony that whilst on duty, he observed, on his video monitor, an alien spacecraft in a safe, stabilised orbit to the rear of the Space Shuttle's main engine pods. A nine feet tall ET was standing upright in the Space Shuttle's Payload Bay and having a discussion with two 'tethered' US NASA astronauts. McClelland also claimed a colleague told him that on another occasion an eight to nine feet tall ET was seen inside the Space Shuttle Crew Compartment.

All major countries are consistently seeking to improve the technology of their aircraft, and designs and experimental vehicles are kept secret as long as possible. It is not only exotic craft which have been covertly developed. There is also the matter of the new weaponry which these craft possess.

One disturbing account comes from fighter pilot and author, Luis Font. In 1953, a highly qualified aviator 'Steinbeck' was summoned to an unnamed air base near Los Vegas to test a one-of-kind interceptor fighter prototype which was armed with an atomic cannon.

He took to the sky, with an unidentified German 'technician' following his progress from the control tower. Witnesses suddenly saw the 'foreign expert's' face blanch as he stared at the radar screen. He immediately ordered the pilot to land, as there were unidentified machines to the prototype's right.

They were closing in at incredible speed, and instead of turning back, Steinbeck fired his advanced weapon at them. Horrified witnesses at the base saw the prototype crash, at high speed, into the desert two-and-a-half miles away.

This was not the only case of strange craft with 'beam' type weapons. Pierre Perry, president of Arizona's Copper Mountain Mining Corp. told of a disturbing incident which happened ten years earlier in the summer of 1943. He was travelling, on horseback, to a remote site north of Prescott. As they were crossing the Agua Fria River, the lead horseman called out; "El Diablo – El Diablo," (the devil.)

Overhead they could see a military plane approaching two stationary large, round bright unidentifiable objects. As the plane neared, the objects moved forward and projected a violent, luminous ray, which Pierre likened to an energy beam. It hit the plane, and as it plummeted to the ground, the two pilots ejected. As they parachuted to safety, another beam hit their parachutes, and they fell to their deaths.

A third UFO joined the other two, and they all sped towards the Mexican border at incredible speed. Soon military vehicles arrived, and Pierre and his two companions guided them to where they had seen the plane crash. There were parts scattered all over the mountainside, and the lead horseman, a Mexican, said he had seen the same thing 'many times before'. Were these deadly beams extraterrestrial – or did they have a more earthly origin?

Tesla was not the only scientist experimenting with deadly beam warfare. Britain had her own 'boffin' – H. Grindell Matthews. Born in Gloucestershire in 1880, Matthews was apprenticed to a firm of electrical engineers, and later served in the Boer War. He went on to be a consultant engineer, where he could indulge his passion in developing his 'aerophone', experiments for adding sound to film, and 'aerial minefields.'

Of particular interest are his experiments with the technologies which UFOs seem to possess. He worked on devices to stop aeroplanes mid-flight by an electric charge, and had already proven he could stop motor cars with internal combustion engines. He invented a mystery beam, which could be used to control pilotless craft, and designed a rocket aeroplane which he claimed would travel at three hundred and sixty miles per minute.

He was certainly involved with experiments for the British Government during World War I, and as a result, was given a twenty-five thousand pound award, which was a lot of money in those days! In the 1920s he experimented with radio waves for defence weapons, and between 1920 and 1935 he registered five patents.

He went to America where he found lucrative work for Warner Bros. in the sound production of films. In 1934, sensing the danger from Nazi Germany, he returned to Britain, and set up his own experimental facility at Mynydd-y-Gwair, a mountain top in Wales, between Swansea and Ammanford.

He had been working on an early type laser beam, and was not very happy at being dubbed 'Death-Ray Matthews'. On 22nd September 1934, he told the *'Western Mail'* newspaper that his work was of 'such great importance to the nation that they cannot be given publicity at the moment." For the next five years he received clandestine visits from European envoys, seeking his advice on how to hold Hitler at bay. He declined a rewarding offer from the French government, remaining loyal to Britain.

In August 1941, when he was planning to move back to the United States, to continue his work, he suffered a heart attack, and died the following month. It was claimed that he destroyed all his plans, diagrams and paperwork during the last few days of his life. I wonder??

British researchers have suggested that Matthews work was very valuable to the British Government, and in 1973 a spokesman for the Ministry of Defence said that if he did top-secret work during the war, it would probably still be classified.

CHAPTER FOUR

UP THERE IN THE SKY

PART ONE – THE EARLY YEARS

There is a growing body of evidence from experienced pilots, air traffic controllers and radar operators as to the existence of UFOs. Declassified government documents reveal that they make reports on a daily basis. Misidentification...? maybe some are...but even the most hardened sceptics would have to agree that these people are the most expert and well-informed witnesses available. They, unlike the general public, are more qualified and aware of whether a strange craft may be the product of our own new technology.

A 1952 FBI memorandum stated that according to Commander Randall Boyd of US Air Intelligence, pilot sightings, especially those that are corroborated by radar records or ground visuals, are 'the most credible reports and are difficult to explain.'

Why then do pilots remain totally silent and non-committal when asked about unidentified phenomena? Pilots spoke of being interrogated, sometimes all night long, 'treated like incompetents, and then instructed to keep quiet'.

One friend, a commercial pilot, told me that if they discuss UFO sightings, it is most certainly going to damage their careers and promotion prospects. Although they would not necessarily lose their jobs, when it came time to renew their medical and endorsement qualifications, necessary for their licences, it would be made extremely 'difficult'. This is why reports are often made once the pilot has retired, decades after the event.

In the early post-war days, the US made it very risky for pilots and air crew to say anything. During the various official 'Committees' and 'Reports', the US Air Force issued *Regulation 200-2* in August 1953. It stated that it was forbidden to release UFO information to the public from Air Force Base Level. A little later, another instruction further added that Air Force, military and sometimes even commercial pilots, releasing UFO Information, would be charged under JANAP-16 which stated that to discuss UFO reports publicly would be 'a serious crime, punishable with fines up to $10,000 and imprisonment for up to ten years'.

Pilots were so annoyed at being accused of hallucinating, or 'having one drink too many', that in 1959 airline pilots held a meeting in Dayton, Ohio and issued the following statement; *'We report cases such as these, and when we land, we are interviewed for hours. We are tired, and want to get home to our families. We are threatened not to make statements, and told that the thing that paced our aircraft for fifteen minutes was a mirage or bolt of lightning....nuts to this 'big brother' attitude, who needs it.'*

Whilst the military have always ensured that their personnel do not publicly admit to UFO sightings, information continues to flood in from the civil aviation sector. We still hear of reports from passengers and crew of many local and international flights. I suspect we only know about relatively few of these airborne encounters with unidentified objects.

One of the people we interviewed, while researching *'The Gosford Files',* lived on Mangrove Mountain, where there is an aircraft beacon. He claimed to be 'an official weather spotter'. He, his son and friends had seen UFOs on several occasions, and had a theory that the objects are attracted by blue metal/basalt deposits.

He regularly monitored VHS 128 Radio frequency which, in those days, was apparently used by Sydney and Brisbane approach aircraft. One Saturday, in mid-July 1996, he was demonstrating radio reception to a friend. They heard a pilot approaching Sydney airport talk of an object in front and to the right, pacing his plane.

Traffic Control asked if any of the passengers had noticed it. When the pilot said the cabin crew had not mentioned it to him, Traffic Control advised him not to bring it to their attention.

My own father was a flight-engineer, who flew many SAS missions over Europe during World War II, and while he, along with many other airmen, confirmed seeing the notorious 'Foo Fighters' during that time, he never elaborated on any details. Later reports indicated that the allies thought they were a German secret weapon. It appears that the Germans were just as mystified, concluding that they were some new American invention.

After the war, it was suggested that these annoying and often feared objects, were the top secret anti-radar 'Feuerball', produced by an experimental centre at Oberammagau in Bavaria. Even if this was correct, not all of them were fast moving balls of light. It didn't explain all sightings during the conflict.

In his book *'Strange Company'*, Keith Chester writes of an incident in June 1942, when Lt. Roman Sabinski and the crew of his Wellington bomber were returning from a night-time bombing mission over Germany. They had left the coast of Holland, and were returning to base when a round, copper-coloured object, about the size of the full moon, approached from behind.

His gunners opened fire, and directly hit the craft. The tracer rounds seemed to be absorbed by the object, as there was no sign of them exiting the other side. The intruder pulled away, and climbed upwards at phenomenal speed.

In 1942 there were many other instances of strange craft and objects over war zones. On 26th February, the crew of the vessel, the 'Tromp', on the Timor Sea, near New Guinea, were scanning the sky for enemy aircraft. A Dutch sailor, William Methort, later told researcher Peter Norris that he and the others on the bridge saw a large illuminated disc approaching at speed.

It was about four to five thousand feet above them, and for the next three or four hours it flew in circles before suddenly, with an unbelievable burst of speed, veered off and disappeared out of view.

In November, the crew of a Lancaster bomber over Turin, Italy, reported an object travelling at approximately five-hundred miles per hour. It was two to three hundred feet in length, with four pairs of red lights spaced equally along the length of its body.

Jacques Vallee, who had been an engineer with US Intelligence in Germany, claimed that by 1943 the Allies were already aware that these 'foo-fighters' had a possible electrostatic effect, and were capable of interfering with internal-combustion engines.

'Flying Saucer Review' and the *'New BUFORA Journal'* 2003 – published an in-depth investigation by Alan Hilton into an incident experienced during a Bomber Command operation over Essen in Germany on 26/27 May 1943. They were at about nineteen thousand feet, and ready to make their final 'run-in', when they saw an object, much bigger than their own plane, in front of them and slightly to the port side.

It was long and cylindrical, silvery-gold in colour, with what appeared to be portholes evenly spaced along the side, and possibly a second row underneath. It was very sharply defined, hanging at about a forty-five degree angle in the sky. Within about twenty to thirty seconds, it suddenly began moving, and climbed away, accelerating rapidly to an incredible speed, until it vanished from sight.

The entire crew witnessed this strange craft, and were amazed at its speed, which they calculated to be thousands of miles per hour. When they returned to base, they reported the incident during debriefing, but didn't know how much importance it was given by their senior officers.

Most of the 'foo-fighters', sighted during the latter years of World War II, were the small fiery-type objects – but not all. In August 1944, a Lancaster bomber (one of the largest planes in existence at the time) was returning from a mission over southern France, when it encountered a disc shaped UFO which dwarfed their aircraft many times over.

The radio operator, Ron Claridge, said that all eight members of the crew saw the enormous disc about three thousand feet away from their plane. It had circular lights, rather like portholes on a ship, and was bright yellow changing to intense white. It was there for about three minutes before it silently accelerated away and out of view.

When they arrived back at base, they were all interviewed, told not to say anything to anyone else, and not to record it in their log books.

Whilst most wartime reports were made during 'sorties', close to enemy aircraft bases and landing fields, the following incident occurred far away from the main arena of World War II hostilities.

Researcher Bill Chalker wrote of a case which occurred in February 1944. At 2.30am, a Beaufort bomber was flying at about 4,500ft above Bass Strait. The plane was travelling at 235mph when a 'dark shadow' appeared alongside, and kept pace at a distance of only some 100 to 150ft. Only about fifteen feet of the rear end of the object was visible to the crew, who could see a flickering light and flame belching out from the end.

All radio and direction finding instruments ceased functioning during the twenty minutes the craft paced the bomber. It finally sped away, and the pilot said its speed was three times that of his own plane.

Not all sightings were made from the air. In mid-July, 1945, about six weeks before the Japanese surrender, Rolan Powell was stationed at the Pasco Naval Air Station, where new pilots were trained for future missions. There were also experienced airmen on standby to protect the secretive Hanford Plant sixty miles away. This crucial facility produced plutonium for atom bombs.

At about noon an alarm sounded. Radar had detected a fast moving object which was now in a holding pattern above the plant. Everyone could see a saucer-like object, which was very bright, very high and extremely fast. Six F6F Hellcats were sent up, but couldn't get close enough to the object, which was above their 37,000ft ceiling. They estimated its altitude as being about 65,000 ft, and described it as being oval shaped, pinkish in colour, and the size of three aircraft carriers side-by-side. It hovered for a further twenty minutes before going straight up and disappearing as quickly as it came.

Many of the upper echelons of the world's military were beginning to realise that we were not alone in the universe. At the conclusion of World War II, General Douglas MacArthur made a very cryptic statement; "The next major war will be an interplanetary one!"

Reports were made by respected pilots long before World War II. In 1917, during World War 1, former German Air Force pilot Peter Waitznik said he and the famous fighter pilot, the 'Red Baron', were flying in their Fokker tri-planes over western Belgium early one spring morning. They saw a 'thing' in the sky, which Peter said resembled the flying saucers reported in later decades.

It was about forty metres in diameter, and had undulating orange lights. Thinking it was a new American craft, the 'Baron' shot it down, and it fell to the ground, shearing off tree branches as it crashed into the woods.

Waitznik said; "Two little bald headed guys, probably battered and bruised, then got out and ran into the woods. When we arrived back at headquarters, we were told never to mention it again."

In April 1929, Edward Pline took a photograph of a 'large, round thing, as big as a very large boulder', which moved through the air above the Ward Sawmill in West Colarado, USA. It made a 'terrible, thunderous bellow', and the ground shuddered. His daughter, who was only six at the time, did not take much interest, but many years after his death, she realised the object resembled a traditional flying saucer and passed the photo on to researchers.

In 1965 the *'Australian Flying Saucer Review'* published an interview with former Air Marshall Sir George Jones. He mentioned an incident in 1930, when he was a Squadron Leader, and was sent to Warnambool to investigate a formation of 'aircraft' seen flying over the coast.

"I went there but could not establish what they were. They were not aircraft belonging to us and, as far as I could find out, they were not aircraft belonging to any other powers. The possibility that they might have been a formation of swans or other birds was always there, but the thing was left open – I could not establish what it was."

He also mentioned seeing a brilliant white light, below a shadowy shape in 1957. It was at 1,500ft, and moved silently, in a purposeful way at about 400mph. He had no other witnesses, and said nothing at the time.

Only a year after the Warnambool incident, in 1931, while flying across the nearby Tasman Sea, on the first solo flight from Australia to New Zealand, (Sir) Francis Chichester saw strange flashing lights, one of which approached his aircraft.

In the 1940s there was the famous case of pilot Kenneth Arnold sighting UFOs. Others were more sinister. Thomas Mantell was killed during a mid-air pursuit of an unidentified craft, and in 1948/49 there was a purported 'heat-ray' attack on an American fighter jet over Walesville, N.Y. State. The pilot ejected safely, but the plane crashed into a house below, killing five people.

Donald Keyhoe, author of *'Flying Saucers from Outer Space'*, investigated many of these incidents. All the sightings prior to and during the early 1950s are important. If the Allies had seconded advanced German technology, or the rumours of a crashed Roswell disc being back-engineered were correct, would the resultant craft have appeared this early? Even if there were a few prototypes, they would not have been as large as the unidentified craft being reported. Neither would they have matched their altitude and speed.

Two incidents demonstrate this contention. The first occurred in the late 1940s over White Sands Guided Missile Base. One large disc was tracked travelling at 18,000mph **56 miles** above the Earth. Another two smaller discs were tracked by five observation posts, and seen to pace a high altitude rocket. After circling it for a moment, the discs speeded up and rapidly out-climbed the Army projectile.

Again, in late February 1950, witnesses at Key West, Florida, saw two glowing saucers, and Naval radar screens tracked two objects **50 miles** above the Earth.

An elderly man recounted a strange event which happened many years before in 1946. A professor and over thirty students were on an educational expedition, in the Carpathanian Mountains in Czechoslovakia, when they saw a yellow dish-shaped pulsating object just over a kilometre away. They could see 'things' walking around it before it shot off into the sky and disappeared. Thinking it may be some new Russian military experiment, they decided not to say anything.

'Flying Saucer Review' received an interesting report from a former member of the RAF, who had waited for the expiry of any 'secrets' embargo, and now felt it was time to speak out.

In August 1949, he participated in 'Operation Bulldog', which was an exercise designed to test British radar and defence capabilities. The witness, who didn't give his own name, identified all the other officers who were on duty that particular day at the RAF Sandwich Radar ACI in Kent.

They, and other radar stations, tracked an enormous object, which was over the English Channel before turning northwards towards the Thames Estuary. It was at an altitude of fifty thousand feet, travelling at 3,000mph, with a calculated size of close to twenty thousand tons, and an echo similar to a large passenger or freighter ship. When it approached Bampton Radar Station it suddenly increased speed and headed upwards. It vanished from their screens after it reached an altitude of one hundred thousand feet.

In those days there were no known aircraft of that size, or capable of such speed. They were all summoned to a meeting with the Commanding Officer, who reminded them of the Official Secrets Act. They were to forget about the occurrence, and not mention it to anyone outside of the RAF.

The servicemen and officers on duty had meticulously recorded every detail, but the following evening they noticed that the incomplete Duty Watch Book had disappeared, and had been replaced with a brand new one.

Other, less publicised encounters were also taking place in the early 1950s. One instance involved a Qantas Super Constellation flight out of Karachi. An unusual cigar-shaped object paced the plane for approximately forty-five minutes. It was travelling alongside – within one hundred feet – and was seen by all the crew and passengers, some of whom were taking photographs. This object also rapidly flew away. The pilot, who is now retired, did not publicise the event, was later promoted to senior positions in the aviation industry.

At 8.25pm on 27th April 1950, a Trans World Airlines DC3 – Flight 117 – was cruising over Indiana at an altitude of two thousand feet. Both pilots and all the passengers saw a strange red disc, fifty feet in diameter, both below and then behind the plane. It was a spherical shape, and moved swiftly as it climbed, overtook the plane, and 'closed in'.

At that stage it resembled a 'blob' of hot metal, which glowed brightly on top. It paced the plane for a while, then dived away at about 400mph before speeding off. The 'glow' seemed to dim as it slowed, and grow as it increased speed.

Major Gordon Cooper, later a Mariner Capsule astronaut, was flying a F-86 Sabre-jet over Western Germany in 1951, when he sighted some metallic, saucer-shaped discs. They were at a considerable altitude, and could out-manoeuvre all American fighter planes. He later admitted that in 1951, during two days of observation, he saw many flights of UFOs. They were of different sizes, and flying in fighter formation, generally from east to west over Europe.

He and his crew submitted a report, and months later the hierarchy replied, saying they were 'probably high flying seed pods', which to Cooper, 'didn't seem very logical.'

Donald Slayton, later a Mercury astronaut, was flying over Minneapolis, testing a P-51 fighter in 1951. He said in an interview that he was at about ten thousand feet on a bright, sunny afternoon when he saw an object he first took to be a kite or maybe a balloon. When he got closer he realised it looked like a saucer – a disc, which quickly moved away.

1952 was a memorable year, and it can be said that, whoever was controlling these unidentified craft was certainly trying to get our attention. It was the year when George Adamski met with the humanoid 'Orthon' in the desert, and several other incidents also stand out in 'UFO History'.

In April, two US Naval planes, en-route to Hawaii, were carrying Admiral Arthur Radford and the Secretary of the Navy, Dan Kimball. Two discs, moving at fantastic speeds, first buzzed one plane and then the second, which was fifty miles behind, before speeding away. The entire incident was filmed by a Navy aviation photographer.

A dispute later arose as to the handling of the investigations. It was while the Navy and the Air Force were in hot disagreement that the CIA moved in to take control of U.S. investigations

At 9.12pm, on 14th July 1952, two Pan-American DC-4 pilots were flying at eight thousand feet near the Naval Base and Air Station at Norfolk Virginia. Suddenly six, one hundred feet diameter, disc-like 'machines', in an 'echelon' formation, flew about two thousand feet under their plane.

They glowed a brilliant orange, like red hot metal, which dimmed when they flipped on edge to make a 150 degree course change and shot away. A few seconds later, two more discs followed.

Less than a week later, on 20th July, an alarming situation occurred over Washington in the U.S.A. These events were confirmed by multiple reports from airline and Air Force pilots, control tower operators, and tracked simultaneously on radarscopes at Washington National Airport and Andrews Air Force Base.

At 12.40am seven 'craft' appeared in the sky and 'separated'. Two were over the White House, one near the Capitol Building, and some near the Air Force Base. They were alternatively described as 'huge fiery orange spheres' – 'five huge discs' and also as 'a large white light'. At first their speed was estimated at only being about 130mph, but then they accelerated at terrific speed and streaked off, making manoeuvres and turns that would be impossible for our conventional machines.

They circled Washington for about two hours until the arrival of F-94 interceptors, when they flew away at speeds up to 7,000mph. As soon as the jets had returned to base, the objects came back and didn't leave until dawn.

There were many more disturbing incidents occurring in the USA in July/August 1952.

On 23rd July, a saucer showing a bluish-green light was picked up on radar over Boston, but when a F94 was sent to investigate, the disc swiftly outdistanced the plane. Three days later, another formation of discs was detected high over Washington. They were tracked on radar, and seen visually from the ground and by airline pilots. Air Force jets gave chase at over 600mph, but the saucers were much faster, and sped away.

Just before 11am, on the morning of 1st August, a thirty feet, round, glowing saucer with a shiny metallic gleam, appeared to be observing the Wright Patterson Field. As in the previous cases, it was tracked on radar and seen by civilians and Air Force pilots. The object was at an altitude of thirty thousand feet, but when two F86 jets were sent to intercept, it climbed and sped away.

Across the Atlantic, only two days earlier, in Britain, RAF pilot Ronald Hughes was returning to base after a training mission over West Germany. He reported seeing a flash of silver light, which rapidly descended towards his Havilland Vampire plane. As it came closer he could see a 'gleaming, silver metallic disc'. It was about one hundred feet in diameter, smooth and seamless, with a highly reflective surface. The strange craft flew alongside of him before disappearing at incredible speed. It was captured on RAF radars, and confirmed at travelling at speeds far greater than any current aircraft.

   Hughes was later summoned by Ducan Sandys, the Aviation Minister, to personally recount the event. Sandys found the report and radar evidence 'convincing'. He referred the incident to Lord Cherwell, the government's chief scientist, who had tended to be very sceptical.

The USA and Europe weren't the only ones to receive a 'visit'. On 5th August, the officers at the control tower at Japan's Oneida Air Force Base, viewed and tracked a dark coloured saucer with a glowing white light in front and a smaller one underneath. It slowly approached the tower, hovered nearby, then suddenly turned away and accelerated at high speed. Radar returns indicated it then divided into three parts, which raced off 'keeping accurate intervals.'

On the afternoon of 21st November 1952, Flt. Lt. Michael Swiney, and his student pilot Royal Navy Lt. David Crofts, took off, in a Meteor jet, from Little Rissington, Gloucestershire for a cross-country training flight. As they punched through a layer of cloud, at around fifteen thousand feet, they were astounded to find three white objects in front of them. They were circular and stationary, and looked like the traditional 'flying saucers' which had been reported in previous years.

When Swiney climbed to thirty-five thousand feet and levelled out, the objects still remained visible. He looked carefully, and noted that there were no discernible signs of propulsion, portholes, turrets or other tale-tale evidence that may have identified them as conventional aircraft viewed at an unusual angle. He decided to advise Traffic Control and return back to base.

Traffic Control had different ideas, and told Swiney to approach the UFOs. He followed instructions, and turned his aircraft, at full power, towards them. As he closed in, one disc turned on its side, and climbed away, out of sight, 'at great speed'.

Meanwhile, authorities at Fighter Command had been advised. It was the height of the Cold War, and since other ground radars had detected the unidentified craft, two more Meteors were immediately sent up, but didn't make contact.

One of the radar operators later commented; "They had entered our airspace going at a fantastic speed, approximately three thousand miles per hour. We had nothing that went that fast, and neither had the Russians nor the Americans."

When the airmen got back to base, they were interrogated for a couple of days, and the episode designated as 'unexplained.' Michael Swiney later rose to the rank of Air Commodore before his retirement from a long career in the RAF. When he was in his seventies, he spoke to British researchers D. David Clarke and Andy Roberts, who conducted an excellent in-depth investigation of the incident.

It was also in 1952 when ANA Captain Bob Jackson was flying into Mascot Airport, Sydney, at about 11pm one night. When he was over the Woronora Dam area he saw a flash of light, and watched as an object, with an orange light at the tail, shot past towards the coast near Wollongong. Mascot Air Control advised there were no other planes in the vicinity or on radar. Two minutes later he saw the object again. This time it made a complete circle around his plane, and then sped back towards the coast at terrific speed. On 5th January

1954, the 'Melbourne Sun' quoted Captain Jackson as saying the experience was 'nerve-wrecking'. He, like many other senior pilots, had not made an official report at the time, for fear of ridicule.

The pilot, crew and passengers of a British Comet jet-liner were not so fortunate on 2nd May 1953. It was dark and rainy when they took off from Calcutta's Dum Dum Airport, and six minutes later collided with an unidentified object. The shattered remains were strewn across five square miles.

No distress call had been received by the control tower, and after careful examination of all the wreckage, the Air Ministry reported that the plane had been hit by an unidentified flying body.

I suspect that, by this time, the authorities were well and truly 'spooked'. In Australia, it seemed everybody, internally and overseas, were 'sticking their noses' into investigations. It started on 16th April 1952, when during a flight of Dept. of Civil Aviation aircraft Drover VH-DHA, a portion of the propeller flew off, damaging the fuselage and two engines. The Captain was injured, and he asked passenger, Tom Drury, to take over. Drury had been a RAAF pilot during World War II, and he was able regain control of the plane, which he successfully ditched in the sea.

This incident brought him some acclaim, and many years later, during interviews, reporters and investigators asked what had been deduced from some photographs he had taken the following year.

On August 23rd 1953, while in Papua-New Guinea, Drury was standing with his family on the coast road, overlooking the Flying Boat Base at Port Moresby. He filmed a silver object, 'a long cylindrical-shaped pointed thing', which came silently out of a cloud, and climbed very fast, leaving a vapour trail behind. A silver 'dart' had come from one corner of the object, and shot away at phenomenal speed.

The next morning he handed the undeveloped film over to ASIO. He eventually got a 'print' of his movie back, with a substantial amount missing. Australian researcher Bill Chalker conducted an in-depth investigation of this incident, and discovered the film had gone to the RAAF, the USA and the British RAF. In fact, several years later, some Australian ufologists had seen prints of Drury's footage, which he himself had never been given.

It was soon established that the projectile did not originate from Woomera Rocket Range. It is still not known if the object was in fact extraterrestrial, or some earthly missile technology of unknown origin. Chalker's pursuit of the facts uncovered just how interested and concerned the authorities were in 1953.

Countries from all around the world were receiving reports of strange inexplicable aerial objects. Even by 1954, it is extremely unlikely we had developed such numbers of advanced craft, even from captured Nazi technology or crashed alien saucers.

The Commander of the Norwegian Air Force, and multiple members of the Astronomical Society, saw two enormous silver/metallic rotating saucers swoop across the sky. They were also photographed from the window of a plane travelling between Oslo and Stavanger.

On 9th January 1954, the Australian 'Melbourne Age' quoted a high ranking RAAF officer as saying that, during the previous months, there was an increase in UFO reports coming from aircraft in flight.

Two days later, on 11th January 1954, the 'Adelaide Advertiser' carried the following headlines on its front page; 'Plane Crew Sees Sky Object'. Capt. Booth, the pilot of an ANA airliner, had left Broken Hill for Adelaide at 6.25pm the previous evening. His First Officer Furness and the rest of the crew also observed the strange phenomena, on and off, from 7.40pm, when they were flying at eight thousand feet, about fifteen miles north of Morgan.

At first Capt. Booth thought it was a north-bound plane, due to pass at that time, but the strange object seemed to move back and forth across their line of flight, as if circling. They thought it was another aircraft...due to the manoeuvres... perhaps the RAAF, but Parafield control room advised that there were no other aircraft in the area. Although it was dead ahead of them, they never caught up with it.

They watched for ten minutes until it became too dark to see the object. Several times it disappeared into the haze and cloud layer while it was circling. Probably mindful of their careers, both men said it must have been an 'optical illusion of some sort'. Furness couldn't explain how it occurred, and Capt. Booth commented that he had been flying for fourteen years, and had never seen a similar sight before.

The island of Madagascar also experienced strange visitors in August 1954. Edmond Champagnac, head of Air France's Technical Services, was with a group of people in the city of Tananarive when a luminous green ball was seen in the sky. At first it was descending, and when it disappeared behind a hill, they thought it was a meteorite.

Suddenly that, or a second identical object, appeared over the hills, and flew horizontally at a slower speed. It curved past the government buildings, and descended to rooftop height. It headed along the eastern side of a major avenue, and drew level with the witnesses, who realised that it was actually two objects.

The lead object was shaped like a 'lentil' and had the colour of 'electric green luminous gas.' One hundred feet behind was a cylindrical metallic object about 130ft long. The surface reflected the rays of the setting sun, and behind it was a plume of orange-red flames. Its speed was estimated to be about 185mph.

The two 'craft' continued in unison to silently fly over the city, only swinging to the west when nearing the airport. The electric lights in the buildings momentarily went out as the objects passed over. Before they disappeared from view they skimmed over the zoo. Although the animals were not normally disturbed by planes from the airport, this time they went into a frenzy and stampeded. Some broke through the fences, and it took several hours for the police and soldiers to round them up.

An inquiry was set up by General Fleurquin of the Madagascar Air Force, and headed by Father Coze, who was the director of the Tananarive Observatory, and had witnessed the UFOs himself. There were thousands of witnesses, but no-one seems to know what happened to his report.

Another well documented Australian encounter (detailed in my book *'Contact Down Under'*) is that of Lt. J. O'Farrell on the night of 31st August 1954, when he was flying a Sea Fury aircraft over southern NSW. The two objects were not only sighted by the pilot, but were also tracked by radar at the Royal Australian Navy Air Station at Nowra. After pacing the plane for some time, the objects took off at an incredible speed. It was unlikely that there were even any secret experimental craft this advanced in 1954.

Late in 1954, radar at British RAF Bawdsey tracked an unidentified craft intruding into the exercise they were conducting. The Meteor NF11s, sent to intercept, reported sighting the 'saucer-shape' object which was too fast for them. The next morning everyone was ordered on parade, where the Commanding Officer told them that the Official Secrets Act applied to the events of the previous night.

Despite a security clamp-down, it didn't take long for the media and nosey journalists to get wind of many of these incidents. On 22nd May 1955, Dorothy Killigen, a well known New York journalist, reported from London that a British official – 'of Cabinet rank' – had told her that the wreckage of a 'mysterious flying ship' was examined by British scientists and airmen, and all indications were that it had been crewed by 'small men, probably under four feet tall'. They were convinced that it was a flying saucer from another planet. The story was later 'hushed up', after Killigen suddenly died. British researcher Gordon Creighton suspected that her informant had been Lord Mountbatten.

In the late 1990s, British researcher, Graham Birdsall, was contacted by Francis Parker, who had been a Senior Air Craftsman with the RAF in 1955. On 20th March that year, as he had flown into Karachi, Pakistan, he and several others on the plane had noticed an orange/bronze coloured 'ball' suspended some distance away in the sky.

Francis and his military colleagues could still see the 'disc-like' object when they disembarked and boarded their bus to take them into town. They were astounded when, after a while, the bus came to a halt, its path blocked by thousands of people kneeling in prayer on the ground.

Everyone was looking up at a huge 'flying saucer', hovering about 125ft above the ground. It was at least 150ft across and 75ft high, metallic bronze coloured metal, with a large black hole on the underside. On the top was a translucent dome, with red, green and blue flashing lights around the outside, and inside a pinkish-red light.

The servicemen watched as the craft made 'whooshing sounds', and every so often, swung from side to side and discharged hot air downwards. Francis thought whoever was behind the controls was experiencing some kind of engine problems. After an hour, his friends were tired, and left to get a meal and a drink. It was not safe to stay there alone, and Francis followed them. Later the strange craft and worshipping crowds had all disappeared.

Major Donald Keyhoe investigated this report in 1959. The incident had happened three years earlier in 1956, when Commander George Benton and Lieutenant Graham Bethune were flying a Navy R7V-2 Super-Constellation transport plane across the Atlantic from Iceland to Newfoundland. Their aircrew passengers were asleep in the cabin.

They were cruising at 19,000 feet, when a huge disc-shaped machine rushed up from below, tilted and angled past their port wing. It then drew abreast, and paced their plane at a distance of about one hundred yards. Some of the passengers crowded into the cockpit, and they all witnessed the amazing metallic craft, which was at least thirty feet thick and four hundred feet in diameter. It looked like 'a gigantic dish inverted on top of another.'

After the UFO pulled ahead, and then quickly accelerated away, Benton contacted Gander Airport, who advised their radar had also registered the huge object. When they landed at Gander, Air Force intelligence officers interrogated and debriefed everybody, and later, when they reached their final destination, they each had to complete a written report.

It seemed the authorities never doubted what they had seen, but could anything so immense be one of our own prototypes in 1956? Six days later Benton met with a scientist from a 'high government agency', who showed him several photographs. Benton pointed to one which was identical to the disc they had encountered.

"Somebody must know the answers," he said, "if you've got photographs of the things."

The scientist locked the photographs back into his dispatch case. "I'm sorry, Commander," he said, and left.

It wasn't just the Americans and Canadians who were seeing unidentifiable craft in the Arctic. If the Americans and their allies were suspecting the Russians were responsible for these advanced craft, the Soviet Union thought exactly the same about their Cold War adversaries.

Soviet pilot V. Akkuchatov was the chief navigator for the Soviet Air Base at the North Pole. In 1956, one of their planes was flying over a strategic ice area near Greenland, when a large disc, resembling a lens with a pulsating edge, closed in from the port side and flew parallel to the plane.

Thinking it was American, the Russian pilot flew back into the clouds for forty minutes, only to find the disc still there. He ventured closer, and the UFO also altered course, and later shot off at tremendous speed to a higher altitude and accelerated out of view.

On 13/14th August 1956, at East Anglia's Lakenheath Airbase in Britain, USAF and RAF army radar detected over twelve white lights darting across the sky at incredible speeds of up to 4,000mph. They covered a distance of more than fifty miles, sometimes in formation, and executing sharp turns. One object was tracked for twenty-six miles before hovering for five minutes then flying away again.

Two RAF Venom fighters gave chase, and when one obtained a radar gunlock on the target, it circled the fighter's tail, and remained there despite all attempts to shake it off. Another aircraft captain and co-pilot reported seeing an object 'tail-chasing' a fighter plane. When the fighters landed to refuel, the UFO headed north, and ground staff reported seeing one or more white rapidly moving objects.

It was officially 'unidentified' and the following observation made; - 'The apparently rational behaviour of the object suggests a mechanical device of unknown origin'. The same night Bentwater Radar Station made three observations at 10pm, about the same time as the Lakenheath incident. They said one object raced across the screen at over 15,000km per hour. Next fifteen objects, led by three more in triangular formation, moved north-east at 160km per hour, followed soon after by another UFO travelling west at 20,000km per hour.

A cable sent from US Air Force Headquarters in Washington warned of their 'considerable interest and concern' at the sightings, and demanded an immediate inquiry. The cable asked if they were linked to a similar scare reported by a British radar station, a week later, on the Danish island of Bornholm in the Baltic Sea.

Researcher David Clark, in collaboration with Graham Birdsall, considered that the incident was treated so seriously by the military that it sparked a Cold War security scare. Apparently, the Lakenheath Base played host to the new super-sensitive American U-2 spy planes, and also provided storage facilities for atomic bombs!

Clark said; "I am a UFO sceptic, but this incident has me baffled. It is just possible that some form of Soviet spy craft was responsible, but difficult to match any of their planes to what was observed at that time."

On 4th April 1957, Wing Commander Walter Whitworth was the Commanding Officer at RAF West Freugh. Five objects were detected on radar at both Balscalloch and Stranraer. They were very real, and gave an echo similar to a ship, rather than a plane. Four were in a line, while the other hovered at fifty thousand feet before ascending to sixty-seven thousand feet within a minute, then quickly descending to fifteen thousand feet, with a trajectory containing a forty-five degree turn and moving off.

Whitworth said at the speed the object was going, no plane could turn that fast. He had copies of letters and newspaper articles from the time, but when he tried to get further details in 1971, the MOD said they had no records prior to 1962.

Dr. Irena Scott wrote about another occurrence in the late spring of 1957, when an unidentified craft hovered over the Ellsworth Air Force Base in South Dakota. It looked like a traditional 'saucer' – silver/metallic in colour, with a dome and portholes on top. Planes and pilots were scrambled, and the object seemed to be 'playing cat and mouse with them'. It would hover until the planes got close, then take off at incredible speed.

A crash was heard, and later, although everyone was told not to discuss the incident, one of the pilots said a plane had gone missing, and the wreckage never found.

Another incident, on 3rd May 1957, does beg the question as to whether or not we had developed our own 'flying saucer' prototype. An object, described as an inverted plate, with a dome on top, hovered close to the practise range at Edwards Air Force Base in the USA. It was a luminous golden colour, with portholes or panels around the dome. Many witnesses took photographs, which were all confiscated by 'Intelligence'.

CHAPTER FIVE

UP THERE IN THE SKY

PART TWO – THE 1960s ONWARDS

By the time 1960 rolled around, identifying UFOs became increasingly difficult. Our own technology was much more sophisticated. We had developed missiles and satellites, and by 1969 would land men on the Moon. Gone were the days when researchers could enthusiastically declare it was most probably 'alien'. They had to examine each sighting and ask themselves if the upsurge in reports was due to our own technology and prototypes, or a growing interest and concern by extraterrestrials?

In 1962 the US were conducting very high altitude flights in the X-15. On 11th May, Pilot Joseph Walker claimed that one of his tasks was to detect UFOs. He was over fifty-five miles above the Earth, and during that time filmed five or six UFOs. During a later conference he declined to speculate on the objects.

A couple of months later, on 17th July, Major Robert White reached an altitude of fifty-eight miles, and spotted an object which was greyish in colour and thirty to forty feet away. He had no idea what it was and exclaimed over the radio; "There are things out there! There absolutely is!"

By 1960, and the height of the Cold War, military bases were established in Alaska and the remote Arctic wilderness. The indigenous Eskimos already had myths and legends about visitors from the skies. They spoke of the 'tinmiukpuk', or 'thunderbird', an enormous eagle which would, with a sound like thunder, come from the sky.

Another story was of a ball of fire, like the moon, coming down, and a large creature, resembling a skeleton, arriving at the village and killing most of the inhabitants. Apparently, some of the 'Visitors' were more benign, seducing some of the women and producing children said to be conceived from the 'moon spirit'. Eskimos who chose to visit the 'Sky Land' were called 'pavungnartut', which may correspond to our definition of a contactee.

Many reports were being lodged by the scattered bases, however some suspiciously resembled rocket type vehicles coming from Siberia. Others were not so easy to dismiss.

On May 27th 1962, the Air Force was unable to explain two apparently controlled UFOs which manoeuvred above Palmer, Alaska. At the end of August 1965, a large disc hovered above Hyder for over eight hours. It then zoomed away in the late evening. On 15th November 1967, an airport weather observer at Fort Simpson in northern Canada, reported an object, with radical speed variations, making right angle turns.

Colin Phillip, (ex-president of UFOR.QLD), investigated a case which happened over Bouganville Reef, just off Queensland, at 3.25am on 28th May 1963. The pilot, co-pilot and stewardess on a charter flight from Brisbane to Port Moresby, reported to Townsville Ground Control that they were being 'buzzed by a flying saucer'. They described the object, which paced the plane for ten minutes, as being a 'round ball with exhaust gases coming from it'. They also advised they had taken photos of the object.

When they arrived in New Guinea the pilot was told not to get the photographs developed. As soon as they returned to Australia he was met in Brisbane, and the film and flight tapes were flown to Canberra. The crew and DCA officials were told they would lose their jobs if they ever discussed the matter.

In his book, *'The Jarrold Listings'*, Phillip Frola has published copies of several contradictory official letters received in response to various enquiries by researchers at the time. While there was an official denial of the incident, confidential testimonies received tend to confirm the sighting and surrounding circumstances.

'The Journal of Alternative Realities' Vol.5 Issue1 1997, published an intriguing article by Wendy Wolfe. The witness had only come forward some thirty-two years later.

Samuel David, an officer in the US Navy, served in the Investigation Section of the Military Police. In 1965 he was sent to report upon an amazing incident which occurred in Florida.

A delta-shaped UFO had been reported by the military, pilots, Naval Radar and civilian witnesses. A military aircraft had been deployed to intercept the object, but in full view of many witnesses it was struck by a beam from the UFO and disappeared.

Two more planes took up positions at the rear of the UFO, but when they fired their ammunition exploded before reaching their target. One of these two aircraft was destroyed, but it was not known if it was due to another beam from the intruder, or their own ammunition deflecting back on them.

The remaining pilot was given permission to return to base, where he was detained and questioned for three weeks, and not allowed to speak to anyone else. Samuel David was instructed to confiscate the cameras and photographs of all civilian witnesses, and swear them to secrecy. Everything he took was handed over to a higher authority.

Samuel was responsible for writing an official report – he said it was the size of a 'telephone directory' – but his superiors were not happy, and instructed him to change it to 'something more acceptable'. He refused and as a consequence lost his position, and was transferred to serving as a seaman on the USS English.

On 16th July 1965, just before 11am, staff at Canberra's Airport Control Tower saw a mysterious glowing object hovering in the sky. It was there for nearly forty minutes. They described it as being a shiny white 'spot' at an altitude of about five thousand feet in the north-east. Several pilots confirmed the sighting, and other people at the airport also saw the object. Several witnesses called Mt. Stromlo Observatory, who could offer no conventional explanation. One officer described it as a circular light, and the meteorologist said it looked like a steel disc revolving in the sunlight.

Reports at the time stated that the RAAF sent a plane to identify the object, but it accelerated away before the aircraft could reach it. It was later suggested that it may have been more than a coincidence that the craft was near Tidbinbilla Space Tracking Station at the time 'Mariner-4' was transmitting reports on Mars. The signals had been 'jammed' at the time of the sighting, and returned to normal when the UFO flew away.

After the air traffic controller had retired, he confirmed the incident, and also that the object definitely appeared to be some type of revolving disc.

The following year, 1966, brought a flood of official reports. It wasn't until 1996, thirty years later, that 'T.L.' contacted us about an incident which occurred at 7pm on 16th April 1966. He was a commercial airline pilot, flying a DC3 VH-EDC (Qantas owned for Fiji Airways). They were tracking from Lauthala Bay and climbing, in gathering cloud, to their safety height of over six thousand feet.

'T.L.' said; "On breaking into visual flight, and approximately thirty nautical miles east of Nandi Airport, we observed an intensely bright white light followed by three amber lights in perfect 'Vic Three' formation about a quarter of a nautical mile behind.

"We immediately called Nandi Tower and requested traffic information. We were told 'nil' traffic but they were also all watching them. (At that time Nandi Tower was still not equipped with radar). Both of us in the cockpit flashed our landing lights. At the same time we extinguished the cabin lights, and called up the purser to also see the 'phenomena'.

"The lights first appeared from the south-west, south of the setting sun. They were four separate objects flying at approximately nine hundred knots, and an altitude of fifteen thousand feet. The Tower said they made no noise, and were probably a rocket or meteorite!

"From our perspective, in the cockpit, they were completely under control, and flew from the south-west to the north-east. When they entered a cloud bank over Vanua Levu Island, significantly the cloud 'swirled' around each object, and the 'Vic' of three orange lights banked in perfect formation whilst still maintaining constant altitude.

"We carried out a normal approach, landing in the gathering dusk, and the next morning the *'Fiji Times'* newspaper reported over two hundred credited observers at the airport had confirmed the sighting.

"An old colleague of mine, currently in charge of Qantas Flight Simulators, Capt. 'J.M.', then second officer on a B707, en-route via Nandi, was on the tarmac at the time, and smoking a cigarette on the aircraft steps. He confirmed there was no noise associated with the over-flight, which was directly above the airport reference point.

"There was a reported French Aircraft Carrier in Noumea Harbour, however it would have been impossible for their aircraft to have flown to Nandi and reached supersonic speed without noise and reporting their positions."

A month later, several unidentified craft were seen around Victoria, Australia. Were they prototypes from a nearby testing ground?

On 1st May, a steady, circular object was seen glinting in the sun near Whittlesea airport. On 8th May, witnesses reported a silver coloured elliptical object with a dark core. They watched for ten minutes as it descended from eight thousand to four and a half thousand feet before being lost from view behind a cloud. Three weeks later it was seen again, but had disappeared by the time an observer took off in an aircraft to investigate.

On 5th May at 7.45am the air traffic controller at Tullamarine Airport in Melbourne, followed an unidentified radar target, with good echo-signal strength. It travelled at approximately eighty-five kilometres for twenty-nine minutes. On the same day the crew of the HMAS Anzac, despite no radar contact being reported, saw four closely grouped objects leaving trails of colour.

On 14th May an Ansett pilot saw lights ahead and below his plane. He was flying south of Wonthaggi in Victoria, and described three objects in an approximate 'V' formation. At first he thought he was overtaking them, but then they seemed to draw ahead of the plane. After about ten minutes he appeared to be overtaking them again, and realised there were two smaller objects in formation with a larger one, which looked like a large jet aircraft with swept back wings. He had been flying at some speed, and observing for fifteen minutes, but this experienced pilot later told the RAAF that what he had seen were in fact 'large metal buildings just south of Dandenong'!

In the British summer of 1967, Captain Graham Sheppard and his crew were cruising along the main flight path from Scotland to London. It was a routine commercial flight, with good visibility, when the received an unexpected warning message from Preston Radar Control; "You have fast-moving, opposite direction traffic in the airway."

Captain Sheppard and his two co-pilots looked out to see a thirty-foot wide disc-shaped craft race into view, and speed within metres of their plane.

Graham Shepherd and his crew had also witnessed another incident in March 1967, when there was a ten minute aerobatic display by two unidentified objects over the Bay of Biscay. In 1993, Graham appeared on a TV program, where he described the incidents. As a result, he was summoned to the British Airways Public Relations office, and told that they would not tolerate 'any talk of UFOs'. He received a formal letter, banning him from any contact with the media.

Eighteen months later he took early retirement and became a freelance pilot. He estimated that about ten percent of commercial and military pilots have had some sort of experience, but are afraid to speak out.

Australian researcher, Keith Basterfield, wrote an excellent review of a case which occurred on 22nd August 1968. Two pilots, Walter Gardin and Gordon Smith, were flying an empty Piper Navajo charter plane from Adelaide to Perth. At 09.40GMT (5.40pm WA) Walter, who was at the controls, woke Gordon, who was asleep in the cabin, and asked him to come to the cockpit to see a 'formation of aircraft'. There was one large craft in the middle, and four or five smaller ones to the right, left and above it.

The Navajo was 130nm east of Kalgoorlie, cruising at 8,000ft, airspeed 190km and tracking 270 degrees magnetic. Gordon said; "These aircraft appeared to be maintaining station with us."

They contacted Kalgoorlie D.C.A. communications centre, and were told neither they nor the RAAF had any traffic in the area. For the next ten minutes they lost communications with Kalgoorlie - just harsh static on all frequencies.

During that time the larger 'ship' maintained the same altitude, but split into two then rejoined, in a sort of cycle. The smaller craft, actually about six in all, stayed at the same level but kept flying left and right, in and out, and then 'formatting' with the two halves of the larger object. There movements were not consistent with normal aircraft, and they did not turn like normal planes.

Gordon said; "The shape of the main ship seemed to have the ability to change, not dramatically, but change from say, spherical to a slightly elongated form, with the colour always remaining dark grey to black. The smaller craft had a constant cigar shape, and were of a very dark colour."

Walter and Gordon said the whole formation maintained the same distance and bearing from their aircraft during the whole sighting. They could not accurately estimate the size of the larger object, except to compare it to a Boeing 707 from about ten miles.

At 09.50GMT (5.50pm WA) the whole formation joined together, 'as if at a single command', then departed at tremendous speed. Within three or four seconds they had diminished in size until out of sight. The Navajo's radio communications were immediately restored, leaving two flabbergasted pilots.

They discussed the matter, and after dismissing all conventional explanations, reached the conclusion that 'the UFOs were in fact aircraft, with the solidarity of aircraft, except perhaps for the fact of the larger UFO's ability to split and change shape slightly'.

This incident occurred near Zanthus, a locality on the East-West transcontinental railway line. Twenty-one years later, on 9th September 1989, trains traversing this route towards, and including Zanthus, also experienced strange UFO sightings. (See *'Contact Down Under'* pp151/2)

On 18th October 1968, an Air Force Hercules aircraft took off from Darwin, and the crew saw a series of white lights they assumed to be from another plane. It did not appear to have any visible fuselage, structure or navigation or anti-collision beacons. Their radar indicated a target at fifteen miles range, travelling at two hundred knots, and at least the size of their own plane.

The unknown craft crossed in front of the Hercules' path, at an estimated altitude of about 2,500ft. Ground radar was not operating at the time, and whilst no unauthorised aircraft were reported in the area, the official report stated that 'a possible violation of our national airspace cannot be discounted'.

Another airline pilot told of an incident which occurred on 24th July 1969. It was just after sunset when, in clear weather conditions, he was flying from Mt. Magnet to Perth, and had been given permission to pass through Pearce Military Control Zone.

About six miles north-east of Pearce they noticed what appeared to be an aircraft taking off from RAAF Pearce. The co-pilot remarked that it was unusual for a civil aircraft to receive clearance for this route when Air Force activity was in progress. They watched as it climbed, and drew closer. Concerned that normal separation standards could not be maintained, they asked the Perth ATC controller as to the 'aircraft's' intentions, only to be told that there was no known traffic in the vicinity.

They were looking at a bright light, similar to an aircraft landing light, with several smaller yellow lights, which resembled cabin lights. They changed frequency to the radar controller and enquired as to traffic on radar, and received the same response that there was no known traffic. When the pilot disputed this he was backed up by another pilot who was flying from Lancelin Island to Perth, and could also see the UFO.

The object was so close, they took precautionary action and quickly turned to the right, intending to pass behind it. As they turned, they flicked their landing lights. The object accelerated with incredible rapidity and in less than five seconds disappeared from sight. The next day newspapers reported accounts of ground sightings from places as widely separated as Perth and Albany. Again, the pilot waited several years before reporting the event to VUFORS in 1978.

By the 1970s, the highly experienced older pilots, who had gained their skills 'by the seat of their pants' during wartime, were still flying. The aviation industry had grown and expanded, and they had been joined by a new generation of young, well trained aviators.

On 28th March 1980, the 'Mirror' newspaper published an interesting article detailing a fatal encounter between an RAAF fighter plane and a UFO.

A retired RAAF technician, who was on duty at Laverton Air Force Base, in the early 1970s, got a message from a transport plane, flying at normal altitude. The pilot reported seeing a cigar-shaped object travelling at the same altitude and speed as his own plane. As Laverton confirmed the object on radar, the pilot radioed that a second object was on his left.

Radar readings then confirmed that several 'cigars' were clustering around the transport plane. The pilot was immediately given permission to land at Laverton, and a fighter plane was sent up to reconnoitre.

The 'Mirror' quoted the technician; "The fighter pilot radioed that the cigars were matching his greater speed. Then the objects moved really close to him, and he started to 'get the breeze up'. He told us he would break from his course and return to base, because he was getting nervous.

"Then suddenly the fighter and the cigars disappeared from the radar screen. My friend later confirmed to me that he had been in the radar room all the time, and viewed the entire event. The plane was reported missing, and its wreckage was found a day or so later.

"What staggered everybody was where it was found – more than four hundred miles from where it could have flown, even if it had been fully refuelled. The pilot's body was never found."

The *'Mirror'* did 'due diligence', and obtained supporting testimony from another ex-RAAF officer who was at the base when this happened.

George Fawcett, a well known US researcher, sent UFOIC, (of which I was a member) an interesting account from 12th September 1972. The sheriff and deputies, at Miami and Palm Beach Florida, reported a large number of domed objects, with small portholes, and red exhaust trails, manoeuvring overhead. One of the craft appeared to be cigar-shaped, and another was described as a 'glowing circular object'.

The UFOs were seen through binoculars, and tracked on three separate radar screens located at Palm Beach, Miami Control Centre and Homestead Air Force Base. They were also confirmed by Eastern Airline Pilots, control tower operators and FAA authorities. Jets and helicopters were sent up in pursuit, but it is not known, and extremely unlikely, if they were able to capture any of the intruders.

On the night of November 30th 1973, Riccardo Marano, the pilot of a Piper Navajo plane was preparing to land at Caselle Airport in Turin, when he received word from ATC that there was a UFO at a height of four thousand feet above the runway, very close to the spot where he was due to land. They had the object on their radar screens, and it was heading in the direction of Susa Valley.

They authorised him to check it out and see if it could be identified, but as he approached it, the 'object' disappeared from their radar screens. Another aircraft informed Marano that the UFO was now behind him, at an altitude of about twelve thousand feet. By then Navajo had climbed to about ten thousand feet, so Marano turned and looked at what seemed to be a bright, white luminous sphere, which was emitting lights of every colour. It pulsated from bright to dim, but never went out completely.

Marano described it as 'flying in a most irregular fashion, making fantastic lateral deviations and sudden vast jumps to and fro'. When the object was below him Marano sped up to over four hundred kilometres an hour, but could not keep up with the craft, which disappeared into the south-east at an estimated speed of about nine hundred kilometres per hour.

Two other pilots also confirmed the sighting. Comandante Tranquillo had just taken off in his Alitalia DC9, and advised the Control Tower that he would not dare approach the 'shining object giving out flashes', and quickly changed his course.

Comandante Mezzalani was landing his Alitalia DC9 from Paris, and saw the UFO as he was touching down. He described it as large and bright, yet dimmer than a star or satellite. A third reliable witness was Colonel Rustichelli, Commander of the neighbouring Caselle Military Airfield. He observed the object on his radar screen, and described it as being solid, with a similar size return as a DC9.

This incident may have soon been forgotten, but it came to the attention of French radio reporter, Jean-Claude Bourret, who was solely responsible for interviewing the then French Minister of Defence, Robert Galley, on the air about the UFO phenomenon. During the interview Galley freely admitted to the existence of UFOs and revealed that the French Government had set up a secret section devoted to studying the topic.

On 19th September 1976, two fighter pilots found their weapons to be useless against unknown intruders. An enormous UFO had been seen visually, and tracked by radar, north of Tehran, Iran. Two F4 jets were sent up, and the first found his instruments jammed when he was about to fire. The second pilot was ready to 'shoot' when a small craft dropped from the UFO and apparently disabled their weapons systems.

Researcher and author, John Pinkney, wrote about another case which occurred at 9.10pm on 4th November 1976. The pilot, who worked for a major airline, told Pinkney that he was fifty miles south of Brisbane when he, along with his first officer and flight engineer, saw a 'cherry-red' object flying at between eight to ten thousand feet.

At first they thought it was a plane with a 're-heater' after-burner, but when it began zig-zagging vertically up and down, they knew it was not a conventional aircraft. They contacted the Department of Transport in Brisbane, who had nothing on radar, and there were no other planes nearby. However, the Coolangatta tower had also reported the object.

The plane crew were more fascinated than frightened. For the next twenty minutes the red object zig-zagged and paced the plane before accelerating and taking off at a speed 'beyond belief'. (The pilot estimated approximately 4,000mph.)

When the crew landed, they were given the standard, confidential form used for all personnel who have seen UFOs. The RAAF mounted a full-scale investigation, and cautioned them all to remain silent about the event. They complied at the time, because they knew of other pilots who had been intimidated into secrecy for fear of losing their jobs.

Issue 109 of New Zealand's SATCU group's *'XENOLOG'* (March/April 1977), featured an article by J. Brill, USA, which detailed a close encounter by a Columbian pilot and crew on 21st January 1977.

The Avianca Airline plane had just left Eldorado Airport, Bogota, and climbed to an altitude of twenty thousand feet. About 9pm Captain Gustavo Ferreira spotted an extremely bright white light about twenty miles away. The object, which was alternatively stationary then moving, seemed to be following a zigzag path of flight.

Whilst there were no reports of any air traffic in that direction, radar operator Jorge Jiminez could see the object clearly on his screen. According to the radar signal the mysterious craft was three times the size of a conventional plane, and travelling at an incredible speed. (Much faster than the Avianca or any other jet.)

The sky was clear, and by this time the five crew members were all in the cabin watching the unusual phenomenon. The pilot turned on his landing lights to indicate his position. Suddenly, the light changed its colour to red. Captain

Ferreira turned his lights on again, and the object responded with green lights. After three minutes the object moved away to the south at a dizzying speed and an angle of ninety degrees.

Another interesting case occurred in about 1977. The details only became available some years later, and the pilot 'Trevor' (a pseudonym) did not wish to make any public comment at that time.

Trevor was a pilot for British Caledonian Airways, and was taking a 747 cargo plane from London to South America. Just off the coast of Africa, Trevor and the other four crew members noticed an enormous object on their radar screen. It appeared to be on the same altitude as the 747 and directly on their flight path. They couldn't believe the size the screen was displaying. They contacted Algiers for verification, and were told that Algiers' radar didn't extend that far. They were given permission to alter course, but Algiers noted that there shouldn't be anything else in that airspace.

As they approached the area, Trevor and the crew were dumbfounded to see an unbelievable object which corresponded to the readings on the radar screen. It was silver in colour, with no windows, and hovering like an airborne fortress. As it came closer it moved around to the side, enough to give the 747 room to pass. Trevor claimed it was like something out of 'Science Fiction'. It seemed to have doors along the side, as if it might have been some form of cargo vessel.

It remained stationary, and did not interfere or communicate with their plane as they flew along the full length – at least **twenty miles**. The crew maintained a stunned silence during the entire encounter. After they had passed the object, the pilot followed Standard Operations Procedures, which entailed opening a small safe box, and handing report forms to the witnesses. Once the reports were completed they were locked back into the box, and the crew instructed to say nothing about what they had seen.

As soon as they landed back in Britain, the crew and locked safe were escorted back to a RAF Base, or similar government establishment. They said they were treated well, but virtually 'imprisoned' none-the-less. The witnesses were separated, and then questioned individually. Each was told they had seen a 'weather balloon', and would have to 'sign this' before they could leave. After three days they wanted to 'get out' and complied with the request.

If the crew's estimate of the size of this object is correct, it is extremely unlikely it originated on Earth. One can only speculate as to its resemblance to the reported 'mother-ships', and it was conveniently over the ocean, out of range of our ground-based radar systems.

On 21st October 1978, Frederick Valentich was flying a single-engine Cessna-182 across the Bass Strait from Melbourne to King Island. In a series of messages to Melbourne Flight Service he advised an unidentifiable object – "not an aircraft" – was hovering above him. Following the transmission of a 'large metallic sound' the radio went dead and neither Valentich nor his aircraft have ever been found,

Just a few weeks later another well documented case occurred in the early hours of 31st December 1978, off the east coast of New Zealand, between Wellington and Christchurch. An Argosy freight aircraft, carrying a television crew, witnessed and filmed a number of bright objects which were also tracked on radar. The film was subjected to scientific analysis by some of the world's leading experts. They concluded that the light sources 'could not be explained by any known means', which was a direct contradiction of official attempts to explain the incident away as some kind of misidentification or natural phenomena.

One of the witnesses on board the aircraft, TV journalist Quentin Fogarty, later wrote the book *'Let's Hope They're Friendly'*. (I have discussed these last two events in more detail in my book *'Contact Down Under'*.)

Ten years earlier pilot Jay Cole, flying a Beech C-45 twin engined utility plane near Ocala, Florida, encountered similar strange lights. One performed aerobatics for fifteen minutes before disappearing, and a second almost collided with their plane before making a ninety degree turn and disappearing. These UFOs were also tracked on radar.

There was another little known incident which also occurred in about late 1978 at Pearce RAAF Base in Western Australia. My informant was only twenty at the time, and completing his initial training. There was a secondary heavy duty runway nearby, and every night two junior airmen were sent there to perform guard duty.

One night there was a terrible kerfuffle when the terrified recruits saw a huge, brightly lit object hovering over the airfield, as if about to land. The senior officers raced out to find the strange craft was gone, but the tarmac had melted and the bush on either side was on fire. The two young airmen were immediately posted elsewhere, and the army engineers called in to effect repairs.

Although we didn't hear about it very often, the Soviet Air Force and pilots also experienced their fair share of inexplicable interference. In 1983 a retired Russian Air Force Colonel told of a case in 1983 where an unknown object had hovered over an intercontinental missile base for four hours, affecting their mechanisms to a ready-to-fire status. This had prompted his government to call for an exchange of UFO information with the West, to avoid a nuclear war being triggered by accident.

He personally knew of forty cases where Soviet pilots had been ordered to follow the unknown craft, and several had crashed whilst in pursuit.

In 1985 Aeroflot airliner Flight 8852, from Tblisi to Tallinn, was 120km from Minsk when the crew and co-pilot noticed a huge, bright yellowish star. It emitted a thin ray of light which suddenly widened into a blinding cone, followed by two more cones.

Passengers said they were surprised to see the streets below them illuminated. The bright light vanished leaving a green cloud that descended at great speed until it came to a halt behind the plane. The 'cloud' changed shape into a circle, then a square, and finally solidified as a giant wingless aircraft with a 'needle-nose'.

The pilot contacted ground control, who advised the UFO was flying behind him at an altitude of 10,000 metres and a speed of 480km/hr. The object tailed the airliner over Riga and Vilnius all the way to Tallinn, when it eventually disappeared. The radar in all these places picked up two targets. The reality of these objects is beyond doubt, when flight schedules showed only one airborne at the time.

In later years, the Russians were a little more forthcoming about UFOs. In May 1990, Gorbachev was reported as saying; "The leaders of our armed services have long recognised UFOs as genuine phenomena, calling for sensitive response. We are alert, but have no reason to believe that these visitors are other than peaceful."

The same year Igor Maltsev, Soviet Air Defence Director, said; "We have scrambled our jets to observe the craft. Our pilots were ordered not to attack, on the grounds that the discs might possess formidable capacities for retaliation. We obtained many photographs of the UFO – and also registered it on thermal and optical sensors."

In 1992, General Yevgeniy, of the CIS Scientific and Technical Committee, stated; "Our air forces have been recording UFOs and scrambling in pursuit of them since the end of the war against Hitler. The reality of these objects is beyond doubt, but what they are and where they come from is unknown. I am not aware of any overt hostility by the UFOs – and our pilots are ordered always to treat them in a peace-loving manner."

Were any of these strange objects ever apprehended? In his article 'When Pilots See UFOs', Steve Gerrard of the Southampton group – SUFOG – wrote of a report in the *'Daily Mail'* 25th June 1990:

'Soviet fighter planes shot down a UFO, but secret police hid the incident, it was claimed yesterday. Scientists attending a conference in Munich said parts of the craft were recovered after it was shot down over the Caucasus Mountains in March 1983. They said a recently leaked picture of the wreckage proved the KGB was hiding something sensational'.

The Chinese were also experiencing a similar problem, and giving the usual nonsensical, mundane explanations. The *'China Daily'* newspaper, on 29th August 1987, told of how an unidentified flying object appeared over Shanghai for seven minutes before it vanished in the East China Sea.

The paper said that Chinese fighter pilots, in military jets, tracked and observed the UFO but were 'unable to corroborate the description given by people on the ground before it disappeared'. Shu Jiaxin, Chief Engineer of the Shanghai Meteorology Bureau said the UFO was probably caused by 'meteoric ice'.

A case in 1985/86 highlighted the need for investigators to follow-up all leads before defining a sighting 'definitely unidentified'.

The newspapers were abuzz with a report that the N.S.W. Premier, Neville Wran, along with one of his government ministers, saw an extremely bright, shiny, spherical object from their chartered plane, while flying over northern NSW at 8am one September morning. The pilot, Gary Elass, had also seen it and taken a photograph.

"It was very high, too high to be properly identifiable," he said. "I don't think it was a balloon, radar deflector, satellite or rocket case. I contacted Brisbane operations that evening, and was told there were no weather balloons in the area at the time." The photographs taken by Capt. Elass showed the UFO as a pin-prick of light on the horizon.

A 77 Squadron Mirage fighter was vectored from Williamtown at 12.30pm to identify a radar contact 250km north of the base, which was suspected of being the UFO. The Mirage pilot, Flight Lieutenant Ray France, was unable to positively identify the object because of its great altitude, some 10km higher than the Mirage.

The pilots of an Ansett Boeing, travelling from Sydney to Brisbane, also sighted the UFO, and reported it to the Brisbane Airport control tower. The Sydney Meteorological Bureau confirmed contact with 'an object' hovering almost stationary 100,000ft above Coffs Harbour. The RAAF report stated that the most likely explanation for Premier Wran's 'UFO', was that it was some sort of research balloon, operated by sources unknown at that stage!

Two days later, veteran investigator, Paul Norman, was visiting friends in Eyre, when he received a telephone call to say that a similar object was seen in several areas, including the incident involving Premier Neville Wran.

Paul Norman and Judy Magee of VUFORS, interviewed many witnesses from Victoria, the Nullabor and other parts of South Australia. They also sent photographs for computer analysis. The Department of Transport were becoming concerned that, what appeared to be a balloon, might become a hazard if it drifted into airspace. The Meteorological Bureau finally confirmed that the 'UFO' was indeed a balloon, but it didn't originate in Australia. Some in depth detective work by Paul and Judy resulted in an identification, however the media still preferred the more sensational 'UFO' headlines!

On the other side of the world, identical reports were being received over South Africa and Zimbabwe. Cynthia Hind, the MUFON co-ordinator for Africa, finally solved the problem. The source of the balloons was a French Space Agency, Centre National d' Etudes Spatiales, based just outside of Pretoria, South Africa, although some of the balloons might have originated from French controlled territory in the South Pacific, to check for radiation in the atmosphere resulting from atomic tests. Reports were also being received by Dr. Willy Smith, CUFOS representative for the Spanish speaking countries, where the balloons were also seen.

But were all sightings balloons? On 22nd July 1985, there was a major incident when a UFO was sighted by scores of witnesses and officials above the Zimbabwe Bulawayo Airport. Several pilots tried unsuccessfully to intercept the object. A Zimbabwe Air Force Air Marshall confirmed the sighting, and Air Commodore David Thorne, Director General of Operations said that he and his staff - "believe implicitly that the unexplained UFOs are from civilizations beyond our planet."

On 17th November 1986, the pilot and crew of a Japanese Air Lines cargo jet – flight 1628 - claimed to have seen two brightly lit and one enormous object which followed their plane for about seven hundred and sixty kilometres.

At 6.15pm they were flying north-easterly, en route from Reykjavik, Iceland to Anchorage. Captain Kenju Terauchi, a 47 year old pilot with twenty years flying experience, saw lights directly in front of his plane shortly after entering Alaskan air space. Fearing a mid-air collision he sought permission for evasive action, and finally 'lost' the objects about one hundred and thirty kilometres north-west of Anchorage.

Yoshio Tsukuda, the plane's flight engineer, was quoted as saying he saw 'two lines of lights which looked like aeroplane cabin windows'. Terauchi described the large craft as a 'mother ship' which looked like 'two aircraft carriers placed back-to- back'.

Terauchi located the object on his own on-board weather radar, and the FAA controller also tracked them, sometimes as close as eight kilometres from the plane, and reported that they stayed with the aircraft during its turns and descents. A Federal Aviation Administration spokesman later attributed the whole episode as being due to 'erroneous data on their own radar tracking system.'

On 23rd March 1989, three major British newspapers all carried the same story; A British Island Airways Tristar, was making an inaugural return flight from Malta to Gatwick Airport. On board were one hundred and forty passengers, mostly holiday industry journalists and travel agents, checking out the new destination.

Capt. BobTaylor, a veteran pilot, first spotted a strange object when cruising at thirty thousand feet above the Mediterranean island of Sardinia. Initially he thought it was another plane, but ruled that out because it was travelling too fast.

"I have never seen anything like it," he said afterwards. "We will probably never know what it was – but it certainly wasn't a plane."

As the mysterious glowing aircraft sped towards it, Capt. Taylor's plane was sent hurtling thousands of feet downwards, but within seconds he was luckily able to regain control.

Passenger Susie Walton said; "I looked out the window and saw what looked like a bright, glistening, multicoloured cloud that left a trail of smoke behind it. Then all of a sudden we plunged and it disappeared from the night sky. I thought it was the end. It was terrifying. Some passengers started praying, and I grabbed hold of the man next to me. I was sure we were going to crash."

Stewardesses toppled over in the aisles, and many passengers hit their heads against the ceiling. There was no way that British Island Airways could keep this out of the media. Their spokesman tried to play it down: "We saw some bright lights in the sky, then we experienced some turbulence. It has been blown out of all proportion."

The British 'Times' Newspaper, 26th May 1995, published an article about the crew of a Portuguese Airlines Skymaster, seeing a long cigar-like wingless object, whilst en-route between Epsom and Dunsford the day before.

The radio officer, Almeida, said that it was long and slim, and travelling at a terrific speed. It seemed to be revolving as it flashed under the nose of the aircraft. The flight engineer, Jose Elika, commented that the object approached from the port side and passed right under their nose. He described it as a 'silver cigar', and noted there was no smoke trail coming from it.

AFU Newsletter' detailed an incident which took place at 4.25pm on 11th July 1995, over Steinkjer in Norway. A Dash-8 passenger plane was travelling from Fornebu to Bronnoysund, at approximately fifteen thousand feet, when the co-pilot noticed an object to the right side of the plane. At first he thought it was another plane, but whilst it was silvery and polished, it had neither wings nor tail fins. Within a minute it slowed down and disappeared.

The weather was fine, with good visibility, and corroborative reports were received from an eleven year old boy, and a seventy-five year old man on the ground. The boy said it was almost as large as the plane, and it disappeared straight up at a great speed. The object was not tracked on radar, and as there was no other known traffic in the area, the military considered it to be unidentified.

Less than a month later, the *'Telegraph Mirror'* reported another incident over Argentina. On 2nd August 1995, an Aerolinas Argentinas jet, carrying over one hundred passengers, was descending for its final landing approach. It had to pull up short to avoid colliding with what witnesses described as a 'space ship'. The pilot, Jorge Polanco, said he saw a 'white light, bearing down really fast, before it halted about one hundred metres away'.

The *'Sun'* newspaper, on 24th November 1995, carried the story that a UFO had been 'buzzing' Edinburgh Airport only a few weeks earlier: *'The object was seen by the control tower, ground control and security staff. The tower had a visual on it, and it showed up on the radar screen'.*

The airport diverted a commercial plane, 'to check it out', and then contacted the RAF. Although the RAF did not admit to the incident, an anonymous pilot source reported that three Tornadoes were scrambled to intercept the craft. They had the UFO in their sights, and were closing in when it suddenly 'shot straight up into the air and 'left them for dead' – the jets just couldn't keep up with the thing!'

At the Australian International UFO Symposium, held in Brisbane - October 1997, one of the guest speakers was James Courant. He had been a pilot, flying DC8, 727 and 747 airliners. He was also an instructor for multi-engined aircraft, helicopters, gyrocopters, gliders, seaplanes and balloons!

He had researched UFOs since 1962, and had three sightings himself within a three year period. He was also in contact with many witnesses in government departments, airlines, astronauts, scientists and the media. As a result, he was convinced that there is a global cover-up of UFO reality.

He recounted two startling cases I had not been aware of before. The first occurred in November, 1962, at an airbase in Greenland. A UFO had been visually sighted and tracked on radar. A jet fighter was scrambled to investigate. The pilot confirmed a visual, and suddenly his plane and the object merged on the radar scope. The plane and its pilot had completely disappeared.

A DC3 search plane took off, sighted the UFO and also vanished off the face of the earth. A rescue helicopter was dispatched to investigate, and the crew reported seeing strange lights before radio contact was lost. The chopper and crew were not found, despite a major search the next day. Some months later the helicopter was found in the same area, but there was no trace of the crew. Their bodies were never found.

James Courant went on to liken this case to one that occurred a year later, when a jet fighter merged with a UFO over Lake Superior. It was seen on the radar, and vanished along with its two man crew. In 1989, over Puerto Rico, over one hundred witnesses on the ground saw a F14 Tomcat jet fighter disappear into a UFO.

He commented that it was no wonder that the US army concluded that aliens were hostile, and developed high energy lasers and particle beam weapons to shoot them down. He said that Col, Philip Corso (Ret) claimed these weapons have had some success, and they are much more powerful than those depicted in the movie *'Independence Day'*.

Professor Sun Shi Li also attended the Symposium, and confirmed that Chinese pilots have also reported UFO encounters to control towers. Graham Birdsall, editor of Britain's *'UFO Magazine'*, discussed the enormous 'black triangle' craft, seen over Europe during the last few years. He discounted the theory that they were advanced secret military aircraft for two main reasons.

First, he considered there was such a large number being reported, they would be beyond the stated defence budgets of governments to produce. Secondly, the 'triangles' were so brazen in publically hovering at such low levels, no pilot of a secret advanced aircraft would ever be allowed to do this.

I am not so sure he was correct in his assumptions. Seven years later, on 5th November 2004, employees at the Bhadha Atomic Research Centre (BARC) Mumbai, India, saw a bright light beyond the windows of the plant's Cirrus 40-megawatt heavy water reactor building.

When they went outdoors, into the parking lot, they saw 'a large triangular UFO hovering silently overhead'. The craft then flew slowly over the plant grounds and hovered over the building containing BARC's Dhruva 100 megawatt heavy water reactor. It remained in view 'for several minutes, making no noise', before it retreated in a north-westerly direction.

In 1998, London journalist David Derbyshire wrote an article about a UFO – 'as big as a battleship' – off the coast of Britain. The RAF tracked it flying in a zig-zag pattern at thirty thousand kilometres per hour over the North Sea. It then accelerated to forty thousand kilometres, and zoomed off towards the Atlantic. The Dutch Air Force also tracked it, however two F-16 fighters, scrambled to intercept, could not keep up.

The Ministry of Defence had also spotted the object at its long-range listening station on Fylingdales Moor in North Yorkshire. They said the unknown object was triangular, about the size of a battleship – 'and, judging by the various manoeuvres executed, definitely under control.'

The Russians still have just as much interest in, and contact with, UFOs as their western counterparts. In their May/June 2003 Newsletter SUFOG published a translation of an article published in the Russian newspaper *'PRAVDA'* on 1st April 2003. Basically, whilst it claimed that attempts to attack a UFO are futile, it discussed events in the USA and Japan, and did not mention instances where its own Soviet forces were involved:

'A very rare documentation, which proves the reality of attempts to attack an unidentified flying object is a tape recording between two pilots who started

battling the objects, which trespassed the airspace of a US Air Force base in New Jersey.

Twelve spherical objects appeared in the airspace above the army base on October 7th 1965. American military men took them for a squadron of spy planes. Three pursuit planes took off from the airbase to destroy the unidentified objects. Pilots described those objects as 'balls', whose speed was a lot faster in comparison with the speed of their battle planes. A pilot said they opened fire on the objects and hit them several times. Bright flashes could be seen on hitting spots, although weapons did not get to harm flying objects at all.

The raid was finished with a failure; UFOs left safe and sound, while flabbergasted pilots had to go back to the airbase with nothing. Luckily, the tape recording of their conversation was preserved at US Air Force archives, and was then exposed to the public.'

The article also detailed another case from 24th June 1999. At 3.15pm passengers on a bus heading for Dallas, saw two planes several hundred metres behind a silvery disc, which was flying at high speed in the direction of Dallas Love Field airport. The pilots opened fire, and flashes could be seen when the object was hit several times. The UFO merely increased its speed and left the 'fire zone'.

The article went on to say that there was unconfirmed information, which said that several encounters between UFOs and pilots ended lamentably for the latter:

'Three pursuit planes of the Japanese Air Force were heading to the Misava airbase on 24th August 1998. All of a sudden, two planes vanished from radar screens at 8.58pm. The pilot of the third plane transmitted a strange message;- ' I can see a large ball of red colour. Two other planes have been downed.' As Japanese newspapers wrote afterwards, the ball that pilots saw was about three metres in diameter, and had produced plasma flashes, which downed two Japanese pursuit planes.

When those planes disappeared from radar screens, the pilot of the third plane managed to avoid a collision with a strange object, and that manoeuvre saved his life. Thirteen patrol ships were sent to search for fragments of the planes in the sea. They only found a small piece of a horizontal stabilizer of one of the planes. There were no doubts the pilots were killed.

Another accident like that happened on 9th October 1998 at 8.02pm. A pursuit plane, with an experienced crew of two pilots, encountered a red ball, not far from the Misava base. As soon as pilots prepared to attack the object, radio contact with the plane was lost. A rescue team managed to find a part of the wing and some documents on the water surface. The pilots of the plane are still considered missing.'

I would submit that while many cases may have been more worldly espionage or surveillance, we will never know. Perhaps there is a conventional explanation for many of the events. We know that unknown prototypes of earthly origin are covertly tested, but at the time the characteristics of some of these strange craft surpassed the most advanced secret experimental technology.

What has really been happening in our skies?

CHAPTER SIX

UFOs: SCOTLAND and FRANCE

UFO sightings occur all over the world, and my Scottish relatives were also very interested in this and other similar phenomena. In the early1950s they had been travelling to the seaside for their annual summer holiday. Suddenly everyone on the train was rushing to the windows, and pointing out a strange saucer shaped object which was buzzing the engine and carriages.

They never forgot the incident, and how excited they had been. For several years they collected articles from the local newspapers regarding UFOs and similar phenomena. When they heard of my research into the subject my uncle sent me his collection of clippings, which had been forgotten and packed away in the bottom of his wardrobe.

I realised that most of this information has probably been lost in the mists of time. It was difficult to determine the actual dates and exact locations of some of the sightings and incidents. Because they had originated in the 1950s it was obvious that most of the reports did not equate with our own known technology of the era.

Many articles described multiple witnesses, from the Glasgow area, seeing 'glittering lights' in the skies. I wonder if these were experimental 'prototypes' being tested over the west coast of Scotland? Perhaps there was some truth in the theory that crashed discs in the 1940s had been back-engineered?

One particular incident, which occurred just before 8pm one Saturday night, involved a fluorescent cigar shaped object which was reported by hundreds of witnesses from the Borders to Oban, Fort William and the Western Islands including the Isle of Mull. The Port Patrick Duty Coastguard described it as having an oblong shape, with a long tail, flying at an altitude of about 4,000 ft.

During the 1950s radar operators were also tracking unidentified objects across the skies of south-west Scotland.

Two civilian employees at the RAF Radar Post, West Freugh, ten miles south of Stranraer, tracked unidentified objects at 60,000 ft. Only two days later a couple of golfers at Rothesay spotted three silvery circular objects, which travelled silently across the cloudless sky, and vanished out of sight without leaving a vapour trail.

In one case two RAF jets were 'left at the post' by mystery objects plotted on radar screens. The Air Ministry issued the following comment; "We are baffled – the objects were not visible to the naked eye." A few days later 'three phantom shapes in the sky' were seen by people as far apart as Rothesay and Cumberland. Two Admiralty policemen also reported a strange object – 'like an airship' – above Loch Lomond.

Glasgow people were still reporting sightings, and the *Daily Record* received multiple phone calls from residents as far afield as Paisley, Clydebank, Carlyle and High Blantyre.

All the witnesses described the same 'things' they had seen at 2am that morning. Circular, soundless, brightly coloured discs – (some people claimed to have seen 'portholes') - were travelling across the sky. A large one was in front, with three smaller ones following behind at a consistent speed. The larger one suddenly shot away from the others, displaying a green flashing tail as it departed.

The newspaper did 'due diligence' and contacted the RAF who said that there were no aircraft in the area at the time. An official at Prestwick Airport was ambiguous, but a little more forthcoming; "There was a small-scale exercise!"

The area around Dunoon had more than its fair share of inexplicable events. On one occasion five bright 'aluminium looking' objects were seen over Dunoon. The students, teacher and driver on the school bus all gave consistent reports, and noted that the objects seemed to be reflecting the Sun's rays.

The Daily Record, October 14 1959, detailed an incident involving the local postmaster and baker's wife. They were driving along the New Cumnock Road, Ayrshire, when Mrs Richmond gulped and said; "Can you see what I see?"

They stopped the car, got out and watched for ten minutes as a strange disc shaped craft moved silently across the sky. It was a solid object, about thirty feet in diameter, dark grey on the outside, and slightly paler in the middle. It manoeuvred in and out of the clouds, sometimes on end, and often as a flat round disc. Suddenly it zoomed upwards into the sky and out of sight.

The *Express* newspaper reported an incident which was not quite so benign. Two teenage girls were walking to their home in Dunoon one evening, when they saw two strange objects in the sky.

The black and white craft were round and tapered to a point at the bottom. The girls became frightened when the objects started moving close towards them, and then backing away, only to return. They left the highway and ran into a nearby field to hide. The craft then descended to telegraph pole height, and were hovering directly overhead.

By this time they were terrified, and raced back to the road to hide in the ditch at the side. They tried signalling to passing motorists, but the 'thing' was still just above them. Eventually a husband and wife stopped and picked up the hysterical girls. They also confirmed seeing two 'big round things' overhead, as did two other motorists who subsequently pulled over.

These reports are not the first similar type incidents occurring in the Scottish skies. During one of the local 1950's 'flaps', a Mrs Edgar of Auldgirth, Dumfriesshire, wrote to the local paper about an incident back in 1925;

"I was going home from the village store when up above seemed to grow quite bright. I looked up and there was 'the thing', as I've always called it. It was passing along about tree-top level, making a hiss-hissing sound. It was quite hot. It kept straight on over the wood where my home was.

"I watched it out of sight. Far away, among the hills, I heard it land with a great 'crump', and the pheasants for miles around set up a screeching. I told my neighbour when I got home, and she had also heard the 'bang'. Later my husband told me it must have been a shooting star, a meteor.

"That was in 1925 or 1926, but it is still fresh in my memory, and has been revived by all this talk of Russian satellites. Makes one wonder if what I saw was a forerunner of a guided missile."

Due to Scotland's proximity to France, the local newspapers also reported on what was happening across the water. A lot of mysterious lights and craft were being reported in their skies.

The French were not happy about these unidentified objects invading their provinces. The mayor of Chateau Neuf du Pape issued a decree banning 'flying saucers' and 'flying cigars' from his municipality, and ordered the rural constable to impound any that might land!

The Evening Times - October 28 1954, carried an article titled – 'Man from Mars Paralysed Me with a Blue-Ray Lamp.' (These were the days of shock and wonder headlines!)

The case itself is quite interesting, and involved Aime Boussard, a 47 year old farmer from Aubusson, Central France, who described encountering a creature about five feet tall, wearing something like a diving suit, with a light green light on either side of its head. It was shining two powerful pale blue lights at him.

"Suddenly I was blown from one side of the road to the other, and stayed there for about ten minutes without being able to shout or call for help. At last the blue lights went out, and the being crossed the road and vanished. I felt pains in my legs and right hand – I can still feel them."

Police who went to the spot found freshly disturbed earth and turf torn up, but no trace of footprints. In the meantime a lorry driver reported seeing a 'flying cauldron' – as big as a five ton lorry – taking off from a meadow by the road to Angouleme, south-west France. He said it left a white trail as it vanished noiselessly into the clouds.

One report my uncle had saved - 'The Boy Who Came in from the Cold' - was fascinating.

A gravestone in the churchyard of Sainte-Miande, south of Toulouse, contains the following unusual inscription: *'March 9 1901. Here lie the remains of the boy who came from nowhere.'*

This particular article, researched and written by John Maklin in the 1970s, really caught my attention. Back in those days, older people in the village still remembered the incident, and some claimed to have actually seen the child.

In September, 1900, during a freak storm which hit the village, a local farmer was awakened by an insistent tapping on the window of his downstairs bedroom. At first he thought it was the wind, but eventually he got a lantern and went to the door.

Standing outside was a small boy, about ten years old. His face was pale, almost luminous, and his hair long and yellow – quite unlike the local lads. His only clothing seemed to be a piece of sacking, which he had wrapped around his shivering body.

The farmer's wife came out, and taking pity on the child, insisted on bringing him into the house to the warmth of their fire. As she wrapped him in a blanket, they had already noticed that he had only three fingers on each of his strange long hands.

He slept on a mattress in front of the fire that night, and the next morning the couple found him some of their son's clothes to wear. He didn't seem to understand what clothes were, or how to put them on. Buttons were a complete mystery to him. The same applied to food. He didn't seem to know what a knife and fork were for, and had to be taught how to drink from a cup.

He was even scared of the cat, and at first the farmer assumed he must be some simpleton or dumb waif. Initially they thought he couldn't speak, but then he started to talk. It was a language they had never heard before.

They contacted the village priest – Father Rene Mouville – who had entered the priesthood at age 50, having previously been a professor at Lyons University. Father Rene took the boy back to his home to be cared for by his housekeeper.

The priest attempted to communicate, to no avail, with pictures and drawings. He sensed that the lad was very intelligent, and tried writing down numbers in the form of clustered dots. Immediately the child took the paper and pencil and began writing dots at high speed. Father Rene was astounded to see that he had worked out the square roots and cubic roots of all the groups of numbers. The child also seemed to be fascinated by physical movements, as if he had never seen them before. He would sit for hours watching birds, the clouds and rippling water.

After a while he began to develop and understand and master some words, and Father Rene took him out on his rounds with him. The villagers began to accept him as part of the community rather than a curiosity.

The priest and his doctor had a sense of foreboding about the boy's physical condition. Apart from the three fingered hands, his hips were extremely

narrow, and his rib-cage an inverted V-shape – quite the opposite to a normal chest structure.

After Christmas the boy became sick with what appeared to be a bad cold, but in a few weeks he seemed to recover. In February his pallor was a deathly colour and he developed a high fever. The doctor was also concerned at the lad's heartbeat – slower than anything he had ever heard and half that of a normal human.

He gradually became weaker, and died in early March. They buried him under an ash tree in the local graveyard, still none the wiser as to who he was or where he came from. Many have since speculated that he was from another world.

France, like most other countries, has its own history of UFO and alien sightings, some dating back centuries. Alencon Police Inspector Liabeuf reported that on 12th June 1790, dozens of peasants, farmers, two mayors and a doctor, amongst other dignitaries, witnessed an amazing event.

A large spherical 'globe', surrounded by flame, and emitting a whistling sound, made some oscillations before slowing and moving towards the top of a hill. It unearthed plants along the slope, and gave off enough heat to set the grass and small trees on fire.

A 'kind of a door' opened, and someone, dressed in a strange tight-fitting suit came out. This person saw all the people, uttered some unintelligible words, and ran into the woods. The sphere silently exploded, throwing pieces everywhere, which burned until they were powder.

All over the world there was immense interest by all governments to obtain the secrets of these mysterious discs – be they extraterrestrial or from a rival nation. In France, after a couple of landings in the 1960s, the Gendarmerie were quite explicit in the detailed reports they required; 'This includes on the type of noise coming from the UFO. We want descriptions of any occupants, including their complexion and appearance. We also want to know about their equipment and the effects on animals, soil and plants near any landing site.' They also advised witnesses to refrain from any use of force and to use caution when meeting or dealing with any occupants.

One of the independent UFO researchers, affiliated with INUFOR, is parapsychologist Sylvie Hoenig, who has brought a welcome French perspective to the whole phenomenon. Sylvie was born in Paris, and later lived in Switzerland, where she experienced some strange UFO related phenomena. Sylvie immigrated to Australia in 1961, where various types of 'UFO happenings' continued.

Looking for answers, she joined the NSW based UFO Information Centre, when the president was the well esteemed Dr. Lindtner. I joined the organisation after his sudden death, however both Sylvie and I dropped out when the group started to disintegrate in the mid 1970s. We had both begun to realise that there was often a strange political agenda within large UFO societies.

A few years later, Sylvie decided to start her own welcoming group for people who needed reassurance and assistance because of UFO related events. She provided therapy, via her UFOLINX group, to help people cope with their ordeals.

She found that group therapy, mutual understanding, encouragement and sometimes hypnosis could benefit those who had all kinds of UFO experiences. During her many years of involvement with ufology and the paranormal, Sylvie developed her own theories and perceptions regarding the experiences of some contactees. She shared her thoughts in the following article, written for a joint INUFOR, MUFON, UFOR NSW Conference I hosted in 1997.

DIFFERENT REALITIES .... Another Way of Looking at it.

The relative connection between UFOs and Other Dimensions.

We at UFOLINX have decided to distance ourselves from the standard ufologists' collective thinking structure. We feel that this thinking is, more or less, a third dimension reality, seeking tangible facts and figures.

If we take a long hard look and analyse all the UFO related research in the last fifty years, comprising of personal efforts, monies expended, risks taken etc., and reduce it to a concise form, the result is bound to be disappointing. We are no closer to solving, clarifying or understanding this very vexing conundrum.

All our most poignant questions are simply leaving us with more new questions. Could it be that all the proof and real tangible data is staring us in the face, but we are unable to perceive or understand what is really going on? Is this because it's not happening on a dimensional level that we can possibly relate to?

Quantum scientists are telling us now that there's strong evidence pointing to the fact that we are part of a multiple holographic universe without some drastic change in our third dimensional concept or thinking.

When I look at some of the very interesting UFO data that has come to hand, I can't help but be fascinated by split second appearances or disappearances, and just as rapid materialisations or dematerialisations. In the majority of instances people seem to dismiss these cases so readily because they say – 'it's impossible!'

However, all of this is not as impossible or incredible as it appears. In line with the recent quantum science thinking, coupled with some of my beliefs, we are about to take part in a huge shift into a fifth dimension.

Let's say, hypothetically, that some of the aliens who thus far have been relating, connecting, communicating, altering and abducting etc., may belong to that fifth dimension. Is it inconceivable that, in our present time, we are quite obviously being prepared for a dimensional shift? Any serious researcher into psychology, sociology, parapsychology or quantum science would probably agree that we are entering a very unusual and different dimensional density.

I have been interested in the inter-dimensional hypothesis for quite some time, and am currently embracing studies of other consciousness, ie. sacred geometry etc.

In abduction cases, where there is a lack of sustainable physical evidence, there seems to be a shift from the physical to a transpersonal, psychological level. Due to their nature, these cases need to be treated with the same response as if they were of the physical kind.

I have once, personally experienced an inter-dimensional shift that lasted approximately one and a half hours. For the last three years, I have been trying to find answers about that experience. I have spoken to numerous people who are well aware of other dimensions, living parallel to our reality at the very same time.

I find it fascinating, very exciting, in fact mind blowing – and well worth the effort and interest to take a different approach in relation to the 'Alien Saga'. This is not to say that we believe all alien interactions belong to inter-dimensional realms, or that we at UFOLINX take this as gospel. We are merely investigating with a new approach, and know we're not the only ones exploring these avenues. UFOLINX dedicates itself to all levels of research, whatever they may be.

As well as her own work, Sylvie enjoyed her continued involvement, on different levels, with MUFON, SOS OVNI, UFOR and INUFOR. In the early days, along with many others, Sylvie always wanted to see a worldwide network system of data and information which was not locked solely within the English speaking countries.

In 1997 Sylvie wrote the following article for the *'INUFOR Digest'*. It was of great interest to me, as the incident in Orolon, involving 'angel hair', was very similar, in many ways, to a case we had investigated at the town of Quirindi in NSW. (See *'Contact Down Under'*.)

UFO HAPPENINGS IN FRANCE

Apart from seeing my family and friends, my recent trip was to catch-up on what was happening in France with regard to the UFO scene. It seemed to be very much 'under wraps'. I contacted CNES and SOS OVNI, and found that it was indeed a 'hush-hush' subject.

Perseverance paid off, and I soon found that there were quite a lot of happenings reported from all over the country. Past and present governments are, of course, totally silent, although I found many scientists, of all statures, highly interested and ready to investigate. This has enabled me to relay some of the up-to-date facts, past and present, on UFO data from that part of the world.

On 12th October 1952, a strange object was observed in the village of Oloron, Sainte Marie, by a local school principal. It was white in colour, tilted at a forty five degree angle and at an estimated altitude of two to three thousand feet. White cloud or smoke seemed to be detaching itself from the top.

The principal looked to the right, and noticed thirty smaller objects behind the craft. They were travelling at a similar speed in the same direction. Grasping his binoculars, he noticed that each of the smaller objects were the shape of a domed saucer with a red central sphere.

They seemed to be travelling in pairs, in swift zig-zag movements. Each pair was linked by what was described as an 'electric arc'. They left long trails of a threadlike substance, which detached itself and floated slowly to the ground, and the people of Oloron and nearby villages found it on roof-tops, trees, street lamps and telephone wires. The threads resembled strands of nylon or finely spun wool. When touched, it became gelatinous, vaporised and then disappeared.

This phenomena was seen by many people, and could hardly be dismissed as an hallucination. The official explanation was given as; 'Threads left by spiders, millions of migrating spiders'! The people were angry at this silly attempt by officials to dismiss this occurrence. Spider webs do not disintegrate within minutes.

The furore had almost died down, when two weeks later, at 5pm on 27th October 1952, two gendarmes and around one hundred residents of Gaillac, another little town in the south of France, saw a repeat performance. This was almost identical to the incident in Oloron, but this time there were only twenty of the smaller objects, which came much closer to Earth. The estimated minimum altitude was fifteen hundred feet, and the thread that was left behind was likened to 'glass wool'. While I was there, I took the opportunity to enquire within the area, but nothing like it has been seen since.

1954 saw another huge wave of UFO sightings, this time in the north-west of France. These were humanoid sightings.

At 8.30pm on 27th September 1954, four children were playing in the barn of their farmhouse at Premanon, in the mountainous Jura region. Their dog began barking, and the eldest boy went out to investigate. Once outside, he was astounded to see a 'rectangular creature on legs'.

He threw pebbles, and then shot a toy arrow at it. When this had no effect, he moved forward and tried to touch it. An invisible force immediately flung him to the ground, and terrified, he screamed as he jumped up and ran away. He looked back and saw the strange being waddle off towards the meadow.

The children ran to the house, and once safely inside, looked out. They described what they saw as a 'red sphere' wobbling over the field around one hundred and fifty metres away. The next day the gendarmes discovered a circle of flattened grass measuring four metres in diameter.

At 7pm on 9th October 1954, in Lavoux near Poitiers, a man on a bicycle found himself face to face with a weird being. He described it as about 1.3m in height, wearing a suit similar to a cloak. He said that the head was like a mass of hair with big eyes shining through. He watched as the creature shuffled off into the adjacent trees and disappeared.

Not surprisingly, this was the subject of hilarious jokes in the French National Press. However, what the journalists didn't know, was that at about 6.30pm, the next day, the 10th October 1954, in the neighbouring village of Pournoy La Chetive, a shiny machine was seen to land in a local field.

It was witnessed by three people, who described a 'kind of man', about 1.2m tall, emerge from the machine. He was dressed in a black sack, somewhat like a priest would wear. They also told of his face being very hairy, and that he had huge eyes, with a glowing sphere in the abdominal region.

The creature uttered a few words which none of the men could understand. They were so frightened that they made a hasty retreat. Looking back, they saw they saw the machine climb very rapidly into the sky.

At about 7.30pm the next day, the same machine was observed by several men on their way to Tapignac. The craft hovered about ten metres above the ground, and the men got out of their car and followed the path it was taking. Suddenly it moved between the trees and disappeared.

The witnesses continued to proceed for about four hundred metres in the direction where they last saw the object, and stopped when they came across the craft which had now landed. Underneath they could see four creatures which were similar to the one they had seen a few moments earlier. They seemed to be busy at some task below their 'ship', and then re-entered the craft, which went through some very rapid colour changes and took off into the sky at great speed.

Another most interesting case was that of Renato Nicolai, an Italian man living in France for thirty-five years. The Gendarmerie has records of the following incident that took place at 5pm on 8th January 1981, in Trans-en-Provence. Renato was working quietly in his garden, when a soft whizzing sound, about fifty metres away, caught his attention.

He described a weird object slowly wobbling down to the ground. Renato approached. It was oval in shape, about 3.5 metres by 1.5 metres, and making no other noise. It almost immediately rose vertically to an altitude of about twenty-five metres.

Renato was in shock. Did he dream this? Was it an hallucination? He walked towards the spot where the object had landed, and found very clear burn marks on the ground. At least he was certain that they indicated he had seen something, but what exactly was it?

He went home and immediately told his wife, who thought he was losing his mind. She spent a sleepless night worrying about her husband, and what was happening to him. In the morning she went to have a look at the spot, and sure enough, the burn marks were still there. She went to speak with Mme Maurin, her neighbour, who knew Renato as a quiet man with a lot of common sense.

She advised the Nicolais to notify the police right away, and after the gendarmes collected the facts, they called the CNES (National Centre of Spatial Studies). Jean-Jacques Velasco, the director of the SEPRA division of CNES, took over the investigation, and reported several interesting facts:

On that day, no anomaly was detected on the radar of the nearby military base. The military were also firm in saying that they most definitely did not have any engines that can manoeuvre in such a manner, and certainly not noiselessly.

Jean-Jacques Velasco collected samples of plants, grass and dirt, which he gave to Professor Michel Bounias, a bio-mathematician and toxicologist, for analysis. Professor Bounias kept the samples refrigerated for thirty days, awaiting permission from CNES to conduct his analysis.

His examination showed, inexplicably, that the chemical components of the leaves and grass from the location were the same as the dirt, but the proportions were inverted. The metabolism of the plants had transformed themselves. The elements found there showed very unusual chemical changes, and an imbalance with the dirt. The official scientific investigation deepened, and the lid of secrecy came down.

After fifteen years, what did the scientists and CNES have to say?

The machine was definitely where Renato said it was. The scientific analysis conducted by biochemists, showed that the propulsion system used by this 'engine' was not carbon based like ours. The tests also revealed that the effect it had on the plants was still evident one month later, however the chemistry of the plants completely reversed back to normal two years later.

I found the French government and military to be just as secretive as anywhere else in the world, but the scientists were more open and ready to admit that we have evidence of unknown phenomena.

On 21st April 1974, Robert Galley, Minister for Defence, admitted on national radio that the French government had been secretly studying UFOs for twenty years. Today, any UFO incident in France must be reported to the Gendarmerie. If they think it is a genuine case, they refer it on to SEPRA and CNES.

I would like to quote a phrase I saw at the SEPRA headquarters;

'Healthy scepticism is a good thing, but we must beware of being so sceptical that we dismiss as nonsense, everything we do not understand.'

———————————————

CHAPTER SEVEN

IT CAN HAPPEN ANYWHERE

UFOs are reported from all over the world, in every kind of imaginable places and circumstances. Often the encounters can be anything but pleasant.

BICYCLES

It is not only cars that are stalked by UFOs. Bicycle riders are much more vulnerable. There is nowhere to hide.

Post magazine detailed the experience of one unfortunate lad in 1956. Shayne was only sixteen, and living on the family farm in Waimo, New Zealand. He had a part-time job, at the bakery, every morning before school, and regularly left home at 2am to cycle to work.

It was always without incident, until one morning when he was cycling down the winding, bushy road, a dense fog engulfed him. He said it was so bright his headlight beam simply bounced off it.

"Then the fog lifted, and I saw a bright cigar-shaped craft, with a fiery exhaust, climbing vertically and almost grazing the mountains." He rode on to his job, but nobody else had seen the object.

Two days later, when he was riding past Sharp's Quarry, he noticed a bright light streaming down from the cliff face. He stopped, and realised that the light was coming from a round ball, about sixty centimetres in diameter. It seemed to be studying the cliff face, but suddenly 'froze'.

Shayne turned off his bike's small, but noisy 'dymo', and the ball seemed to continue as before. He didn't want to be late for his job, and continued on his way, only to find that the ball had left the quarry and was 'keeping pace' with him.

The next thing he remembered was kneeling at the bakery door, covered in blood, and crying for help. His nose was pierced, all his teeth were missing, and his lip was torn away. Thinking he must have been hit by a car, the boss took him to hospital, and then set about looking for Shayne's bicycle. It couldn't be far away, as the lad had arrived at 2.30 am, his usual starting time.

Eventually it was located in a creek, seven kilometres away. The frame was bent, and the front wheel buckled, but the police could find no paint scratches which would indicate a collision with a car. Shayne had no lacerations on his knees or legs, which would be consistent with falling off his bike.

Shayne is convinced the UFO 'took' him during his fifteen minutes of 'blackness'. In the following thirty-seven years he has developed psychic abilities, has some unknown 'task' to perform that is related to the UFOs, and has been 'protected' several times in his life.

Paul Norman from VUFORS, investigated a rather harrowing case which occurred near the Victorian town of Wodonga on 24th August 1967.

Mr. Hydes was travelling at about 70kph on his motorbike along the highway, when he was engulfed by a brilliant bluish/white light which nearly blinded him. He stopped, and closed his eyes for a moment.

He said; "When I opened them, I could see a disc-shaped object about one hundred feet away, to my left and just off the road. The object was silver on top - quite a high polished silver - and either a very dark grey or black underneath. It was just like two inverted saucers."

The object was hovering three or four feet above the ground, and he decided to go over and have a closer look. A passing car diverted his attention, and when he glanced back, he could see two figures beside the craft. They were about five feet tall, and dressed in metallic overalls which closely resembled the colouring of the craft itself. They wore helmets that looked like 'fishbowls they had just popped on their heads'.

Hyde continued; "At this stage, starting to get a little frightened, I took a step forward, to see what would happen, and they did the same. Then one of the figures took another step forward and beckoned me over. I panicked and just dived on the bike, whose motor was still running, and took off down the road. I intended to put as much distance between myself and that object as possible.

"Suddenly, however, I heard a humming noise, and straight away I knew what it was. Looking up, I saw the UFO following me at about one hundred feet altitude and one hundred and fifty feet away. I tried to flag down a couple of cars, and point the object out to them, but none responded."

By this time the craft had overtaken Hydes, who was now scared that it would cut him off. He reduced his speed to three or four kilometres per hour, and watched the UFO, awaiting its next move. To his relief, it tilted its base towards him and shot up into the sky at a forty-five degree angle. It vanished from view in a matter of seconds.

You would think that in Asia, where bicycles are a major mode of transport, there would be many more similar cases. I only found one, although I'm sure there are many more.

This undated incident was reported by the Chinese UFO Research Society, CURO. A teacher, from eastern Tianjin, was cycling around the park one night when he noticed a 'shimmering ball' overhead. He lost consciousness, and came to by the park gate. His watch was now an hour behind the actual time. Although he had no memory of what had happened, a month later he had 'flashbacks' of two short beings, in unidentifiable space suits, abducting him onto a strange craft.

Researcher Ron Edwards wrote about an incident which happened in Brazil in July 1970. Joao Marcelino used to leave his bicycle at the bus stop, five miles away from his home in Papagaios, Catarino. He alighted from the bus, and started pedalling his bike along the rough road. A bright light appeared in the sky, and he suddenly found himself surrounded by a narrow beam.

He and the bicycle were lifted up and suspended in mid-air for several minutes. He felt as if he was paralysed by some unseen force, and could not jump off and 'make a run for it'. He was lowered back onto the road, and began pedalling as fast as possible. It didn't help, and the beam of light raised him up again and held him motionless above the ground. Once he was back down on the track, he frantically pedalled like a 'madman' and eventually managed to escape his mysterious abductor hovering overhead.

In *'The Alien Gene'* I discuss the case of Lydia, who was abducted with her children, in Manchester, UK, in 1979. At the time, they had been coming back across the park after farewelling James, a visitor who was going back home on his bicycle. He also was abducted that evening, but decided to only confide in Lydia and a couple of other people due to the unwelcome attention the case was receiving.

He claimed they had done something to his pineal gland, which didn't make a lot of sense to me until I read an article by Australian investigator, Matthew Favaloro, in 2004. He quoted psychiatrist Rick Strassman, who researched human brains, including the use of psychedelic and hallucinogenic drugs.

N,N-dimethyyltryptamine, or DMT, is naturally produced by the pineal gland, and excessive production can lead to 'mystical experiences'. DMT is also found in plants around the world, which were often used by shamans and other religious leaders to promote spiritual and other experiences.

I am not for one minute suggesting that abductees were having some form of 'high' – more that perhaps the 'visitors' are able to manipulate the pineal gland in order to facilitate telepathy or inter-dimensional interaction.

SCHOOLS

Are extraterrestrials interested in our children, or is it just coincidental that there have been several cases of craft landing in close proximity to our schools. Whilst some cases have involved interaction with alien beings, I suspect that others may have involved test flights of our own prototypes. Regardless of the origin of these UFOs, it must be remembered that schools usually have level, clear playing fields, which make ideal landing sites.

Welsh researcher, Margaret Fry, investigated the 1955 case of nine year-old Rae Fountain, who attended a boarding school near Leighton Buzzard in Bedfordshire. At about 3.55pm, on 30th June, he was going to play in a school football match. As he walked down the muddy country track, with bushes on either side, he noticed some footprints which were unusual and very close together.

He looked up and saw two odd men ahead. They had closely cropped dark brown hair, were dressed in one piece overalls, and walking with very small foot-strides. He said he started 'stalking them, the way children do, by hiding behind the bushes.' The men were stopping all the time, and seemed to be picking up pebbles and vegetation, which they placed into something in front of them.

Suddenly a 'thing' swished down across the path ahead, and hovered a few feet above the ground. It was roughly a flat 'bell-shape', with a protruding rim just before the rounded top. The nearest Rae could describe the exterior was that it seemed to be a bluish-tinged metallic grey. In fact he had never seen anything that exact colour before.

A door on the top half slid open, a concertina type ladder came down, and the two men climbed in. Rae was close enough to see inside the craft, and noted someone there at 'some sort of wheel or instrument'. The door closed, and the object went straight up and swept across the sky. As it left, the schoolboy could see it had a flat bottom with three 'ball-like' wheels.

Rae didn't remember anything else until he woke-up in the dark with the headmaster shaking him, and several other teachers and pupils looking down as he lay on the ground at the side of the muddy lane. The headmaster was angry, as everybody had been out searching.

They took Rae back to school, and put him to bed. The next morning the headmaster did not believe him, and said the child must have had a bad dream. Rae knew he had not fallen asleep on the road, but could not account for the missing time.

In 1996 I was interviewing witnesses following many sightings of strange objects on the N.S.W. Central Coast. Alan, a conservative man, approached me and related an incident which happened in 1963, when he was a small, frightened eight year-old.

Due to a broken family and ill-health, Alan was temporarily living in a boys' home in Parramatta, part of Sydney's western suburbs. It was winter, and a holiday weekend when fireworks were permitted on the Saturday night. The boys were all keyed-up, and sent to their rooms at 6.30pm, ready for an early rise the next morning.

At about 8pm, Alan and his room-mate heard a humming sound outside their second floor window. There were only trees and fields behind the home, and their initial reaction was sheer terror. They huddled together under the bed, and after about ten minutes gathered up enough courage to peek out of the open window.

The night was clear, with the moon and stars quite visible. For the next thirty minutes they stared in awe at an object hovering to the north-east, about 150 feet above the ground. It was 'cigar-shaped', pink in colour, with a red light on top. Suddenly the humming became louder, and the object's brightness increased in intensity as it 'shot off like a bullet'. Just as quickly, it came to an abrupt halt behind the home and descended behind some nearby trees.

The next morning, several of the boys were sent out to collect wood for that night's bonfire. Alan and his friends made their way to the spot where they had seen the object come down. The trees had broken branches, as if something had been 'pushed down from the top'. The grass underneath was flattened in a thirty feet diameter circle. Whilst the surrounding grass was covered with frost, the circular patch was quite warm.

A few days later, there was great excitement at the home, with several reporters congregating at the gates. Apparently they wanted to interview Alan and his room-mate regarding the Friday night sighting. The two boys were standing in the driveway watching, when they were approached by a housemaster and uniformed policeman.

The officials did not mince their words. The boys were asked if they ever wanted to see their families again. If they did, they must not talk to the reporters or relate to anyone what they had seen. Alan and his friend were pressured into silence.

"When one is a small boy," he said, "large police officers and housemasters can be very intimidating."

Do UFOs have a covert interest in our schools and children? Sometimes we do not even know they are watching. In 1991, at Wyong, on the NSW Central Coast, a mother was picking her son up after football practice. Everyone else had gone home, and she and her young lad stared in astonishment at the huge object hovering about ten feet above the local school.

"It was bigger than the school itself, - the size of as football field," she said. "It was silver-grey, a classic flying saucer shape. There were no seams, windows or lights. We watched for a while, but concerned for my son's safety, left soon after."

Further south, the Australian city of Melbourne received a couple of 'school visits' over the next few years.

MUFON received a report from 1964, when three hundred students at a Catholic school were on playground 'clean-up duty'. Just before the bell sounded at 12.30pm, they looked up to see three discs, in 'tripod formation', hovering in the clear blue sky, about eight thousand feet overhead. The object in the front turned on its side and then shot off at an incredible speed.

Twenty seconds later, it came racing back, and resumed its original position. The other two craft then performed an identical manoeuvre. The sun reflected off their apparent metallic surfaces as they eventually took off in different directions to the north south and west. The teachers cut-short their lunch break, and ordered everybody back to their class rooms.

The next year there was an even more spectacular incident at Westall, which I detailed in *'Contact Down Under'*.

On 6th April 1966, the students at both the Primary and Secondary schools were astounded to see several 'flying saucers' buzzing around in the sky overhead, one being followed by a small plane. Many students and teachers witnessed the event, and described the craft as being metallic discs with a clear dome on top.

They saw one disc descend behind some pine trees, only to rise again a short time later. There were circles of burnt grass, where the objects had landed, and soon the military arrived. They burned the entire area, and used a bulldozer to remove all the vegetation and top-soil, which they took away in trucks.

There was a 'special assembly' at the school, where all the pupils were told not to speak to the press, or anyone else, about the incident.

In 1977, fifteen students at the Welsh Dyfed school of Broad Haven were enthralled when a UFO landed in a nearby field on 4th February. They first saw it at lunchtime, when some of the boys were playing football. It was a little obscured by trees and bushes, but the lads were able to note the object was shaped like two saucers, one on top of the other, with a small dome and flashing light on top. Some saw three or four windows around the edge, and others thought they heard a humming sound.

They ran in to tell the headmaster, Ralph Llewellyn, but he didn't believe them. After school finished at 3.30pm, at first they thought the strange object had gone, but then they saw it rise into the air from behind a bush.

Most of the children were a little scared, and went home to tell their parents. One rang Welsh researcher Randall Jones Pugh, but by the time he reached the site, it was getting dark and raining heavily.

A fortnight later, one of the teachers saw a large silvery object glide away from the same spot, and other witnesses also reported unusual craft in the area. By this time, Ralph Llewellyn had second thoughts, and isolated each one of the pupils, getting them to write down and draw what they had seen. Their accounts were remarkably consistent.

The same year there were other 'school sightings' in Britain, but not with so many witnesses. Only six days later, on 10th February, two twelve year old boys saw a UFO, flashing a blue light, in a field near Haverford West Grammar School. It was about forty metres away, and 'took off' when the boys threw rocks at it.

A week later, on 16th February, a thirteen year old boy, saw a bright metallic object hovering over Pembroke School, when he arrived earlier than usual one morning. Young Graham Howells said the object, which resembled a revolving 'plate', had a dome in the middle, which remained grey most of the time, but flashed a dazzling white every five seconds.

ZIMBABWE

On 14th September 1994, there had been multiple reports of bright lights and objects traversing the night sky over Zimbabwe. Most were attributed to either a meteorite shower or the re-entry of one of the stages of a Russian satellite. Due to the massive discrepancies in the size, speed and altitude of the objects, investigator, Cynthia Hind, doubted both of these explanations.

The Ariel School was a private primary school, about twenty kilometres from Harare, and taught students from a variety of races and cultures. Two days later, on 16th September, all sixty-two pupils were on their morning break in the playing field.

They noticed three silver balls of light moving in the sky, and suddenly one came much closer, and appeared to land about one hundred metres away, from where they were standing on the edge of the school grounds. This area was very rough, and out of bounds, due to the thick vegetation, thorn bushes and snakes, spiders and other less than pleasant wildlife.

The older children were very curious, and described seeing a small man, about four feet tall, dressed in a shiny, tight fitting, black suit, appear on top of the object. He had a pale face, huge eyes, shoulder length black hair and a long scrawny neck. He walked a little way through the bush, and upon seeing the children, promptly disappeared. Either he, or someone similar, re-appeared on top of the object, which soon took off very rapidly and shot away into the sky.

The younger children, having been told legends of 'tokoloshies' eating them, ran back to the school building calling for help. All the teachers were at a meeting, and didn't come out. The mother in charge of the tuckshop didn't believe them, and later said she was not prepared to leave the food and money.

Cynthia took several investigators to the school four days later, and interviewed many of the students. In advance of her visit, Mr. Mackie, the headmaster, had over thirty drawings from the pupils. Some were better than others, but many depicted a typical flying saucer. Some mentioned three or four smaller objects in the sky above.

Despite an extensive search, the investigators could find no radiation or other traces on the 'landing site', and Cynthia wondered if the object had hovered just above ground level.

In early December, Dr. John Mack along with colleague Dominique Callimanopulos visited the school and interviewed the children, whom he believed. Many, who were standing at different vantage points in the playground, reported telepathic messages, or 'feelings', that mankind was not caring for the planet. Since the children have attained adulthood, their memories and evidence have remained consistent.

WE MAY NEVER KNOW

There are some accounts of possible UFO/Alien interaction where we may never learn the truth or full details, and are left to speculate.

On the 5th February 1979, police in Hobart, Tasmania, found a man driving through the city with no headlights. He appeared to be incoherent and disorientated, and did not know who he was, where he was going or where he lived. The police found his personal papers and address, and took him home.

His father and son, concerned that he was still dazed, and seemed to be in a state of shock, took him to the local hospital. His pulse rate was a high one hundred, and when the nurse shone a light in his eyes, he seemed scared and backed away.

His car was also a mystery. The battery was flat, and the oil level very low. The cut-out switch to the alternator needed replacing, and also some of the wiring, especially to the headlights. It was 'bubbled' as if overheated. This did not make sense, as it was the first time the car had been driven since it was checked out three or four days earlier.

The man recovered some, but not all, of his memory, and told them of how he was driving near Lawitta, forty-two kilometres from Hobart. At first his radio died out, and he got no response when he pressed all the buttons. Seconds later an intense white light seemed to envelop the car, and he couldn't see past the end of the bonnet. At the same time his headlights went out and the engine stopped. He recalled trying to start the car, but after that his memory was vague until stopped by police in Hobart.

He resisted any attempt by researchers to find out more about what happened, saying he didn't want to know, and had no interest in the UFO phenomena.

TIMES OF WAR

There are a multitude of cases, reported during wartime, where unidentified discs or craft are sighted over a battle-zone. They could be enemy spy craft, or interested or concerned aliens. We don't know, but in some cases a more direct contact is made.

I worked with a Vietnam veteran I will call 'Warwick', who suffered from PTS, and sometimes just wanted someone to confide in. One day he opened-up about an inexplicable incident which occurred during his second tour of duty in 1969.

"We often saw strange craft in the sky, which we knew didn't belong to us or the enemy. They would hover, sometimes high up, often much lower, but would quickly disappear if any jets arrived. Nothing prepared me for what we saw early one morning when I was on patrol with D. Company.

"We had initially been bedded down, with sentries on watch, in an ambush position. Suddenly all us men were gathered together and moved out. We travelled through the jungle on foot, and came to a banana plantation. In the middle of the 'settlement' was an old pagoda type church, which had been bombed out.

"There were no Vietcong in sight, but sitting in the middle of the clearing, about eighty yards away, was a huge 'egg-shaped' elliptical object. It was about ten feet high, nearly twice the length of a bus, and had no wings or tail. It was like a dark, dull silver-grey shape, bathed in a shadowy misty light.

"Our leader pulled us back a little, and then deployed two segments of troops to encircle the object in a 'bull-horn' manoeuvre. As we moved in, the silence was rent with a very loud whirling sound. After a blinding flash of very bright colour the craft was 'gone', apparently straight up into the sky. We didn't tell the officers. If anyone mentioned UFOs they would just laugh and tell us that they didn't exist and we didn't see anything."

Apparently opposing troops didn't fare very well either. The *Australian UFO Bulletin* published a 2001 report by Erich Aggen, which told of an incident in the summer of 1965. A special unit of two hundred Russian soldiers, stationed near Hanoi, fired upon a UFO which appeared in front of their headquarters. It retaliated with a laser-like weapon, and the Russians were 'completely dematerialised.'

Aggen also detailed a similar incident, during the Korean War, in the spring of 1951. The American troops fired upon a metallic craft, which responded with a pulsating ray. Three days later the men suffered symptoms of radiation poisoning, and had to be evacuated by ambulance. The Allan Hynek Centre for UFO Studies also investigated this case.

In late 1970, William English was stationed, in Vietnam, with US 'Special Forces'. They were ordered to infiltrate the jungle of neighbouring Laos, to recover survivors and flight recorders from a B-52 bomber which had reportedly come down following a report that it was under attack by a bright light.

After four days they reached the plane, which was sitting on its belly on the ground. There was no apparent damage to the surrounding jungle, which tended to rule out the 'crash' theory, and it still had a full load of fuel and bombs. The soldiers, who had to 'blow' a hatch to gain entry, were appalled by what they found inside.

The crew, all dead, had injuries which we now know were reminiscent of the later 'cattle mutilations'. The horrified troops took photographs and collected whatever items they could, before they placed explosives which destroyed the doomed plane and its occupants.

'Nexus' magazine, December 1998, contained an article by Linda Mouton Howe which discussed an incident the next year, in September 1971. A US Army unit was on a routine mission into Cambodia, when they entered a clearing to see a spherical, metallic craft, about a hundred feet in diameter, and as tall as a 'five storey building', suspended close to the ground on four legs.

There were about sixteen to twenty 'humanoids' around it. They were no more than five feet tall, with greyish-white skins, and wearing one-piece silver jumpsuits. There was one, possibly the 'leader', who was taller, perhaps five feet six or seven.

A young corporal panicked, and thinking one of the aliens had a weapon, fired. The being fell to the ground, and the taller 'humanoid' walked over. He put up his hand, in a sign of peace to the platoon, and struck the corporal across the face. Both the corporal and the injured alien appeared to recover, and the humanoids picked up their equipment and returned to their craft which lifted straight off the ground.

In April 1982, during the Falklands War, Roman and his platoon of Argentinean soldiers, sleeping in the El Condor ranch house, were woken in the early hours of the morning by the sentry banging on the door. Outside was a gigantic oval craft, whose intense brilliant lights illuminated everything around.

They stared up at it for fifteen minutes, before it swiftly vanished over the hills. They were all transferred to another building, and after being debriefed, sent into another room. They met with some very disorientated conscripts from another unit, who had experienced a terrifying event, just after Roman's sighting.

They had been in a troop transport, driving along the highway, and suddenly found themselves scattered on the ground in an open field. In an instant, they had been 'transported' three kilometres away from their original position, and the truck was nowhere to be found. As is normal procedure, in most military cases around the world, the soldiers were immediately split-up and sent to different locations.

There was another case, reported by VUFORs, which referred to an unconfirmed CNI News item, that in 1993, eight British soldiers were on a stake-out in Northern Ireland. They were hoping to surprise some IRA gunmen, but instead, 'three or four small, grey figures in human form' appeared. They all stared at each other for a minute or so. The small entities vanished, and the soldiers, who subsequently fled, saw a brief flash of light in the sky.

I don't really know what the Army would have made of their garbled report. Their unit commander was furious that they had abandoned their post. Although he didn't believe them, he passed the information on to British Intelligence. When I heard about this I thought to myself maybe it wasn't so strange. The Irish have always talked about 'the little people'!

Sometimes we at INUFOR, and other sane researchers, receive reports which are beyond belief. However, since we don't know all the answers, it is unwise to dismiss what people have reported.

Journalist, Chester Quinn, published a fascinating article on the 16th April 1985. A Boeing 727 pilot was cruising at an altitude of 27,000ft on a flight from Delhi. Many of his passengers were children, who had been seriously injured in an industrial accident in Northern India, and were being taken to a medical centre in Bombay.

Suddenly a blinding white light ripped through the plane, which started to rise straight up, as if in a vacuum. The pilot did not have time to react, and he saw his altimeter needle spinning out of control before it hesitated at 53,000ft then dropped to zero. The 727 came to a complete mid-air halt! Passengers and flight attendants were screaming and grabbing for oxygen masks and seatbelts.

The pilot reported that the plane was suddenly bathed in a brilliant blue light, which changed to green, red and yellow before going back to blue. He looked through the windscreen and claims he saw human-like faces a few feet from the plane. The pilot looked at his watch - 3.15pm - and the plane suddenly plummeted straight down, settling softly at the original 27,000ft.

Ground control was on the radio, asking where his flight had come from. The pilot looked at his watch again. It was now 7.15pm. He checked on his passengers, and found nothing short of a miracle. When the children had boarded the aircraft, they were a pitiful sight and he could hardly bear to look at them. Now he couldn't see a scar, laceration, burn or broken limb. The attending physician was speechless, and medical officials confirmed that the youngsters showed no sign of injury or trauma after the flight.

The pilot said; "I can't tell you what happened up there. For several hours we were part of another time, another place. There's nothing in my experience to compare with this. The faces were human, but no bodies were attached. Was it a UFO? A time warp? Did we pass through an invisible door into another dimension? You, my friends, tell me."

At the time of Quinn's article the Indian Aviation Authority were still investigating the incident. A spokesman said; 'We have yet to determine what happened up there – perhaps we never will. But something did happen. Of that, there can be no doubt, because we have proof – and lots of it."

Another case of mysterious 'healing' was related to John Pinkney by 'Anne L.' of Mt.Waverley in Victoria. Her brother-in-law, Ian, who was a doctor in Adelaide, noticed his sight was getting fuzzy. A specialist confirmed his worst fears. His problematic eyesight was deteriorating, and he would eventually go blind.

He sank into the depths of despair, which wasn't helped when he would wake in the night to hear strange whisperings in the wall and coloured lights shining into his bedroom. One night, after being woken by a tremendous noise, he felt compelled to go out into the back garden.

A violent wind seemed to be shaking the trees, and he could see a mass of dazzling, multi-coloured lights. Within them was a small domed object which had apparently landed on the lawn. He stood on the back porch, staring at the UFO. It began to spin at such a speed he became dizzy and nauseous.

He had no memory of what happened after that, and didn't recall going back into the house. The next thing he knew was that he was back in bed, and it was morning. Throughout that day he suffered further nausea and violent headaches. On his upper left forearm was a mark which looked like a 'full moon intersected by a crescent moon.'

Several days later he was astonished to find that his eyesight was rapidly improving. His specialist ran tests, and couldn't believe that there was no evidence of his previous eye disease or the deterioration of the corneas.

There are many cases of 'alien healings' and my colleague, Margaret Fry, investigated one which raises far more questions than answers.

Royston was born in 1928 and lived in the small, rural Welsh coal-mining village, of Penywaun in the Abadare Valley. In 1936 he suffered from rheumatic fever. In those days it was a serious complaint, leaving several life-long health problems. He spent many months in bed, and during that time had out-of-body experiences.

In 1944, when he was sixteen, he was waiting for the bus to go to work in Cardiff. It was early morning, and he watched for five minutes as an unusual 'black cigar' type object, surrounded by 'white ovals of light', moved silently over the slag heap. He remembered his childhood out-of-body experiences, and felt that somehow he had been programmed and 'controlled' by alien entities.

He suddenly developed the ability to see into the future and 'predict things to people'. He was not happy about this, and it would certainly have raised suspicions with his deeply religious 'Army' Welsh community.

In 1987, when Royston was fifty-nine, he was admitted to Cardiff hospital for a hip-replacement. After the nurses administered the pre-op injection, he had another out-of-the-body experience, but this time recalled going through the ceiling and being placed on a bed of 'mercury' where a strange tall being rectified all his bodily problems, (mostly caused by the rheumatic fever?), except for the hip replacement.

Later the theatre sister and trainee nurse said they had seen his 'body' rise in the pre-op room and go through the ceiling. They were frozen in terror, until after a few minutes they watched it come back again and re-enter his body.

In theatre he floated out of his body again, and hovered near the ceiling. He heard the surgeon saying to the students around him; "This man has healed his own body!" The surgeon later visited Royston in the ward, confirmed talking about the miraculous healing, and also noted that before recovering, Royston had been 'babbling about aliens and UFOs'.

Margaret and her fellow researchers believe Royston, who does not confuse these episodes with his religious beliefs. They noted he had minimal education, did not read and had little exposure to television due to his membership of the Salvation Army.

Researcher John Carpenter wrote about several humorous accounts, which indicate that despite their advance technology aliens can also make mistakes. Many abductees have woken up in the wrong clothes, and even the wrong bed! Others have found themselves outside their homes, unable to get back in through the locked front door. On a couple of occasions the poor victims were totally naked!

Donald Shrum (his real name), spoke at a MUFON meeting in California in 2005, to 'set the record straight' regarding the reports of his frightening encounter at Cisco Grove in 1964.

That evening twenty-eight year-old Donald had been separated from his hunting party, and it was getting dark. He knew his friends would not search for him at night, and followed the normal practice of climbing a high tree until daybreak, to escape any animal predators.

Later that night, he saw a white light zig-zagging at a low altitude, and thinking it was a rescue helicopter, jumped out of the tree, and lit a fire to attract its attention. The white light turned towards him and stopped about fifty yards away. It was like no craft he had ever seen before, and as a precaution, he climbed back up into the tree.

After a while, two five feet tall humanoid beings, wearing tight-fitting garments with hoods, and a metallic-looking 'robot' approached. Donald could see other beings, at a distance, apparently gathering something, possibly plant samples, from the surrounding area.

The three entities, now below and at the base of the tree, seemed intent on getting Donald down. A battle of wits and cunning went until daybreak, when the creatures left. Whenever the beings approached, Donald would shake the tree, and they would retreat about twenty-five yards, only to regroup and try again.

Donald used his belt to tie himself to a strong branch. He soon realised these aliens were frightened of fire, and proceeded to light matches and throw burning pieces of clothing and paper down on them. He even broke off branches of his pine tree, and sent them flaming to the ground.

Donald also had his bow and three arrows with him, and he shot two at the creatures. One hit the robot in the chest, and Donald said that it fell on its 'proverbial metal ass.' Although the aliens did not retaliate, or appear to have any weapons of their own, the robot emitted a peculiar 'gas', which on one occasion left Donald gasping for air.

Near the end of the siege, a second robot appeared, and together they emitted a large volume of mysterious smoke, which caused Donald to lose consciousness. When he recovered, he was still tied to the top of tree, and there was no sign of the aliens.

After daybreak he climbed down and located his hunting party. They had also seen strange lights overnight, and later investigations showed 'ground traces' which supported Donald's account.

It does appear that perhaps our alien visitors do not approve of humans hunting and killing defenceless animals. In 'Contact Down Under' I relate the case of a Tasmanian man, George, and his 16-year-old son Peter, who were out one night, in 1985, shooting possums. A huge object descended from the sky, landed, and attacked them with a form of 'heat beam' which caused them to drop the carcasses and run.

George obviously did not heed the warning, and in 1986 went kangaroo shooting with his daughter, Sally. This time, a huge saucer, well over 150 metres in diameter, dive-bombed them as they fell face-down on the ground. They raced for their vehicle, and as they sped home, the craft reappeared from behind and moved overhead before departing.

Perhaps they were lucky they only got a warning. Charles Bowen published the following accounts from Brazil, however he noted that there was no way of actually verifying this information.

This report came from the *National Enquirer* in 1981, and quoted the local police chief, Geraldo dos Santos Magela, who insisted a UFO was responsible for all four deaths of local hunters.

"The men died while the UFO was directly overhead," he said. "The other hunters with them were terrified, and came to me asking for help."

The first death occurred when friends Ferreira and Boro were hiding up trees, waiting for the game to come. A huge light descended from the sky, and hovered above them. Ferreira climbed down, and watched as the spinning object shone a light on the screaming Boro. He ran home, and the next morning went back to the spot with Boro's family. They found his body, deathly white and devoid of blood.

The second event was when Anastacio and his friend Raimundo were in the woodlands, and a large object, with a beam of light, descended from the sky. They started to run, but Raimundo tripped and fell. Before he could get up, the light surrounded him. Anastacio kept running, and the next morning Raimundo's totally white body was found.

A third victim, José Vitorio, was lying in a hammock, with his hunting companions nearby. Suddenly a flying object descended over the hammock, and 'shone brightly'. His companions ran for help, but when they returned José was dead.

The last fatality was a hunter seen on the top of a hill. An object suddenly appeared and shone a beam of light down upon him. He rolled down the hill, apparently went crazy, and died on the third day.

Another hunter, Todd Sees, was found dead in Pennsylvania in 2002. Two days earlier he had gone up the mountains to look for pre-season deer. When he didn't return, a search party was mounted. They found his '4-wheeler' near the power line at the top of the mountain, but the tracking dogs could not find his scent around it.

Later Todd's body was found in a hard to reach wooded area. He was emaciated, deathly pale, and had an expression of horror on his face. He was only dressed in his underwear, and the rest of his clothes were missing.

Several farmers said they had seen a large, bright, round light silently hovering over the powerlines at about the time Todd disappeared. One witness claimed it moved a few hundred feet to the east, and shone a beam of blue and white light onto the ground. He saw what appeared to be a man, suspended in the light, and being pulled, head first, into the bottom of the craft, which then sped out of sight. Three fisherman also reported what seemed to be the same object.

Friends of mine, a married couple who live on a property in the Great Dividing Range, west of Sydney, took twenty years to confide a similar disturbing incident that also happened just after the turn of the Millennium.

They had gone to bed for the night, and their dogs were safely tucked up beside them or in the lounge. Suddenly they found themselves outside the front door, with the dogs beside and in front of them.

Across the valley, on a nearby hill, they could see their neighbour's house. The husband and wife, along with their two children were also standing outside. Above them was a huge saucer, which projected a beam of blue light and raised the entire family into the craft.

My friends and their dogs seemed to be paralysed – none of them could move, and the next thing they knew it was morning, and they were back in their respective beds. At least the family across the valley were returned, but they did not fare very well. The wife committed suicide, and the daughter, now a young woman, suffers from psychological problems.

Twenty years later, the experience is still as clear to my friends as if it happened yesterday, and they are still questioning was it a dream or real?

The indigenous, Aboriginal population of Australia, have a long history of interaction with 'visitors from the skies'. Across the entire continent, all the tribes have similar myths and legends of 'Gods' coming down from 'lands in the sky'. Often they would carry off men and women back to the 'Sky World'.

Research of Australian Close Encounters, detailed an interesting report, which dates back to New Year's Day 1920. The informant detailed some incidents that occurred to the family;

"My grandmother saw UFOs her whole life, and told me of this before she died, aged 77 in 1991." Granny lived in a very isolated area, on a property owned by her father. Sometimes other relatives would stay with them, before travelling on.

When she was about six, her elders told her that there are flying saucers which will take some people – lifting the motionless victim off the ground and taking them inside an opening underneath. Older people had been taken from around the region, and nobody went out after sunset. One night, her grandmother's first cousin was still playing outside after dark.

Granny started yelling at her to come home because the 'flying saucers' would get her – but she didn't listen. Suddenly, out of nowhere, an object appeared overhead. The family screamed at her to run for the house, but it was too late.

As it started to lift her up from the ground the entire family, and other witnesses were running out yelling and throwing things at the saucer, but it had no effect. She was taken inside the opening underneath, the 'door' closed, and she was never seen again.

There are many reports and legends within the aboriginal community, and in the majority of cases, abductees are never returned. There have been several exceptions. Rex Gilroy told of two cases from the early twentieth century, when the involvement of humans or an earthly craft was unlikely.

The first, in 1921, occurred on a dirt road some distance from Charters Towers in Northern Queensland. 'Delma', a nineteen year-old aboriginal girl, was dragged into bushland by two strange tall men wearing unusual clothing.

At the same time a large, round brown-coloured flying machine appeared above and silently landed. 'Delma' was screaming for help, but they dragged her inside, to be met by four other men of similar Asian appearance.

She could not describe the interior of the craft, except that it was dimly lit and there was 'a lot of machinery she didn't understand'. She recalled being held down on a table, and injected with a long needle attached to a large box.

She thought she must have 'fallen asleep', because the next thing she remembered was waking, naked, on the floor of another bright blue oval room. Her clothes were piled beside her, and as soon as she had dressed, a round door, about six foot in diameter, slid open. She could see it led to the outside, and quickly made her escape. The craft rose high into the air, and shot off to the west at an unbelievable speed.

The second case, from 1933, involved 'Nellie', an aboriginal woman who was with her tribe gathering bush tucker, in Australia's Great Sandy Desert. They all scattered in panic when a 'large shining egg' descended to about one hundred feet overhead.

Nellie tried to hide in the Mulga scrub, but grey skinned man-like beings emerged from the craft, which had landed a hundred feet away. One of them pointed an object at her, and she was unable to move. They carried her back to their ship, and strapped her down on a metallic table. She said the interior was aglow with light, and lots of apparatus she didn't comprehend.

Two or three of the beings prodded her all over with metal rods, and a huge glass plate descended from the ceiling. It covered her whole body before rising up again. Nellie remembered nothing else until she woke, lying alone on the ground. The mysterious craft and its humanoid occupants were gone.

Brisbane's *Sunday Mail* published an interview with Muriata, a Girrigun elder, in 2002. The aboriginals called UFOs 'chic a bunnahs', or 'devil men', and Muriata's grandmother had told him that if he got caught by one he would die.

In the 1930s he was a small boy, playing with his friends one night on the banks of the Tully River. A huge ball of light had descended from the sky and zoomed along the waterway. He and the other children ran as fast as they could back to their camp and mothers. It was not the first time strange craft had been seen in Australia's tropical north, however all over the country sightings are commonly reported by the indigenous community.

'UFO Encounter Newsletter' January-March 2005 received an interesting report from the Nullarbor – where many unusual sightings and experiences have occurred. Unfortunately there was no mention of the year or month, and any follow-up with the witnesses would be near impossible.

Two men, one a fettler and the other, Abdul, an aboriginal co-worker on a Nullarbor property, were driving back from a mate's place late one night. They had to be up for work at 4.30am the next morning, and as a consequence only had a couple of drinks.

They were driving through the scrub, when suddenly the ute's headlights 'died' as did the engine. There seemed to be no life in the battery, so they got out and raised the bonnet. Their torch wouldn't work either. There was a lot of colourful language, and as the fettler was groping about in the dark, trying to feel his way around the battery, Abdul tapped him on the shoulder and pointed to the sky.

About one to two hundred feet above them was a 'gargantuan' object, which seemed flat, like a dinner plate, from their vantage point. It didn't make a sound, and had a set of lights, green, red and yellow, revolving around the bottom. Abdul's brown face had turned white, and both men felt pure terror. Neither of them twitched a muscle, and felt that they couldn't move even if they had wanted to.

The object hovered for what the witnesses thought was about ten minutes, but was in fact, an hour. The huge craft then began to move slowly away before accelerating at an incredible speed. The ute started without any problem, and the two men drove home without speaking a word. Because they lived in a small community, the next day they agreed not to tell anyone. It was only due to the fettler confiding in his ex-wife that the incident came to light.

TANAMI

Meaning no disrespect to the unfortunate witnesses, our first reaction to this piece of sensational journalism was great mirth.

We were unable to determine if there was even a fraction of truth to the following report, however it was published in the *'Weekly World News'* March 1996 by reporter Ben Gold, and quoted the local policeman, whom he named.

Tanami is a small outback settlement in Australia's Northern Territory. It is 72km due west of Banka Banka, off the Stuart Highway in the Tanami Desert. Up to forty-nine of the residents had, over the previous two years, been experiencing unwanted alien intrusions and abductions of their citizens.

They claimed the 'spacemen' came in a 'star-ship with red and blue lights'. They would usually corner their prey at night and immobilize them with a special light ray. The victim would then be given an injection, which would render them unconscious, before being 'beamed' aboard the craft for several hours of experiments and examinations.

(This part of the article gained my attention – many abductees reported an 'injection' of an implant, but not so much of an anaesthetic/ sedative. The abductees also described 'horrible mutilations' and emotional trauma, with one dying from the injuries inflicted by 'alien scientists'. Again, this was not consistent with the majority of cases we've investigated – so what was going on? Did these cases have a human or alien origin?)

The townspeople were on constant alert for these unwelcome visitors, and one night they spotted a three-foot tall entity trying to snatch a little girl. She was only two blocks away from the public library, and the local constable and two deputies 'snuck-up' on him and made an 'arrest'.

"Just because we're out here in the middle of nowhere, these space freaks think they can buzz our town and experiment on us like we were lab' rats," the local policeman said. "Well, we're showing them that we aren't going to take that kind of treatment.

"We've got one of their 'little green men' and they're going to have to negotiate to get him back. I want them to feel what it's like to have a friend in the hands of strangers from another planet."

When Ben Gold interviewed the policeman and witnesses three weeks had passed, and they had seen nothing of the UFO. I wondered if anyone would make contact or try to retrieve the strange creature they were holding captive. Perhaps they were not holding a 'real live alien'. It may well have been a biological robot, of earthly or extraterrestrial origin.

At the time, G.Stewart of UFOtec, was an INUFOR contact. Originally from New Zealand, he was familiar with the 'harmonic' research of both Bruce Cathie and Richard Hoagland. We forwarded the details to him for an opinion. He completed his calculations, which we published in the *'INUFOR Digest'*. He noted that the location was extremely close to the latitude location of 19.5 degrees, which well-known investigator, Richard Hoagland, considered very significant.

Mr Stewart also commented; "Collectively, the values that are evident at this location in the Tanami Desert indicate the possible presence of what science refers to as 'Ripples in the Space/Time Continuum'. An excellent description of this phenomenon is written up in the book called *'Wrinkles in Space Time'*, along with some remarkable photo images captured by the Cosmic Background Explorer (COBE)."

He then proffered some 'speculations'; "If we consider the possibilities that the Tanami position is in fact some sort of ripple or distortion in the space/time continuum, then it may well have a direct link with the anomalous activities that are continually reported in the general vicinity. These include strange lights, weird sounds, electronic equipment failure and even alleged alien abductions. It is quite conceivable that extraterrestrial craft could use this type of space/time distortion to literally materialise from other dimensions.

"It is also highly likely that certain members of our scientific elite are well aware of the unusual harmonics present at the Tanami location. Furthermore, we cannot rule out the possibility that this peculiar area has been 'created' deliberately as part of some on-going covert scientific program.

"This being so, it adds a whole new perspective with regards to the various unexplained activities that are continually reported in the area, especially the 'drop-outs' of electronic equipment. Whatever the answer turns out to be, it is certainly an area to keep close watch on. I would not be at all surprised if other strange happenings are seen and reported in this vicinity."

Our Northern Territory representative, Keith Douglass, had spoken to the indigenous population of the area on several occasions. They all claimed some knowledge of 'extraterrestrials', and maintained that the ones to the east of the town were okay – but the ones to the west – 'not so nice'.

In regards to 'portals' and the 'distortion' of the space/time continuum, this is not the only area of interest in Australia. One colleague, who often visited an 'experiencer' in rural NSW, was astounded to see a humanoid 'being' materialise near his property. His clothes were not the current norm, and his physical features altered as he came into view.

Her friend, who was a very wise and 'knowing' elderly man, indicated that this was not the first time he had met with similar visitors coming through a portal, but he did not want his identity or location ever disclosed.

Sometimes valid information comes elusively close to being revealed, only to disappear again under a veil of secrecy. The late Graham Birdsall published this intriguing account from July 1990.

Six US military personnel, from the 701st Army Intelligence Corps, went missing from their German Base. The authorities reported them missing and in possession of US Army property. A week later, the five men and one woman arrived in Gulf Breeze, Florida, where numerous UFO sightings had been reported in previous years.

One of the servicemen walked into the sheriff's office, and after admitting he was a deserter, was promptly arrested. He also claimed the group had stolen military computer chips and documents, which would prove 'alien beings' had, and still were visiting this planet at will.

He and his colleagues were determined to make this public if the government did not admit to these facts. The police arrested the other five, and despite promising safety from the government, notified the military once they were in custody. Fifteen government plain clothes intelligence and uniformed military personnel interrogated the six detainees, and the media 'descended in droves'.

At the same time, an anonymous message, including UFO documents and photographs, was received by all the major news agencies. It stated that full contents and disclosure would follow if, and only if, the six miscreants were not released immediately and granted immunity from prosecution.

Instead of being charged not only with desertion, but also stealing and revealing classified information, they were all released and given Honourable Discharges from the US Armed Forces.

CHAPTER EIGHT

UFO CRASHES and LANDINGS

PART ONE – USA and AUSTRALIA

In 1968, when Ted Phillips accompanied the legendary Allen Hynek on a couple of investigations, Hynek advised him to concentrate on the most valuable, which were landing cases, especially those with physical evidence.

Allan Hynek was one of the most knowledgeable investigators in this field, so I will also take his advice, and discuss a few of the many cases involving UFO crashes or landings.

There is much controversy regarding the 'crashes' of UFOs. Did they happen at all, and were they alien or one of our own craft? If they did occur, all nations would be desperate to learn not only the nature and intentions of the occupants, but also how to replicate the advanced technology.

There are many reports of saucers, and their alien occupants, crashing on Earth. Cases like Roswell are 'overdone', and nothing much can be added to what has already been written. Personally, I tend to believe the witness testimony and documentation that determined investigators have unearthed. It must, however, be remembered that New Mexico was a testing ground. On January 1st 1947, the *Waco Times-Herald* carried the headline – 'V-2 WARHEAD HAS VANISHED'. As of that time, despite extensive searches, nobody had located where the 2,000 pound object had come back to earth.

Graham Birdsall's *UFO Magazine* highlighted one of many disputes among respected researchers. Dr. Michael Wolf, who claimed to be a member of the scientific group within MJ-12, wrote a book – *'The Catchers of Heaven'*, in 1996. In it he confirmed the retrieval of two extraterrestrial spacecraft – one from Roswell and the other from Socorro in 1947. He also mentioned captured aliens and a technological exchange in the 1950s.

Stanton Friedman and John Carpenter investigated a separate incident which occurred on 5th July 1947. Gerald Anderson, a former police chief and County Deputy Sheriff, was only a young lad when his uncle drove his family into the desert 150 miles east of Roswell. They were going to fossick for moss agate, but found far more than they expected when they rounded the corner of a dry creek bed.

Stuck on the side of a ridge was a silver disc. It had a gash in the side, as if it had been crushed in. Anderson later thought that the contours of the vehicle would fit the gash perfectly. He speculated that maybe two of these discs had a mid-air collision, with one falling at Roswell, and the other crash landing where they found it. (In hindsight, this makes sense. Later reports state that a high powered government radar, which had been set-up nearby, interfered with the controlling mechanisms of the saucers.)

There were four bodies on the ground, shaded by the wreckage from the hot sun. Two were lifeless, one apparently injured, and a fourth obviously terrified. A professor, Dr. Buskirk and his five college students arrived, curious to discover what they had seen crash from the sky the night before.

While Buskirk was trying, unsuccessfully, to communicate with the frightened alien, another witness, civil engineer Barney Barnett, arrived in his pick-up truck. Anderson had telepathically sensed the creature's terror, and felt great empathy. Just as it seemed to calm down, the alien 'went crazy' at the sight of a contingent of armed soldiers that suddenly arrived.

The civilians were manhandled, told it was a secret military aircraft, and threatened if they ever divulged anything about it. After they had been ushered back up the hilltop, the witnesses saw more military arrive, including trucks and planes which landed on the blocked-off road. Whilst Anderson and the others were pressured into silence, they all knew what they saw was not a crashed weather balloon.

I was, however, left wondering by a paragraph contained in a 1997 letter sent to the Victorian UFO Research Society by MUFON investigator George Fawcett; He referred to the fact that the balloon and dummies, officially blamed for the Roswell incident, were not deployed until several years later; *'I was amazed to find that the Air Force used time travel and a space warp to explain the Roswell incident in that dummies dropped from high altitude, not only missed the crash site by seven years (1954) and seventy miles, and that a check on U-2 and SR-71 spy plane flight schedules in the 50s and 60s, showed they accounted for a few radar and pilot sightings at best.'* ??

Going back to a more popular theory, an interesting comment, allegedly made by Edgar Hoover, in a letter to Clyde Tolson, dated 15th July 1947, throws some light on the mystery: "I would do it, (study UFOs), but before agreeing, we must insist on full access to **discs** recovered. For instance, in the L.A. case, the Army grabbed it and would not let us have it for cursory examination."

In *'The Alien Gene'* I detailed the amazing 'air battle' over Los Angeles in February 1942. For hours ground based ordinance, fired multiple rounds at as many as fifteen unidentified craft which appeared over the city.

In 2010, MUFON published the text of some very revealing documents, which throw a lot more light on the incident.

On the 26th February 1942, G. Marshall, Chief of Staff, sent an initial memorandum to the President, detailing the Los Angeles incident.

The next day 'FDR' sent a memorandum to the Army Chief of Staff. This was very different! It mentions 'the disposition of the material in possession of the Army that may be of great significance toward the development of a super weapon of war.' He talks about 'the study of celestial devices', and precludes any sharing of information with the Soviet Union.

On March 5th 1942, G. Marshall sent another memo to the President. This time it mentions an 'Interplanetary Phenomenon Unit', and makes specific reference to the **Navy** salvaging one unidentified airplane off the coast of California – *'it had no bearing on conventional explanation. The **Army Air Corps also recovered a similar object** in the San Bernadino Mountains, east of Los Angeles, which cannot be identified as conventional aircraft.*

'This Headquarters has come to a determination that the mystery airplanes are in fact not earthly, and according to secret intelligence sources, they are in all probability of interplanetary origin.'

(This correspondence alludes to two different crashes. Dr Michael Wolf may have provided the answer when he claimed that the first UFO came down in 1941, into the ocean west of San Diego, and was retrieved by the navy. He explained that was why the US Navy claimed a prominent role in UFO matters.)

Two years later, on 24th February 1944, Franklin Roosevelt sent another memo to 'The Special Committee on Non-Terrestrial Science and Technology'. Basically it stressed the necessity of learning all the secrets of this alien technology. Super weapons were needed to win the war. Dr. Bush and Professor Einstein were to initiate a separate program for this project.

On 5th July 1947, Vannevar Bush wrote to the President Truman, and in referring to the 1944 correspondence, discussed furthering and developing the previous research and committees. If these documents are genuine, it's quite obvious that alien craft were recovered long before the 'Roswell' incident!

It is also possible that Vannevar Bush was also responsible for the exclusion of the elected government and other authorities from knowledge of ongoing weapons development and 'back engineering' projects. In 1949 he wrote in *'Modern Arms and Free Men'* that; *'Competent scientists and engineers must be enabled to get at it, without constraint by those who profess to know all the answers in advance. There is nothing more deadly than control of the activities of scientists and engineers by men who do not really understand, but think they do.'*

Another interesting fact takes us back to 1947, and those famous photographs showing the unusual 'metal' of the debris. Details about this metal are not often discussed, however there was an interesting excerpt in the *MUFON UFO Journal* Sept. 2004.

In 1970 an Air Force witness claimed that several pieces of metal from an alleged alien craft had hieroglyphs on them. Although the metal was light and bendable, it was virtually indestructible, and couldn't be cut or drilled through.

He said an owner of a drill company in Florida had been asked to come to the base with his best drills. Once there, he was taken into a hanger with three saucer-like craft inside. He used his best equipment to try and drill into one of them. After fifteen minutes there was no heat or colour change, nor any marks where the drill had been working.

In 2004, some fifty-seven years after 'Roswell', *Discover* magazine has reported that scientists in Pasadena have developed a new material, called 'amorphous metal', which can build lighter, stronger versions of many things. Called the 'structural material of the future', it is as thin as aluminium foil but cannot even be severed by wire cutters. The atoms in this metal have been rearranged so that it reacts differently to heat, and it would be difficult to penetrate, even with bombs. If the strange metallic material, reportedly found at

Roswell, was manufactured on Earth, surely it would not have taken all those years to be 'discovered' and utilised.

More information, regarding the 'memory metal' from Roswell, was discussed at length in the July 2009 *MUFON UFO Journal*. Researcher Anthony Bragalia outlines how in the late 1940s Wright Patterson AFB sent samples of a new 'morphing' metal alloy to Battelle Memorial Institute, in Ohio, for further study. This material could be crumpled or deformed, and would return itself instantly and seamlessly to its original state.

Perhaps a statement, reportedly made by President Clinton in September 2005, sums up the situation nicely.

"When I was president in my second term, there was an anniversary observance of Roswell....People came from all over the world, convinced that the government had buried a UFO, and perhaps an alien, deep underground, because we wouldn't allow anyone to go there.

"I can say now....this place in Nevada was really serious, and there was an alien artefact there. So I sent someone to figure it out.....If there were any secret government documents, they were concealed from me too. I wouldn't be the first American president that underlings have lied to. There may be some career person sitting around somewhere, hiding these dark secrets, even from elected presidents. But if so, they successfully eluded me....and I'm almost embarrassed to tell you, I did try to find out."

Regardless of which reports are accurate, in his book, '*The Day After Roswell*', Col. Philip Corso, who progressed to Army Intelligence after distinguished service during World War II, discussed the actions he, and others, took in 1961.

They did, indeed, have parts recovered from crashed discs. His boss, General Arthur Trudeau, did not trust the CIA or his Navy or Air Force counterparts. Part of his mission was to see if any of the harvested material could be used technologically for future programs, especially in advanced weapons. Corso helped send them to trusted Army development labs, with the cover story that they had come from Germany. The contractors were offered the patent rights for their 'discoveries', and the reverse engineering became part of recorded reality.

New innovations included laser technology, highly integrated circuits, fibre optics and much more. It is also obvious that other agencies and corporations have been devising ways to duplicate the electromagnetic and anti-gravity secrets of the alien craft.

The CIA was obviously not happy about initially being kept out of the loop. In a 1952 memorandum to the National Security Council, the then Director, General Walter Smith wrote; *'The Central Intelligence Agency has reviewed the current situation concerning unidentified flying objects, which have created extensive speculation in the press, and have been the subject of concern to government organisations......*

'Since 1947, approximately two thousand official reports of sightings have been received, and of these, about twenty percent are as yet unexplained. It is my view that this situation has possible implications for our national security which transcend the interests of a single service. A broader co-ordinated effort should be initiated to develop a firm scientific understanding of the several phenomena which apparently are involved in these reports '

Several incidents have been well publicised, however there are others which are lesser known.

USA

The rumours and testimony about crashes of UFOs in the United States are many and varied, and the modern day saga actually begins in the late nineteenth century. Around that time a lot of mysterious 'airships' were seen all over the world, and it is arguable as to where they originated.

A couple of cases, however, are worth mentioning. On January 25th 1878, the *Denison Daily News* told of Texan farmer, John Martin, who saw a dark object, high in the sky, which was moving towards him. Its shape and velocity caught his attention. Initially it appeared to be the size of an orange, but by the time it was overhead, it had increased considerably in size. He could actually see it was solid and possibly 'back-lit', and although he equated it with a possible 'balloon', travelling at incredible speed, he actually was the first to coin the phrase 'flying saucer' when describing the anomaly.

Nexus magazine published an excerpt from the *Dallas Morning News*, several years later on April 17th 1897. The report came from Aurora in Wise Co. Texas.

It details an airship which sailed over the town, *'collided with the tower of Judge Proctor's windmill, and went to pieces with a terrific explosion.'* The craft, fifty feet in length and weighing several tons, was badly wrecked, but appeared to have been *'built of an unknown metal, resembling somewhat a mixture of aluminium and silver'*.

The remains of the small pilot were buried the next day. Witnesses stated that, although badly disfigured, *'he was not an inhabitant of this world'*. Papers found on him were written in unknown hieroglyphs, which could not be deciphered. (This raises the interesting question as to why, if he was from a technically advanced society, would he need notes on paper? Was he in contact with unknown human allies?)

The debris was scattered over a large area, and 'souvenirs' were collected by many people. The episode was all but forgotten for seventy years, and while some researchers dismissed the entire event as a hoax, there were four 'old-timers' who remembered the incident from when they were children.

At the time some interested parties had wanted to dig up the entity's remains, and the locals, not wanting strangers interfering with their cemetery, had removed the small headstone marker. In the 1970s several pieces of alleged 'metallic debris' were submitted for analysis, but the results were varied and inconclusive.

Fragments were analysed by Dr. Tom Gray, a physics professor from North Texas University, and also by one of the nation's leading aircraft manufacturers. The professor couldn't identify it, and the aircraft company stated the alloy could not have been manufactured before 1920, long after the crash.

Tests had shown the material, which had been quickly molten in the air, had slowly cooled while in contact with the soil. Its internal structure was similar to a metal sample recovered from the coast of Brazil, in 1957, where a UFO was seen to explode

---

MISSOURI

Several researchers investigated a case in the spring of 1941. A non-human manufactured craft, along with a non-human, dead alien creature inside, purportedly crashed at Girardeau. Rev. William Huffman, of the Red Star

Baptist Church was called out to the site of what the local police thought was a crashed plane.

Instead he found himself looking at a wrecked disc, with three dead or dying entities. He dutifully performed the equivalent of the last rites for these strange beings, which certainly didn't appear to be human.

They were about four feet tall, with a 'soft' structure and long three fingered hands. Their eyes were oval, the mouths just a slit, and the ears almost non-existent. Their bodies looked like crinkled aluminium foil, but he couldn't tell if they were wearing suits or it was just 'skin'.

Although, when the military arrived, he was sworn to secrecy, Huffman talked about it to his family. Many years later his widow spoke of it just before her death. His granddaughter contacted researchers who were investigating UFO crashes, and others have confirmed the report.

NEW MEXICO

There was a report regarding three craft recovered in New Mexico. Little was proven until a single page was posted on the FBI's 'Vault' – the bureau's electronic 'reading room', which was launched by the agency in 2011.

Associated Press, in a subsequent article, commented that this 1950 Office Memorandum, sent to the then FBI Director J. Edgar Hoover, had already been viewed nearly one million times.

'An investigator for the Air Force stated that three so-called flying saucers have been recovered in New Mexico. They were described as being circular in shape, approximately fifty feet in diameter, with raised castors. Each one was occupied by three bodies, of human shape but only three feet tall, dressed in metallic cloth of a very fine texture. Each body was bandaged in a manner similar to the blackout suits used by speed flyers and test pilots.

'According to my informer the saucers were found in New Mexico due to the fact that the Government has a very high powered radar set-up in that area, and it is believed the radar interferes with the controlling mechanism of the saucers.

No further evaluation was attempted concerning the above.'

If this correspondence is referring to the alleged crash of discs at Aztec, some caution is recommended. In 1975, Mike McCllenan, an APRO investigator, researched the entire incident, and strongly suspected that all the previous reports had been generated by second and third hand information, which had been sensationalised for publicity reasons.

However, in August 2004, MUFON published the results of a lengthy investigation where first-hand witnesses were located. Although they were now very elderly, with one on his deathbed, they clearly remembered the incident.

Early in April, 1948, Ken Farley and a friend were driving to San Diego, when they followed a lot of trucks and a police car going down a dirt road. They came to a mesa, where a lot of ranchers and oil field workers were gathered near a large disc, sitting silently on the ground.

It had no noticeable damage, and was perfectly smooth on the outside, with no seams or markings except for around the middle of the craft. Some of the oil field workers were climbing on top of it, with other older witnesses shouting at them to "get off".

Finally, the military arrived, interviewed the witnesses who were 'threatened with their lives and sworn to secrecy.'

El Paso Gas Company employee, Doug Nolan, and his boss Bill Ferguson raced out to Hart Canyon at 5am that morning. They had been alerted to a brush fire, but when they arrived other workers told them it was under control, but there was something else they needed to see.

Doug saw the disc on the ground, and described it as being large and metallic with no noticeable seams, rivets, bolts or weld marks. He said it looked like it had been moulded. Both he and Bill also climbed up on the craft, and looked through what appeared to be a broken 'porthole'. They could see two bodies slumped over what they thought was a control panel.

Soon a military helicopter started circling overhead, which Doug clearly remembered, as it was the first time he had actually seen one. Doug and Bill spoke to the two police officers, one of whom said he was from the nearby town of Cuba. He had followed the low-flying disc earlier on, and tracked it to the area of Hart Canyon Road.

Other witnesses have been interviewed over the years, most of whom were not at the actual crash scene, but involved in the later 'clean-up' site or analysis of the debris. In these reports there is a slight discrepancy in the dates, but it is evident that the crash occurred in late March – early April 1948.

In March 2004, Graham Birdsall published an interesting report, based on evidence from two elderly gentlemen, Jose Padilla and Remigo Baca, who had been aged nine and seven in 1945, when they lived on a ranch in New Mexico.

In August that year, at the same time our first atomic bombs were being tested and detonated over Japan, the two lads had set out on horseback to find a cow and her newly born calf. A bad storm came up, and while they were taking shelter, there was a brilliant light and the ground around them shook. The storm had already passed, and they thought it must have been another test at White Sands.

A short time later, they saw smoke coming from the next canyon, and upon climbing to the top of a hill, saw a gouge in the earth, 'as long as a football field', with a circular metallic object at the end of it. They waited until the burning vegetation had cooled, and climbed down to the wreckage site.

There was a huge litter field, and they picked up a piece of thin shiny material. They said it was like the tin foil in old cigarette packets. When folded 'it spread itself out again'. They approached the craft, and could see strange looking creatures moving franticly around inside – 'shadowy and expressionless, but definitely living beings.'

They raced back home, and told Jose's father, who felt it must belong to the military, and obviously didn't want to get involved. He did, however, advise his friend, Eddie Apodaca, who was a local policeman, and the boys took him to the crash site on 18th August. When they arrived, they thought the wreckage was gone, but then they spotted it, hidden by dirt and debris. The policeman and Jose's father went into the disc. The entities were gone, and it looked as if as if someone had attempted to clean up the area and camouflage the craft. Before they left, the lads were cautioned to say nothing to anybody else.

Two days later the military commenced a recovery operation, and an army sergeant visited the Padilla home, and insisted that what they had found was a weather balloon. Tight security was installed around the ranch, and the family was told not to tell anyone. They watched as soldiers, with camouflaged flat-bed trucks, removed the disc and most of the debris.

Jose and Remigo both commented that if this were some form of extraterrestrial craft, it was, in hindsight very crude and rudimentary, given our modern technology.

On 24th April 1964, policeman Lonnie Zamora was in his patrol car, just south of Socorro, when he saw a bright bluish/orange flash, accompanied by a roaring sound. He turned off the highway, onto a side gravel road, to investigate.

In the distance, he saw what he thought was a small, overturned car in a gully. Beside the vehicle he noticed two indiscernible small figures, in white overalls, standing nearby. Before he reached the scene, his car engine and radio temporarily failed. The 'beings' had disappeared, and the craft rose about twenty feet into the air. It was oval, with a long horizontal axis, and sort of shiny white, like 'aluminium'. Zamora noted that it was smooth, with no visible windows or doors. The strange object emanated the same blue flash and roaring noise as before. The light and noise subsided, and it moved silently away, angled sharply upwards and disappeared into the distance.

Bushes around the landing site were smouldering, and due to the proximity of an old dynamite shack, Zamora called his police headquarters. Two other officers arrived at the scene, and one immediately took photos of the imprints of four 'landing gear', where the craft had been on the ground. Military authorities arrived, and confiscated the film before it had been developed. Alan Hynek, who arrived a few days later, intimated that the film had been 'fogged', possibly by radiation. Apparently, this incident was categorised as 'Unexplained' by Project Blue Book.

Over the next couple of weeks, other interested people visited the site, and also witnessed the remnants of the charred brush and fading scorch marks. A large rock, which had been directly underneath the craft, had melted in two. Due to the publicity at the time, Zamora and his family were subjected to a multitude of unwelcome phone calls, and he left the police force two years later.

NEVADA

Dr. Willy Smith, from the UNICAT Project, wrote of an interesting case, sourced from the Project Blue Book Files.

On November 23rd 1953, Lt. Joseph Long was travelling from Stead AFB. At 6.30am he was tired, having driven all night, and without warning his car began to fail, and finally stopped. He couldn't restart it, and as he got out of the vehicle, he noticed a high-pitched whining noise.

About three or four hundred yards away, to the right of the highway, he could see four very unusual objects on the ground. He walked over, until he was about fifty feet from the first one. He later reported that all four craft were identical – disc-shaped, about fifty feet in diameter, with a transparent dome in the centre of the top. They glowed brightly, apparently emitting their own source of light, and had a darker, rotating ring around the outside.

As soon as he approached, the pitch of the noise intensified, and all four objects lifted off the ground and moved slowly away until they disappeared behind some hills to the north.

Long went over to the landing site. Although he could not detect any heat or disturbance on the ground, there were impressions where the landing 'gear' he had observed had been. He returned to his car, which started without any problem, and drove to Indian Springs, which was the closest Air Force Base.

He was a respected officer, and his report was believed by the C.O. and his adjutant. A report was prepared by Capt. Benjamin Kenyon, who concluded that the objects 'were not of this world.' Later, the Blue Book files tried to put another spin on it, suggesting a psychological evaluation of the witness.

TEXAS

In their book 'The Other Roswell', Noe Torres and Ruben Uriate write of a little known incident which occurred in 1955.

Initially, an unknown object, flying inland from the west coast of the USA, was detected by both ground radar and several bombers and their fighter escort. One of the fighter escorts requested permission to investigate.

Col. Robert Willingham, in his F-86 Sabre jet, left the formation and followed the radar contact. He finally made visual contact as the unidentified craft descended into a crash landing, just over the border in the Republic of Mexico.

He was short on fuel, and after returning to his Texas base, he rented a small private plane, and returned to the crash site over the border. When he landed, he surveyed the unusual disc, but by then, the Mexican military had already arrived on the scene.

Two years later, on the night of 2nd-3rd November 1957, a farm worker, driving four miles west of Levelland, saw a glowing object down in a field just north of the road. It rose up into the air, and passed over his truck, causing the lights and motor to temporarily cease functioning.

Several minutes later, another motorist, four miles east of Levelland, encountered an object on the road ahead. It rose vertically, then shot to the north at an incredible speed. Thirty minutes after that, another truck driver reported a similar object on a farm road north of Levelland.

By one-thirty in the morning, the local Sheriff, Weir Clem, and his deputy, Pat McCulloch, had received multiple reports from around the area. Most witnesses had described the object as being a large oval craft, which was glowing bluish/green when on the ground, changing to bright red when lifting off.

Clem and McCulloch took to the road, and they, along with three individual police officers, sighted the craft in the nearby sky. They, and other witnesses, experienced EM effects on their vehicles. The next day there were black cars, full of 'FBI or Air Force investigators' all over the town. The sheriff was told not to say anything about what he had seen.

Many years' later, MUFON's Don Burleson, thoroughly investigated the event. He found many more interesting aspects to this case. Most of the newspapers from the following week were 'missing', and apparently similar incidents had occurred before that particular night. I wonder whether the craft was of alien origin, or one of our own prototypes on an irresponsible 'test run'.

ARIZONA

Author/investigator Raymond Fowler was approached by a man, who said he was using a pseudonym due to the sensitive information he was imparting.

He claimed to have been an engineer at Wright-Patterson Air Force Base, and later at the Atomic Proving Ground in Nevada. On May 21st 1953, he and other military personnel travelled for four hours in a bus with blackened windows, meaning they were not sure where they were when they arrived. He thought it may have been Arizona, and they saw what appeared to be an oval shaped object that looked like – 'two deep saucers, about thirty feet in diameter, with one inverted upon the other.'

He was told that this was a super-secret Air Force vehicle. Everybody was sworn to secrecy, and his job was to determine what speed it was travelling at when it hit the ground. Whilst there, he noticed a tent, and when he looked in, he saw ' the dead body of a four-foot human-like creature in a silver metallic-looking suit'.

Before he left another airman told him that he had seen the interior of the craft, where there were 'two swivel seats and instruments and displays.'

Researcher, Leonard Stringfield, received what could have been corroborating evidence, when a former Air Force metallurgist told him of being flown, blindfolded, to a 'hot and sandy area' in the spring of 1953. He said that he was asked to participate in the recovery of a vehicle much like the one Raymond Fowler's informant had described.

UTAH

Author/researcher Kevin Randle investigated a case which happened on April 18th 1962, over south-western USA. Multiple witnesses had watched a glowing red object, at a very high altitude, moving across the sky. After a while, it came closer, and people described hearing a roaring sound.

It appeared to land, for a few minutes, at Eureka, Utah, before resuming its flight. The 'Las Vegas Sun' on April 19th reported that a large explosion was heard, and whatever it was disappeared from radar screens seventy miles north-west of Las Vegas. Very little more was known of the incident, until the 1980s when Randle interviewed some of the witnesses. The information was slightly inconclusive as to whether there were two objects that night, one in Utah and another in Nevada.

Later, one man, who had been stationed at Nellis Air Force Base at the time, claimed that he and other soldiers were loaded onto a bus with 'closed' windows. After being driven for some time, they arrived at a site in the desert, where they were told to collect the pieces of what looked like a 'flying saucer'. All they were told was that the craft was secret.

CAROLINA

Some objects merely landed, then after a short interval, flew away. One such case happened at Bakersfield, on 18th October 1927. Richard Sweed was driving was driving through the outskirts of the town when he spotted a bluish-grey disc resting on the ground not far away. It was about sixty feet in diameter, with a row of round windows around the edge.

After a few minutes it rose into the sky, at a 45-degree angle, then flew off making a 'humming, swooshing' sound as it went. Another incident occurred at Greensboro, North Carolina, in the 1930s, also long before we had any similar craft of our own.

One clear spring day, two retired, well educated professional women, and two other witnesses, saw a dark coloured disc land in their garden. They described it as resembling a 'child's toy top', about forty feet wide at the centre and tapering off at the edges. They could see the head and shoulders of an 'occupant' inside. After a few minutes it rose straight up, and moved silently and smoothly away. The witnesses noted that, once in the sky, the craft also hovered and moved both perpendicularly and horizontally.

FLORIDA

The NICAP organisation investigated another case which occurred in the Everglades. On March 14th 1965, James Flynn, was camped after spending a day training his dogs. It was after one in the morning when he saw a bright oscillating light. What was it, out here in the wild? He got into his swamp buggy and drove closer to investigate.

Proceeding the rest of the way on foot, he saw a landed object. It was large, about one hundred feet in diameter and thirty feet high. It looked like a shiny, metallic 'inverted top', with a bank of lighted ports or windows. He could not see any sign of occupants, and thought it safe to approach.

An invisible 'sledgehammer blow' knocked him to the ground and he lost consciousness. When he recovered the craft was gone. He staggered to a nearby Indian village, and was taken to Fort Myers hospital. He later took investigators to the scene. The tops of the trees were seared, and a round, burned area, seventy-two feet in diameter, was on the ground.

PENNSYLVANIA

On December 9th 1965, a fireball followed by a flash of light was seen by multiple witnesses over Pennsylvania and Illinois. A forest fire, near Kecksburg, resulted in the area being cordoned off by police. The military arrived, and placed a strange object and debris into several trucks.

Witnesses described an 'acorn' shaped craft, which was suspiciously similar to 'Die Glocke', ('The Bell'), an experimental aircraft developed by the Nazi's just before the end of World War II. Many researchers believe the object which crashed was not extraterrestrial, but rather a further development of this revolutionary invention.

Was this an extraterrestrial craft? I don't think so. On that very same day the Russian spacecraft Kosmos 96 came crashing back down to earth. The Americans would have been anxious to analyse and investigate all the Soviet technology. To admit recovering it would have required them to give it back as soon as possible.

I am not about to enter into the debate about aliens we may have captured or have as our 'guests'. There are countless books, articles and documentaries about this topic. One lesser known report came from George Filer III, when he was based at McGuire Air Force Base in New Jersey, USA.

On 18th January 1978, George arrived at 4am to be told that UFOs had been flying over the base all night, and one had landed or crashed at neighbouring Fort Dix. Later reports confirmed that about twelve bluish-green lights had been seen in formation above the base.

An Army MP at Fort Dix reported that a UFO had been hovering close to his vehicle when – 'out of nowhere a 'thing' – a 'being' – appeared right in front of his vehicle. It was four feet tall, greyish-brown in colour, with a huge head, long arms and a slender body.'

The soldier panicked, and fired five shots into the 'creature' and one more into the object floating above him. The wounded entity fled, and the UFO joined the others hovering overhead. Two more soldiers and a State Trooper joined him in the search for the wounded intruder, and when they reached the inactive McGuire runway, 'their headlights revealed, about fifty feet ahead, a motionless figure lying prone on the cold concrete.'

Researchers Leonard Stringfield and Richard Hall, who also investigated this case, said one of the security police officers commented that there was a strong scent of ammonia, and described the entity as 'a smelly, slimy creature that appeared to have an almost snakelike texture.'

George Filer was told that a C-141, from Wright Patterson Base, Ohio, was on its way to pick up the alien's body. When he asked what country the intruder was from his commander replied; "No, not a foreigner – an alien from outer space."

Within thirty minutes, a heavily armed recovery team, with no identifying insignia, arrived. They sprayed something on the corpse, put it into a crate, and flew off with it in their plane. George had a lot of questions but no answers. As normally happens in these cases, all witnesses were debriefed, sworn to secrecy, and within days retired or transferred to various other bases.

It was this and other incidents which prompted Filer's lifelong interest in UFOs, and led him to become a serious investigator in his own right and also a member of MUFON and their New Jersey State Director.

VIRGINIA

Researcher, Rufus Drake, a US pilot and Air Force veteran, spent many years trying to discover whether the government had any crashed saucers in its possession, and interviewed over a hundred potential witnesses.

One interesting case was related by retired Lt. Col. William Anderson. In the summer of 1952, he was piloting an F-94 when he was asked to divert to a remote swamp in a Virginia tidewater region, where there had been reports of a crash.

Anderson said; *"When I arrived, I circled overhead at 1,000 feet, and looked down at a saucer-shaped craft which had burrowed into a mud flat and partially disintegrated. It had knocked over several trees on its way in. There were signs of activity around the wreck, impressions in the mud, and apparent scorch marks.*

'I was told that the area was being sealed off, and that teams were en route by helicopter. Yet according to the radio traffic, rescue teams had not arrived yet. Low on fuel, I was also told that they didn't need my help, after all.'

Drake spoke to another Air Force officer, who remembered the flurry of activity, and helicopters 'coming and going'. Apparently the helicopters retrieved the saucer only to find that its crew had been pulled out, by an identical saucer seen on radar at the crash site before any aircraft arrived. The saucer was taken to a guarded hanger at Andrews Air Force Base, and ground crews scoured the crash site for days, recovering debris and detecting signs of radioactivity.

HAWAII/CALIFORNIA

An unusual report starts in June 1973, when a US destroyer was sailing from California to Hawaii. A strange craft had flown over the ship, and it crashed into the sea after being targeted by a missile. The UFO was later recovered, from a depth of 350 feet, by the 'Glomar Explorer'. It was then shipped to Honolulu and taken from there to a naval base in Chicago.

Three months later a navy seaman, on guard duty outside a building at the Chicago Great Lakes Naval Base, was told not to let anyone inside, as it contained highly top secret material.

A courier arrived with documentation which required a receipt, and the guard went inside to get a signature. He was escorted down a corridor and entered a large warehouse area. He noticed a very unusual craft, about thirty-five feet wide, and twelve to fifteen feet high at its thickest part. There were no windows or seams, but it had a flange running along the topside.

After getting the signature, the seaman was escorted out, and warned to never say anything to anyone about what he had seen.

ALASKA

In May/June 1991, Jerzy Faron and the crew of a fishing trawler accidently netted a black capsule they claim had broken away from a crashed 'starship'. They found an injured alien inside, and notified authorities. The creature was apparently about five feet tall, human looking, but had no hair or teeth, and only three fingers.

While the coast guard admitted hearing rumours, they had no knowledge of a UFO crash or the recovery of an alien astronaut. Jerzy and his crew were monitoring radio dispatches, and said the alien was taken to an undisclosed hospital under 24 hour guard. Doctors and scientists were gathering to try and keep the being alive, while the military were trying to locate the main body of the 'spaceship'.

AUSTRALIA

On 24th May 1965, just after midnight, three guests, on the veranda of the Retreat Hotel, near Mackay in Queensland, were startled to see a strange, glowing object closing in from the sky above.

J. Tilse who was a veteran airline pilot, proved a very competent witness. He said it was about three hundred yards from them when they first noticed it. The craft was solid and metallic, at least thirty feet in diameter with a bank of about twenty-five spotlights below a circular platform.

It moved across the treetops, with bright tallow/orange lights shining down. When the object came to a small clearing on the ridge, it settled gently to earth. The lights dimmed a little but were still quite brilliant.

Tilse and his friends were a little apprehensive of approaching, and watched the motionless craft from a safe distance. After thirty minutes it started to rise over the tree tops, and they could see three massive tripod-type legs, which they assumed to be landing gear. Each leg had a light on it, but they disappeared by the time the craft reached an altitude of three hundred feet, and they assumed they must have been retracted.

The object then began to pick up horizontal speed, rapidly accelerated and vanished into the north-west. All three men were questioned by the RAAF, who could not identify the mystery craft.

In *'Contact Down Under'*, I have written about a wealth of Australian UFO reports. But not all crash landings are UFOs, and can have perfectly rational explanations. In the late 1990s, something came down into the dam at Guyra, in northern N.S.W. The impact was recorded on the seismograph at nearby Armidale, and there was much public speculation about a UFO. In fact it was a meteorite, larger than a golf ball, which could have done enormous damage had it struck a building, instead of hitting the water.

CHAPTER NINE

CRASHES and LANDINGS

PART TWO – GREAT BRITAIN

Britain has always been one of the world's leaders in aeronautics. It boasts many RAF Bases, and hosts US Bases on its soil. Sometimes, when prototypes crash, it is convenient to blame it on 'UFOs'.

ENGLAND

On 29th December 1968, in Northumbria, Britain, an incident involving an apparently unmanned craft occurred.

William Robson wrote to the Air Ministry claiming that at about noon, while on patrol along the Roman Wall, he saw a silent silvery disc coming down very fast. It was spinning and trailing smoke. At first he thought it was a plane, but when was about 1,000ft from the ground, it levelled off and went north. He followed it for about twelve miles when it suddenly nose-dived out of sight.

Night falls very early during British winters, and not wanting to walk the moors in the dark, William decided to return the following weekend. On 5th January he set off early, and by lunchtime, after walking about ten miles, reached the top of a hill from where he could see what appeared to be the wrecked craft.

Between two hills, in a marshy piece of ground, was a silver disc, sticking half out of the bog. He hurried down and was surprised at the size of the object – like a huge 'spinning-top', about one hundred feet in diameter.

He noticed a doorway and walked in. The walls were a mass of equipment, apparently still working. There were lights flashing and weird noises, but not a sign of life. He noticed the door was starting to sink into the bog, possibly because of his additional weight, and he jumped out to safety. By the time he left it had sunk to the extent that only two feet was left sticking out of the marsh.

A week later he wrote the letter to the Air Ministry. They, in turn, contacted the local police, but it appears there had been some telephone conversations apart from the official correspondence which suggested the report was a little 'far-fetched'.

Robson was unable to locate the site when taken there by police over three weeks later. It must be remembered that it was in a very remote area, and the remaining two feet of the craft, sticking out of the marsh, may well have sunk out of sight.

I wonder what was said in those undocumented telephone conversations? Suddenly, under 'police caution' he wrote a 'confession' saying that although he had seen the object in the sky, he had not gone to any crash site.

British researcher, Andy Roberts, a bit of a sceptic, was gloating over the fact the others had been fooled by a 'hoax'. But had they? William had not sought publicity or contacted the media, and seemed more intent on doing his patriotic duty by alerting the authorities. It would have raised suspicion if the MoD had persuaded him to 'retract' his statement, and I wonder how much pressure was he under when he signed that 'confession' under 'police caution?'

It appeared there was some very sophisticated 'gadgetry' on board this empty craft. Was it remote controlled? Ours, another country's, or alien? At that time, the Apollo Moon Missions were on their way, apparently with the minimum of modern technology – nothing like what we have today.

Philip Mantle investigated a case which occurred in Normanton, West Yorkshire, during the summer of 1979. Mrs Westerman was doing the washing while her children were playing a ball game in the garden. Suddenly her eight year-old daughter came running in, saying an aeroplane had landed in the adjoining field. The children had seen it hovering just above some electricity pylons before it slowly set down in the field.

She went outside to see a dull silver-grey object, with a rim around the perimeter, similar to a 'Mexican hat', lying on the ground a few hundred yards away. Around this strange craft were three very tall men, dressed in silver suits, who were pointing a dark instrument at the ground. Mrs Westerman, along with six children, walked over to the field, and stopped at the fence.

At this time, one of the men looked up, and obviously saw the woman and youngsters watching them. All three quickly walked to the rear of the object, after which it rose vertically, stopped in mid-air, then quickly and silently, shot off at an angle into the sky.

Omar Fowler investigated an interesting case from Hampshire, which occurred on 12th August 1983. An elderly retired man. Alfred Burtoo, was fishing in the Basingstoke Canal near Aldershot. It was after one in the morning, and he and his dog were relaxing and enjoying the peace and quiet.

He noticed a bright light travelling fast across the night sky. It approached, at a very low altitude, and silently hovered only a few hundred yards away. He watched as it started to descend behind some trees, and wondered if it was going to come down on the railway bridge.

His dog began to growl, and Alfred could see two small human-like figures coming along the path towards him. They were only about four feet tall, dressed in some kind of one-piece overall, with helmets on their heads. They stopped a short distance away, and one beckoned Alfred to follow them.

For some unknown reason, he went after them along the tow-path until they reached a large metallic looking circular craft. There was a row of illuminated 'windows' around the circumference, and a 'cowl' arrangement around the top section. Alfred estimated the vehicle to be about forty-five feet in diameter, and fifteen feet of it was overhanging the water.

They led him up a ladder, with handrails, into an open doorway. It was quite dark inside, with only faint illumination. The first figure entered a corridor and a room on the other side, while the second stood in the doorway. He could see a large column, about four feet in diameter, coming out of the floor, and two further figures standing to the side, next to what looked like some type of 'Z' shaped handle. Although there was some panelling along the walls, there was no sign of nuts, bolts or welded seams.

After a while he heard a voice that reminded him of broken English. He insisted it was not telepathic. He was told to go and stand under an amber light across the room. He obliged and found himself facing a panel under the small glowing bulb. He thought that the light/panel was scanning him.

One of the beings asked his age, and when he said seventy-eight next birthday, a voice said; "You can go, you are too old and infirm for our purpose." He hastily exited the craft, and started back to his fishing spot. He heard a faint hum and turned around to see the 'cowl' on top of the craft start to rotate. A vivid light shone out from the bottom, and it began to rise from the ground.

When it was about three hundred feet up it shot off at an incredible speed. He returned to his fishing, and despite deteriorating health did not put too much emphasis on the event. However, after he died, his family were instructed to bury him under a table-top headstone. Omar wondered if he was worried 'someone' might want to retrieve his body!

On November 12th 1987, 'something' crashed in the Kirkby area, south of Mansfield in Nottinghamshire. Was it alien, from a foreign power, or one of our own prototypes? I don't think we will ever know! British researchers Jim Mills and Michael Howard investigated this case, and it produces more questions than answers.

At 1.30am an object was seen slowly zigzagging across the cloudless sky. It was making a strange 'winey noise' as if it was in trouble. Later evaluation calculated the craft as having a diameter of about sixty feet. Several witnesses reported seeing two more objects closing in, and apparently colliding with it mid-air.

At that stage, the original craft seemed to come down in a nearby wood. It apparently exploded upon impact and 'bounced' to a second site, where the wreckage came to rest. There was an enormous shockwave which caused a tremendous amount of damage in a seven to eight miles radius of the surrounding area. Powerlines came down, TV aerials were split in two, and houses suffered structural damage. Some windows exploded, whilst others imploded.

At about 2.15am seven military helicopters were seen scanning the area with powerful search-lights, and soon after the police cordoned off the impact site where a fire was burning. Later, the top soil was removed down to a level of about nine inches, and replaced with new soil over a clay base. Even new trees were planted – but by whom and why? Was this one of the reported crashes ot the military's own new prototype planes?

Army personnel were at the 'wreckage' site for three or four days. Armed guards were positioned and government officials and heavy military trucks arrived.

One man, whose house was virtually destroyed, was visited by two men from the Department of Scientific Intelligence, who took samples of some 'metallic dust' in his garden, and warned him to keep quiet about what he knew. Other witnesses reported receiving threats about saying anything about the incident.

SUFOG - the Southampton UFO group, published an interesting account in 1996: On 19th April 1993, the radar at Air Traffic Control, Prestwich, picked up an object, at 33,000ft, which was travelling more than 5,500mph. When it approached the Pennine range, it turned right and headed due south. NATO's early warning system had also tracked the object, and two RAF Jaguar aircraft were scrambled to intercept.

Eighteen minutes later, at 8.37pm, the radar screens at Gatwick airport registered what was assumed to be the same object, now at an altitude of 10,000ft, and only travelling at 250mph. They monitored it, heading west, for three minutes, before they lost it from the screens.

This incident may have been insignificant, given the hundreds of reports received every year, but a letter from Captain Fodoala Parc, of the Royal Egyptian Army Intelligence Corp., threw more light on the matter.

'I was on military manoeuvres with the British Army at Salisbury Plains, England. On 19th April, at 8.45pm, we were instructed to go to Blackheath, which is approximately six miles from where we were. This apparently was because we were part of intelligence operations and had security clearance.

On arrival at Blackheath, we found a cylindrical object, measuring about sixty feet by forty feet. This had four hydraulic legs, two of which had been damaged on landing – the object was lying at a thirty degree angle. It was made from what looked like metal and carbon fibre material which appeared highly polished and seamless – its colour was a dark charcoal. About one third down the side was an opening, measuring about two feet by four feet.

On entry to the object, we were met by three USAF high ranking officers, and were told to secure the area until recovery personnel arrived. I also noticed, on what I would call the 'flight deck', two other persons which I could only describe as extraterrestrial beings. From what I saw, they were about three-and-a-half to four feet tall, with greyish smooth complexion. Their heads were extreme proportion to their bodies compared with humans, with slanting eyes and thin arms. At no time did they speak.

I immediately left the vessel and secured the area as instructed to do so. Within fifty minutes an USAF Sikorsky chopper came from USAF Woodbridge in Suffolk, to where the object was taken, complete with crew. I later found out that the two Jaguar aircraft from RAF Coltishall, were intercepted by USAF aircraft, and returned to base after being told that the object was a USAF test flight.

I have since returned to Egypt and told not to repeat anything that I saw that evening. Also my security clearance has been lowered and I no longer have access to any of the information from that evening.

I have since learned that there have been similar UFO sightings in that area of the UK, and also that the USAF have been working in conjunction with aliens on designing high-tech military aircraft.

If anybody has more information regarding these sightings, or any information in respect of the USA military and alien connections, I would very much appreciate knowing.'

(Personally I think this whistleblower was using a totally false name and origin, however it doesn't necessarily make the information incorrect. The details indicate this was more of a forced landing than a crash.)

In 2003 BUFORA received another report from the early 1990s, but cautioned that because they could not follow-up the correspondence or other witnesses, it may be a hoax. I was intrigued, because the details were similar to other reports of crash retrievals. Also, the witness had obviously waited until leaving the RAF before saying anything.

'In April 1994 I was in the RAF, employed as a movement controller with the mobile air movement squadron based at RAF Lynham. At very short notice, I got an order to fly, in a C 130 Hercules, with two other military personnel, to an airbase in Iceland to pick up a class 'A' cargo to return to RAF Mildenhall.

'When we arrived in Iceland, I was amazed at the amount of security on the base....like I had never seen before. When we arrived eight armed military police boarded our aircraft...and we were escorted by bus to a small hanger...there, waiting for me and two Icelandic movers, was a standard Hercules pallet with a wooden crate on top.

'......Once I had secured the crate into the aircraft, four armed military policemen guarded the crate on the return trip to England, and shadowed my every move until it was safe in a hanger. Waiting there were ten USAF staff to take charge of the crate. While exchanging paperwork with my American counterpart, I asked him what was all the security about?

'He said, in a very matter of fact way that it was 'Non-terrestrial material'. I asked if it was a crashed satellite, but he replied; "No – satellites originate on Earth. The material in that crate does not come from this planet."

'Any other time, I would have thought it was a joke, but not this time. It was a very bizarre trip, and not one I ever repeated in all the days I was in the RAF.'

Another interesting case was featured, in 2011, by the UK's 'Northern Echo' following an interview with seventy-six year-old Robert Hall, whose case had been investigated by researcher Richard Hall. The elderly grandfather's sister said that although he was teased at school, he has stuck to the same story all his life.

In 1940, and wartime, when five year-old Robert was playing with his friends at the Tyneside terraces in Gateshead. Earlier he had noticed something whizzing over his head, and he left his friends and wandered off around the corner. He was confronted by an aircraft 'the like of which he had never seen before'. It was an elliptical shape with a metallic surface and a bright light.

He was astounded to see some strange figures standing in the back lane. Their appearance and clothes were unusual. Three were small, only two to four feet in height, but built like human men.

The other children were terrified, and tried to get over the barbed wire next to the railway tracks. Some got cut and were screaming. Robert stayed, and the creatures spoke to him in perfect English. They asked if they could examine him, and took blood from the back of his neck. He also recalled they had a short, white hand-held device, which could subdue or immobilise someone.

"I kept my eyes shut, and was so frightened I was shaking," he recalled. "After twenty minutes I was up that street like a shot. My parents thought I was kidding, and so did the soldiers. The next day two men in black suits came, and warned me if I said anything I would disappear."

It was only a few days later that a grey being, with big eyes and a large head, grabbed him in the street. Robert fell over the kerb, hurting his toe. His Uncle Ernie saw what was happening, and 'bashed the creature's head in' with a coal shovel.

Robert said he was sent to find the local policeman, Sgt. Brookes, while they put the alien's body in a coal sack. The Army was called, and they removed the corpse to the local church. Robert also recalled that afterwards, strange small triangular marks appeared on his left cheek. They remained until he was about twelve or thirteen, when they disappeared without a trace.

WALES

My friend and colleague Margaret Fry, had mounted her own investigations into the controversial reports of a crashed disc in Wales some years before, and to her dismay could not get her subsequent article published in the main Welsh UFO Newsletter. Since Margaret was one of the researchers included in our Independent Network, we agreed to publish this article in our own June 1998 *'INUFOR DIGEST'*.

1974 WELSH CRASH

BERWYN MOUNTAIN 23rd JANUARY 1974 INCIDENTS

By Margaret Fry

The Berwyn story ranks with Rendlesham Forest and Roswell in the duplicity of Governments in covering up the UFO phenomenon at any cost. I first read of it through Eileen Buckle, when her article appeared in 'Flying Saucer Review' February 1974. She was one of the first BUFORA (British UFO Research Association) investigators. Titled 'Welsh Mountain Explosion', she detailed finding a number of witnesses for that night, who saw strange objects in the sky from Holyhead, and Betws-y-Coed to Gobwen, near Shropshire.

Apparently there were newspaper reports about people seeing strange things in the sky, but as usual, most were explained away as a meteorite etc. I have only, in this month of February, 1998, seen copies of these reports. One or two lend further credence to what I have independently gathered over the years.

I had received in Dulwich, London, several reports of a mile-long cigar-shaped object, with numerous portholes, flying low over houses. This was about an hour before a UFO landed on Berwyn. Wales was a remote little country to me, and I did not know the place names. It was not until 1979 when my daughter's family shifted to North Wales, that I started meeting local people. Farmers told me of seeing a 'large orange globe' on 23rd January, 1974, either over Berwyn or other parts of North Wales.

Welsh names were unpronounceable and soon forgotten by me. By the time I came to live in North Wales in 1983, I just assumed these places were near my area of Llandudno. Many of these village names were repeated in the same County.

My friend, David Clayton, had written to the Bala newspapers about an earthquake, explosion and meteor crash at Berwyn. David had a hunch there was more to this than the official explanation, and asked people to contact him if they remembered the incident.

Mrs. Pat Evans and Mrs. Rees-Pritchard wrote to him. In October 1991, we drove down to Bala. All reports I previously had 'clicked together', as I now knew where Berwyn was. Berwyn is quite a remote and desolate area of high mountains, just outside the surrounds of Bala town and lake.

Mrs. Rees-Pritchard had written that in 1974 she worked in the bar of a hotel in Bala. When the 'earthquake' came all the glasses in the bar had fallen. Then there was an explosion.

I had checked with the Edinburgh British Geological Survey, Seismology Department, and they told me the earthquake was on the 23rd January 1974, at 8.31 pm, and registered 3.5 magnitude on the Richter Scale. The curious thing about it was that some reported an explosion immediately after, and others did not hear it at all.

The morning after, 'suited strangers' were booked into the hotel, and for a whole week they went up to the mountain every day. The staff had tried, without success, to ask them... 'why'? I was unable to contact Mrs. Rees-Pritchard at the time, and when I did, she had moved away. What she wrote to me proved a valuable piece of information.

It was not until October 1995 that I was able to go to Bala again and interviewed Mrs. Pat Evans, who was a nurse. At about 8.30pm she and her *two daughters also felt the earthquake and simultaneously heard the explosion at Llanderferel village. They thought a plane had crashed on the Berwyns, as there had been crashes there before. She rang Police HQ at Colwyn Bay, offering her services as a nurse. Her two girls were in the St. John's Ambulance Brigade, and also wanted to help.*

When they parked their car opposite the mountain, they first thought there was a fire. Then they realised it was a huge, pulsating egg-shaped craft, glowing pinky-red. It was on a ridge, just below the mountain side. They stayed there for twenty minutes, during which time small white lights zig-zagged up to the object. Thinking these were the police or military, they decided they could do nothing. They turned around by a small, roughly hewn car park on the Berwyn to go home. This took fifteen minutes, and during all the time, there and back, they saw 'not another soul'.

The area was so wind-swept - bleak in muted shades of brown and grey/green with approaching winter. Cader Berwyn and Bronwen, both stood out, treeless, in shades of deep and light browns. As we all stood there on the high mountains, in October 1995, approximately two miles from where the UFO had landed, it was not difficult to imagine the eerie sensations they must have felt.

Two years earlier, Miss Catherine Wynn's family, and another witness in Wrexham, had also told me of that night. They had felt the earthquake and heard the explosion. They saw the red glow in the sky over Berwyn. They headed their cars from Corwen and through Llandrillo village to the council forestry road.

They went on the narrow dirt track through the woods in winter, due to ice and fallen trees. It peters-out a short way up the mountain. It was at this point that police turned back all the many cars that had gone up there. On that narrow track it took the cars a while to turn back. Everyone saw the huge pinky-red pulsating object through the trees, up on the Berwyn mountain side.

I then began to receive numerous reports from people all over North Wales, which seemed to back-up these accounts. A particularly interesting one was from a Bangor family who had stood on Bangor station at 6.30pm on 23rd January 1974. A round pinky-red object came and hovered just a few hundred feet above the platform, and swayed silently from side-to-side. They watched this until their train came in, and they had to depart.

An abduction took place the same night at Bala, when two long distance lorry drivers lost four hours of time. Clearly none of these people had been seeing the reported 'meteor'.

In May 1996, Tony Dodds of Quest International asked me if he may use all the material I had collected for an article in his magazine. I agreed, but the times and two paragraphs were left out. Consequently, the article was inaccurate.

Surprisingly, this did bring me astonishing information from a couple of military informants, local farmers and people living in the area at the time. Tony Dodds had been informed by a high ranking retired army officer, with the pseudonym 'James Prescott', that the military authorities had known for three days previously, that a UFO would land on the Berwyn range of mountains. They were shifted from the south of England, through Birmingham to Chester on the border, and then to Llangollen to await orders to proceed to the mountains on the night of 23rd January 1974.

This officer had been told to proceed from Llangollen, with his unit of four men in their military lorry, to Llandeferal. Presumably, they then had to take the road cutting through the mountains, the B4391, and wait there. Presumably again, they waited in the small hidden car park on the mountain-side.

It was well past 11pm when soldiers brought two long boxes down to them, which they were ordered to proceed with to Porton Down in Wiltshire – without stopping. When they arrived at this underground establishment the boxes were opened in front of them. To their horror and astonishment, they contained five to six foot tall thin, almost skeleton like beings. There was no mistaking they were aliens. At Berwyn they had seen no UFO. They had heard later that some of the Units had taken alive aliens to Porton Down, and also retrieved pieces of a craft.

The first military man who contacted me, said all the foregoing had to be correct. He had discussed it with a mate of his from that Unit. They recalled getting a phone call from North Wales Police saying; "It's big, orange and pulsating, and we don't know what it is."

An officer came into the room and took over the phone, saying he knew all about it, and they were ordered to leave the room immediately. Nobody below the rank of NCO went to Berwyn, and none of the people who apparently took *part in it, talked about it afterwards. He and his friend now felt it must have been a deliberate operation to destroy the UFO.*

I asked how it was that some of the farmers and locals heard no explosion, but saw the craft's slow descent to the mountain. I was assured they had the technology, even then, to destroy such a craft, without causing any sound or outward explosion.

What puzzled these military men was that the officer commanding their particular unit, Staff Sergeant James Prescott, was later killed in the Faulklands War in 1982. Why had Tony Dodd's high ranking military informant used his name? Was he a government stooge, or just someone so desperate to share this information now, that he deliberately chose a name that would draw the attention of the military men who had been in the same unit, and encourage them to come forward?

Nick Redfern, a well known fellow UFO investigator, was also contacted by a military informant, who told him that on their way out to the Faulklands, there were some fifty or sixty men in their unit. James Prescott was one of these men, and he was killed. They had discussed the Berwyn incident, but none of them believed it. It seemed too horrifying. He then said he remembered this when he recently saw a program on Sky TV, and wondered if it was true. That is why he was contacting Redfern.

One of our earliest UFO investigators, Terry Hooper, also contacted me. He was also told the same story about oblong boxes being taken to Porton Down, and that some units had taken dead and live aliens. He was told this as far back as 1990. Not knowing that area of Wales, he had put his notes aside, hoping to do something about it at a later date. When he heard I was investigating the incident, he sent me his notes. One point made was that the unit that went up the mountain wore night goggles, which had just been developed in America and requested by their military authorities to test them out in Britain.

A gentleman from the village of Glyndyfrdwy and his mother gave supportive evidence for the military involvement. At 9.30pm to past midnight, they had watched closed military vehicles rumble through their village to Corwen.

Another lady had a most bizarre experience. In mid-January 1974, leaving work at 3am, she was detained in an electric sub-station at Bethel/Pentir, which is further up the A5 arterial road, which also services Bala. Twenty minutes later, three armed military lorries came into the sub-station. Two of these vehicles contained armed soldiers, and the other – two stone oblong boxes. When they left she was escorted home by military police, and given no explanation. A month later a 'man-in-black' visited her, and asked 'very strange questions'.

Mark Saville was living outside Llandeferel village, on a mountain opposite Berwyn in 1974. There were two other farms there. The night of the earthquake they all rushed out and joined each other. They heard no explosion, but saw the pinky-red egg shaped craft slowly and silently descend to the Berwyn mountain side. It sat there, pulsating, for three quarters of an hour. It diffused no light at all, and then just blacked out! Everything had been deadly quiet – no sounds at all. This account and their experience was verified in 1997 by the family of his neighbours.

Huw Lloyd, his sister and family, on a farm then near to Berwyn, felt the severe earthquake and heard an explosion. Their animals were terrified. He and his neighbour, Enoch, decided to go up the mountain to find out the cause of this. Just then a policeman came into their yard, and asked them to drive him up into the council forestry road.

They did this in the pitch dark, with a car load of strangers following them. When they reached the spot where the road peters-out, and there is a gate on the mountain side, they got out. To his knowledge, no one ventured past the gate.

It was a clear, dry night, but winter, and freezing cold. Suddenly a blue arc of light appeared from ground level, spreading right across the mountain range and lighting up the whole area like daylight. This was not seen by the farmers on Llandeferel mountain, or indeed by the Evans family, who were standing on the B4391 on the opposite side of the mountain.

Huw and Enoch stayed about fifteen minutes, and left the police and strangers there; "The police later came down and were given cups of tea by Mr.William's mother. The Chief Constable wrote thanking her for her consideration. They have kept the letter, which I was shown in the summer of 1997. Yet the Colwyn Bay Police Headquarters today deny any knowledge of the incident or the police involvement." Huw's family felt there was a definite cover-up.

Huw told me the Berwyns are impossible to cross at night, particularly in winter. It is an exceedingly rough terrain, with pot-holes and rocks covered in ice. He also said there were other tracks, from the Corwen side, through the forested area, which the military could have gone on. They would not have been seen from Llandrillo village. To their knowledge, no villagers had seen military personnel that night.

The military involvement does seem a mystery. Whilst they may have got to the lower slopes of the mountain range from Corwen, how did they cross the tops of the mountains and the rocky ridge in those adverse night conditions?

Mike Orton, my fellow UFO investigator, had belonged to the Rhinog Mountain Rescue Team in 1974. He said there were numerous rumours at the time, when they had not been called out to the supposed crash. Yet again, the Lloyd family told me they had gone up to the mountain the following day, and numbers of people were there. This contradicted other witnesses who told me over the years that the area was sealed off for a week, and no-one was allowed in the vicinity.

The other puzzling factor is that so many people saw different shapes and types of UFO that evening and night in the area. A man from Cynwyd village, near Llandrillo, told me that at about 8.30pm to 9pm, he saw a purple egg shaped object from the Corwen road. It was bouncing across the tops of the mountain peaks, and then settled on the mountain side. A short while after it took straight up into the sky again.

A good report given me in November 1997 was from farmers. The father and son's farm was opposite the Berwyn mountain range. They were out tending their sheep when, what the son described as a small 'well defined cake tin', and the father drew as a square, passed less than one hundred feet over their heads. It went very slowly and silently, and they watched it fly directly to Cader Berwyn.

I asked what happened then, and what was the time? They had turned away to tend their sheep, and didn't know whether it went over the mountain top or landed. Their animals had a set routine, so they knew the time exactly – it was 11pm.

They had experienced an earth tremor earlier in the evening, and this was reported in the local paper, so they knew the date was 23rd January 1974.

They had spoken amongst themselves about the incident, but never to anyone else. They had recently seen a report of a UFO on 8th November 1997. They decided to ring me because the article had mentioned the Welsh Federation of Ufologists, and given my phone number.

In the summer of 1997, two military personnel contacted us. One said he was in the unit that took dead aliens to Porton Down. The other, who claimed to be a high ranking officer, suggested we ask our military contacts if they knew about the Ashford connection, the Cambridge Unit or Aberstwyth. If they knew what this meant, they would be genuine.

We ufologists, in Wales, know of the Aberstwyth incident of 1984. It was very similar to what occurred at Berwyn in 1974. I personally had never heard of anything happening at Ashford, Kent or Cambridge. I intend to check with the other ex-soldier who came to me via my farming community.

Today we are told the USA and Russian orbiting satellites can monitor all kinds of things, including meteors, and UFOs etc. coming into the Earth's atmosphere, and can accurately predict where they will fall. Did this happen in regards to an already stricken UFO that landed on Berwyn Mountain? Or did the authorities deliberately destroy it on arrival? Were the aliens dead on impact, or were they also destroyed?

It seems to me, from all the reports I have received, that if what we've been told is correct, this military operation was very successful in being covered up from the local people. Many years later it is still a mystery, and despite all our combined efforts, I think it will continue to be.

I have met various young investigators, new in this field, and very often just 'armchair' researchers at that, who say we should have hard evidence. To date, I have been a field UFO researcher for thirty-three years, and as far as I am concerned, the only evidence and tools we have to work with, is the word of our fellow man. As a good investigator, you carefully ascertain, from various sources, that your witnesses are genuine people who are telling you the truth as they saw it. There the moral obligation ends. There has to be a point where you start trusting your fellow man.

I consider that the investigation of these Berwyn Mountain incidents to be ongoing as long as I continue to get reports. Bits of new information are coming to me at the present time. Maybe, if there was a government cover-up, we will never learn the whole truth. To date, it seems to me to be as important a case for ufology as Roswell, Bentwaters and many others in various countries.

I thank Moira McGhee for giving me this opportunity of telling you about this ongoing very important Welsh case.

Margaret Fry

Official representative of Contact International UK in Wales

& Co-Founder of the Welsh Federation of Independent Ufologists

February, 1998

This case is still very controversial in the UK. Was there one craft or more? Did the craft have an accident when attempting to land, or was it brought down by a hostile action? Was it one of our own prototypes, from another less friendly nation, or of extraterrestrial origin? If the latter – did they come in peace? If the witness who called himself 'James Prescott' was telling the truth, how did the military know, three days in advance, that a UFO was scheduled to land?

Other UFO researchers also investigated this incident, and their reports differed in some of the details. In a later article, Margaret pointed out some confusing issues.

When Mrs. Pat Evans and her daughters first saw the small white lights zigzagging up to and under this enormous object, they assumed it must be military men with lanterns. Margaret dismissed this possibility, and felt they were associated with the craft itself. There was insufficient time, given the rough terrain and gorges, for soldiers to have reached there.

Margaret then asked was this in fact a 'crash'? In addition to her many first-hand witnesses, there were other reports that the villagers of Llangynog saw this object take off between 9pm and 10pm, and pass over the village. That night, there were UFOs seen both at the same time and for hours after all over North Wales.

Margaret also had some doubts about Tony Dodd's mystery military witness, who claimed military lorries went to the landing site at about 11pm; "How on

Earth could soldiers manage to take vehicles across the uninhabited Berwyns in the pitch dark? Neither could the RAF or military have flown to the site by helicopter – not in 1974."

Although none of Margaret's witnesses had mentioned seeing the RAF, Mike Orton later told her that the RAF, from the Valley, Holyhead, Isle of Anglesey had spent three days on the mountain following up the incident.

In 2011, MUFON published an excerpt from *The North Wales Chronicle*. Researcher Russ Kellett claimed that he had a Coastguard document which detailed a military exercise – Operation Photoflash – was underway, from Liverpool Bay to the North Wales coast, the night of the Berwyn incident.

Kellett claimed that depth charges were used to locate one alien craft at Puffin Island, another off the Anglesey coast, and a third near Bangor. They shot out of the sea, and into the air. Kellett said that one of these craft crashed into Lake Bala, and caused the Berwyn Mountain incident. He also claimed another had crashed on a roadside near Llandrillo, and it was this second disc, which a group of men chanced upon, that may have accounted for the other-worldly beings.

The witnesses saw some slim, grey-skinned humanoid creatures emerge from the crashed ship. They were about five-and-a-half feet tall, and wearing jumpsuits. The men watched as soldiers loaded the aliens into a vehicle and drove away. Kellett claimed to have several fragments of one of the craft, presumably given to him by one of the witnesses.

There was another incident near Bala, which happened in mid-January 1974, although it is not known if it was directly related to the crashed UFO.

Two long distance lorry drivers were travelling from Lincoln to their homes in Meanwrog on the other side of Bala. Only an hour away from their final destination, they saw an enormous, black cigar-shaped object, with lights down the side. They watched it in the sky, and it soon flew away.

They arrived at their local hotel, to enjoy a drink before closing time, and found it was after 1am. Where had three hours gone? They didn't know!

Margaret also wrote about the incident at Aberstwyth, which occurred ten years later in 1984, and was initially investigated by a different group of researchers. In similar circumstances, something had come down in a pine forest on a local farm. It completely demolished the trees, causing a large swathe of destruction, and was then followed by an explosion.

Despite being on his property, the farmer said the military quickly arrived and cordoned off the area for over a week. They brought in a mechanical earth digger and removed a large amount of top soil, however it seems they didn't recover a craft as such – only small pieces of debris.

While various researchers still heatedly argue the merits of this case, I suspect that it is unlikely we will ever know the truth regarding what happened at Berwyn Mountain on 23rd January 1974.

Seven years after the Berwyn Mountain incident, another startling and controversial event occurred in Britain.

RENDLESHAM FOREST

In late December 1980, (27th-28th-29th), a series of incidents occurred in the UK at Rendlesham Forest, which bordered RAF Bases Woodbridge and Bentwaters. It sparked an enormous controversy, which still exists today, within the UFO investigative community.

The events exploded into public interest after Larry Warren, previously a United States Air Force Security Policeman, accompanied by several investigators, including Peter Robbins and Tony James of the East Midlands group, EMUFORA, revisited the area. He subsequently published the book 'Left at East Gate'.

Having only arrived at Bentwaters on the 1st December 1980, Larry Warren's testimony commences less than four weeks later, on 27th December, when a police patrol reported lights being seen in the tall pine Rendlesham Forest.

The three man patrol, from 81st Security Police Squadron, comprised of servicemen Jim Penniston, John Burroughs and Ed Cabansag. What Col. Halt did not say in his official report, was that Jim Penniston claimed he got close enough to the small metallic craft to notice strange markings on the side. He likened them to 'Egyptian Hieroglyphs' and made some sketches in his police notebook.

Two nights later, on 29th December, Larry Warren's own security group was called out to the area, and Deputy Base Commander Colonel Halt and Lt. England were on board their truck. I personally have heard a copy of the tapes purportedly recorded by Col. Halt as he made his way through the forest that night, but instead I will first adopt a more conservative approach and rely on the supposed official report he made to the US authorities.

A Copy of the famous 'Col Halt' Memo. (Courtesy of OVNI)

DEPARTMENT OF THE AIR FORCE

HEADQUARTERS 1ST COMBAT SUPPORT GROUP (USAFE)

APO NEW YORK 0/755

13 Jan 81

REPLY TO ATTN OF: CD

SUBJECT: *Unexplained Lights*

TO: *RAF/CC*

1. *Early in the morning of 27 Dec 80 (approximately 0300L) two USAF security police patrolmen saw unusual lights outside the back gate at RAF Woodbridge. Thinking an aircraft might have crashed or been forced down, they called for permission to go outside the gate to investigate. The on-duty flight chief responded and allowed three patrolmen to proceed on foot. The individuals reported seeing a strange glowing object in the forest. The object was described as being metallic in appearance and triangular in shape, approximately two to three meters across the base and approximately two meters high. It illuminated the entire forest with a white light. The object itself had a pulsing red light on top and a bank(s) of blue lights underneath. The object was hovering or on legs. As the patrolmen approached the object, it manoeuvred through the trees and disappeared. At this time the animals on a nearby farm went into a frenzy. The object was briefly sighted approximately an hour later near the back gate.*

2. *The next day, three depressions 1 1/2" deep and 7" in diameter were found where the object had been sighted on the ground. The following night (29 Dec 80) the area was checked for radiation. Beta/gamma*

readings of 0.1 milliroentgens were recorded with peak readings in the three depressions and near the center of the triangle formed by the depressions. A nearby tree had moderate (.05-.07) readings on the side of the tree toward the depressions.

3. *Later in the night a red sun-like light was seen through the trees. It moved about and pulsed. At one point it appeared to throw off glowing particles and then broke into five separate white objects and then disappeared. Immediately thereafter, three star-like objects were noticed in the sky, two objects to the north and one to the south, all of which were about 10 degrees off the horizon. The objects moved rapidly in sharp angle movements and displayed red, green and blue lights. The objects to the north appeared to be elliptical through 8-12 power lens. They then turned to full circles. The objects to the north remained in the sky for an hour or more. The object to the south was visible for two or three hours and beamed down a stream of light from time to time. Numerous individuals, including the undersigned, witnessed the activities in paragraphs 2 and 3.*

CHARLES I. HALT, Lt Col, USAF

Deputy Base Commander

Although there were some similarities in their reports, there were also **significant differences.** British researcher, Omar Fowler, sent me an interesting article written before the actual release of *'Left at East Gate'*. Larry Warren mentioned many other servicemen and personnel being present at the site of a 'hovering object' which lit-up 'Capel Green' below. In the centre of the field was a huge light, somewhat like 'solidified mist', about one foot in height and fifty feet across. It was self-illuminated, although you could see through it at times.

He also mentioned a red light, about the size of a 'basketball', which moved quickly over the trees, then stopped and hovered about twenty feet off the ground. He said it suddenly exploded, showering light down on the original 'thing' down below.

In place of the mist was now a brilliantly lit, more solid looking object. It was about thirty feet across the base, and the sides rose up sharply to about twenty-five feet in height. Except for delta appendages coming out of it, there were no windows, markings, flags or country of origin.

Larry Warren claims that there were a lot of people present, and the object was surrounded by security police at about ten foot intervals. A light moved out of the side of the object and split into three.

"In each light you could make out what appeared to be individual beings of some kind. I saw clearly what looked like eyes, facial features, clothing and some other device. I couldn't make out the legs and lower extremities. It was almost as if the light was translucent at that point."

Wing Commander Lt. Col. Williams apparently conversed with his group of senior officers, and approached these three 'beings', one of whom raised his head. There were no words spoken, and after what Larry Warren described as a 'face-off' the three retracted under a 'delta type of thing' under the craft.

Larry Warren claimed there were a lot of debriefings, where they were told they were mistaken, and hadn't seen anything untoward. Some personnel suffered post-traumatic symptoms, and many were posted to other bases around the world. One shot himself a couple of weeks later.

Countless researchers investigated the incident, and interviewed new and existing witnesses. Some believed all the events as described, and others were totally sceptical, and claimed all the servicemen had seen were lights from a ship and the nearby lighthouse. Radar records proved confused and inconclusive. Investigations were so contradictory that many researchers still experience on-going hostility due to their differing opinions.

One assertion, which would not go away, was that the UFOs had shot their beams of light down over the underground storage areas of Woodbridge Base. These apparently penetrated the 'hardened' nuclear storage bunkers, affecting the weapons, rendering many of them useless.

In 2010, Leslie Keane published his book *'UFOs'* and Chapter 18 was devoted to the incident at Rendlesham Forest. Col. Halt, who had since retired, contributed quite a lengthy segment in the chapter. He would have preferred to remain silent about the whole incident. The audio tapes he had made on his pocket tape recorder at the time, had been copied and distributed without his knowledge or consent, and his memo to the Air Force was released under the Freedom of Information Act.

Col. Halt wrote of how, over the years, he had heard privately from many other witnesses. He said personnel in the weapons storage area tower had seen an object which went into the forest near Woodbridge Base. The air traffic control tower operators had seen something cross their radar screen at extremely high speed – up to three or four thousand miles per hour. All these additional witnesses had been ordered not to speak about it to anyone except their senior officers.

Col. Halt also made some astounding accusations, including that five young airmen were 'harshly interrogated', and even 'brainwashed' during that time. Other witnesses had health problems which had continued to the present day. He speculated at possible exposure to radiation in addition to stress related issues.

He finalised his article by saying; *'I still have no idea what we saw that night. It must have been something beyond our technology, judging from the speed of the objects, the way they moved and the angles they turned, and other things they did. I do know one thing, without a doubt: These things were under intelligent control.'*

Five-star Admiral, Lord Norton-Hill, formerly the UK's Chief of Defence Staff, took particular interest in the case. Did the US have a large 'nuclear arms dump', stored at the time, at RAF Bases Woodbridge and Bentwaters? (Both Bases are now closed). Lord Hill-Norton's letter, sent to a UK Defence Minister, seems to indicate that this may have been so. He also shared a copy of part of this letter with investigator Leslie Kean, (author of the book - *'UFOs'*).

"My position, both privately and publicly, expressed over the last dozen of years or more, is that there are only two possibilities, either

> *a) An intrusion into our Air Space and a landing by unidentified craft took place at Rendelsham, as described. Or;*
> *b) The Deputy Commander of an operational, nuclear armed, U.S. Air Force Base in England, and a large number of his enlisted men, were either hallucinating or lying.*

Either of these simply must be 'of interest to the Ministry of Defence', which has been repeatedly denied, in precisely those terms."

Lord Hill-Norton was not about to let the matter rest there. He had been interviewed by David Jack of the *'Sunday People'* in December 1994, who attributed following comment to the retired Chief of Defence Staff: *"A series of chilling encounters with alien spacecraft have been covered up"*.

The newspaper reporter then went on to elaborate on the 'Rendlesham Forest' incident: *"On December 27th 1980, radar operators at RAF Watton, near Norwich, picked up an unusual 'blip'. As RAF Phantom jets closed in on the object, pilots reported seeing intense bright lights in the sky."*

"Former radar operator Mal Scurrah said: "As the Phantoms got close, the hovering object shot upwards at phenomenal speed – monitored at more than 1,000 mph."

Three years later Lord Hill-Norton raised the issues in parliament. The answers he received were totally inadequate, and only fuelled speculation that there was one massive 'cover-up' of the entire incident.

A REPORT FROM 'HANSARD' ON QUESTIONS RAISED BY LORD HILL-NORTON ON THE 'RENDLESHAM FOREST' INCIDENT.

14 OCTOBER 1997

Lieutenant Colonel Charles Halt; Memorandum

Lord Hill-Norton asked Her Majesty's Government:

Whether the Ministry of Defence replied to the 1981 memorandum from Lieutenant Colonel Charles Halt, which reported the presence of an unidentified craft that had landed in close proximity to RAF Bentwaters and RAF Woodbridge, witnessed by United States Air Force personnel: and if not why not; and

How the radiation readings reported to the Ministry of Defence by Lieutenant Colonel Charles Halt in his memorandum dated 13 January 1981 compare to the normal levels of background radiation in Rendelsham Forest.

Lord Gilbert: *The memorandum, which reported observations of unusual lights in the sky, was assessed by staff in the MoD responsible for air defence matters. Since the judgement was that it contained nothing of defence significance, no further action was taken.*

There is no record of any official assessment of the radiation readings reported by Lieutenant Colonel Halt, from a Defence perspective some sixteen and a half years after the alleged events, there is no requirement to carry out such an assessment now.

---

23 October 1997

HIGHPOINT PRISON

Lord Hill-Norton asked Her Majesty's Government;

Whether staff at Highpoint Prison in Suffolk received instructions to prepare for a possible evacuation of the prison at some time between 25 and 30 December 1980, and if so, why these instructions were issued.

Lord Williams of Mostyn: *I regret to advise the noble Lord that I am unable to answer his Question, as records at Highpoint Prison relating to the period concerned are no longer available. The governor's journal is the record in which a written note is made of significant events concerning the establishment on a daily basis. It has not proved possible to locate that journal.*

---

28 October 1997

RAF BENTWATER'S AND WOODBRIDGE'S

NUCLEAR WEAPONS ALLEGATIONS

Lord Hill- Norton asked her Majesty's Government;

Whether the allegations contained in the recently published book 'Left at East Gate', to the effect that nuclear weapons were stored at RAF Bentwaters and RAF Woodbridge in violation of UK/US treaty obligations are true.

Lord Gilbert: *It has always been the policy of this and previous governments neither to confirm nor to deny where nuclear weapons are located either in the UK or elsewhere, in the past or at the present time. Such information would be withheld under exemption 1 of the Code of Practice on Access to Government Information.*

Lord Hill-Norton asked her Majesty's Government:

Whether they are aware of reports from the United States Air Force personnel that nuclear weapons stored in the Weapons Storage Area at RAF Woodbridge were struck by light beams fired from an unidentified craft seen over the base in the period 25-30 December 1980, and if so, what action was subsequently taken.

Lord Gilbert: *There is no evidence to suggest that the Ministry of Defence received any such reports.*

Lord Hill-Norton asked her Majesty's Government:

What information they have on the suicide of the United States security policeman from the 81st Security Police Squadron who took his life at RAF Bentwaters in January 81, and whether they will detail the involvement of the British police, Coroner's Office and any other authorities concerned.

Lord Gilbert: *MoD has no information concerning the alleged suicide. Investigations into such occurrences are carried out by the US Forces.*

Lord Hill-Norton asked her Majesty's Government:

What information they have on the medical problems experienced by various United States personnel based at RAF Bentwaters and RAF Woodbridge, which stemmed from their involvement in the so-called Rendlesham Forest incident in December 1980.

Lord Gilbert: *Information on medical matters relating to US personnel is a matter for the US authorities.*

Several years ago I was given a copy of a heavily redacted letter, purportedly sent by the Ministry of Defence. I cannot verify the authenticity of this document, so advise extreme caution regarding its contents.

It mentions an OSI report on *'the landing of a craft of unknown origin, crewed by several entities near RAF Bentwaters on the night of December 29/30 1980. – the craft was not damaged but landed deliberately as part of a series of visits to SAC bases in USA and Europe'.* The entities were described as being approximately one-and-a-half metres tall, with claw-like hands with three fingers and an opposable thumb. They wore what appeared to be nylon-coated pressurised suits, but no helmets.

'Tape recordings were made on which the entities are heard to speak in an electronically synthesised version of English, with a strong American accent. Similar transmissions intercepted irregularly by NSA since 1975.' This begs the question if, and only if, this document is genuine, were the 'entities' in fact biological robots?

It is obvious that neither the British parliament, nor the public, will never know the true facts of this or many other incidents which have occurred.

CHAPTER TEN

UFO CRASHES and LANDINGS

PART 3 – THE REST of the WORLD

UFOs are a global phenomena, and incidents occur in every nation around the world. Some countries suppress the evidence, whilst others are more forthcoming with the information.

ITALY

Even before World War II, and the world's first nuclear bomb, incidents of strange objects crashing to Earth were being reported. On June 13th 1933, an unconventional craft had come down. Some reports say it crashed near Magenta, Milan, and others claim it was near Maderno, Lombardy. It was apparently a circular, grey metal disc, about fifty feet wide and seven feet thick.

It was taken to an aircraft hanger in northern Italy, where Italian scientists concluded it was not made on Earth, and had come from a more advanced civilisation elsewhere. Later that decade scientists from Nazi Germany were allowed to access and inspect the disc.

SPAIN

Italy was not the only European country to experience a landed UFO prior to World War II. Scott Corrales detailed how one hot summer morning in 1938, Mario, a young boy in Munico was tending the family cows. He heard a buzzing, droning sound, and saw a silver object descend to the ground nearby.

He hid behind some trees, and scrutinised the round, eighteen metre diameter craft. It had a small dome on top, and coloured lights flashing on and off all around. A 'door' opened and three figures descended. One stayed near the door, and the other two walked a short distance away, and appeared to be taking samples of the soil or vegetation.

Mario got a glimpse of the interior. Through the opening he could see lots of devices he didn't understand. He crept closer, and the being at the door fired a 'bolt of light' at him. He fell down, and retreated to the safety of the trees. He tried a second time, only to have the same thing happen. Soon the two 'sample collectors' returned to the object, the 'sentry' waved at Mario, and the object lifted off. It was spinning on its axis as, at a very low altitude, it headed away.

There were other similar craft reported in 1938, during the Spanish Civil War, but, at the time, most witnesses assumed that they were new German machines sent to assist 'Generalissimo Franco'.

These days it is almost impossible to determine if something that has crashed is space debris, a test prototype or many of the other objects that fall to earth. We may never know if it was something of extraterrestrial origin. The authorities are skilled at 'covering-up', and the aliens are much more careful when traversing our skies.

In October 1992, the Canarias Astrophysical Institute stated that a very large object, possibly a spacecraft or warhead, had fallen in the Las Canadas nature reserve. It had caused a massive 450 ton rock to break off a lava flow. Investigator, Antonio Ribera, reported that the Spanish Air Force mounted a major recovery. Local witnesses said the area was barricaded off for twenty-six days, and they saw a number of strange, 'never before seen', container type vehicles. Ribera also claims a number of scientists at the Astrophysical Institute were threatened with dismissal if they issued any more comments.

ARGENTINA

Leonard Stringfield followed up an interesting account after the witness, Dr. Enrico Botha wrote to him and the Aerial Phenomena Research Organisation, five years after the event. On 10th May 1950, Botha was driving through a remote part of the Pampas region of eastern Argentina, when he saw a metallic looking disc on the ground, not far from the side of the road.

It was about thirty-two feet in diameter, and had a six feet by seven feet circular tower section with a flashing light on top. The craft was lying in an inclined position, with no visible 'landing gear'. Botha went over and looked through a small open hatch on the side, but could see no signs of life or activity.

He crawled inside, and saw three small men sitting inside the tower area. They were about four feet tall and very 'human looking'. They had dark, bronze skin, bright eyes and short grey-chestnut coloured hair. Their clothing was identical – tight fitting grey overalls and boots. Once he realised, due to their rigid bodies, that they were all dead, he took the opportunity to look around.

There were screens, a large panel of bright instruments, a transparent rotating sphere and two levers in front of one being, who appeared to be the pilot. The other two 'men' were reclined on couches which curved along the circular walls. One couch was empty, and when Botha left after five minutes, he wondered if there was a fourth, missing crew member.

He drove seventy-five miles back to his hotel, and informed several friends, who decided to accompany him back to the spot the next morning. When they arrived there, the disc was gone, and in its place was a pile of warm grey ashes, which turned their hands green upon contact.

In the sky above was a large cigar-shaped object, with two smaller discs hovering nearby. The two discs moved towards the larger craft, and seemed to 'coalesce' with it. The 'cigar' then turned blood-red and quickly disappeared from sight. Botha took some photographs, which he later gave to Leonard Stringfield. This is reminiscent of other cases around the world, where other UFOs have appeared after a crash. Could they be on a 'retrieval mission' of their own?

Argentina has always hosted a plethora of UFO activity, and forty-five years later another crash occurred, but due to the passing of time, we have to query if this incident had an alien origin, or was caused by one of our own prototypes?

George Brownie compiled this report for the *Ufologist Magazine:* It happened in the rainforest area Anta, near the Sierras Colouradas. On 17th August 1995, Tony Galvano, along with 'thousands' of other witnesses, saw a huge, bright metallic 'flying saucer', about 250 metres in diameter, speeding across the clear sky from north to south. It was followed by two other objects, thought to be missiles, which impacted with it. The disc plummeted to earth, followed by a powerful explosion, which shook the ground around a three hundred kilometre radius. A thick column of black smoke rose into the air.

Tony ran to the airstrip, and took to the sky in his Ultralight-Flystar. The thick smoke impeded visibility for miles around, and he could not locate the crash site. Two days later, he tried again, and this time saw what appeared to be a crash area on top of a plateau. There was impact damage and a furrow, cutting a trail, five kilometres long by six hundred metres wide. There was massive damage to the trees and vegetation.

Suddenly his own aircraft motor began to malfunction, and he was lucky to survive an emergency landing on the side of the mountain. He managed to gather up some strange white dust, which was all over the scene. Later analysis, by the University of La Plata, determined that it was a potassium compound, with a 98% purity, not found on this planet, and the remainder an unknown material.

About two weeks after the event, several men, dressed in black, arrived in four wheel drives and on terrain motorcycles. They took over the investigation. They said very little, but knowing Tony and his friends were planning excursions into the area, one of them said; "Forget it, Galvano, what's coming down is very heavy!"

The terrain at the crash site was mountainous, with impenetrable foliage and dangerous packs of wild boar. It is not known if Tony and his colleagues ever had any success.

Despite intense speculation, not all crashed objects are alien craft. On May 6th 1978, a huge object roared across the sky, and crashed into a hill, in rugged terrain, just over the border in Bolivia. There was a massive explosion, followed by a sonic boom which shattered windows thirty miles away.

Police, military officers and scientists, from near and far, searched for the remains of the object. They found evidence of an impact and rockslide, but apparently no actual debris. Despite official denials, the rumours were that the crash was caused by an American or Russian satellite, re-entering the Earth's atmosphere. Retrieving the remains of these, and other 'space debris', is of utmost importance to all of the world's major governments and intelligence agencies.

BRAZIL

One lesser known incident from Brazil occurred at Ubatuba Beach in September 1957. Several fishermen saw a disc-like object descending towards the sea at an incredible speed. They braced themselves for the impact, only to see it make a sharp turn and speed back up into the sky.

They watched in amazement as the whole craft exploded into flames, and disintegrated into thousands of sparkling fiery fragments which fell to earth and into the sea. The men collected some of the pieces, and three were given to APRO and Brazilian ufologist Dr. Olavo Fontes for analysis.

The results were to a certain extent inconclusive, but revealed that the very lightweight material was very pure magnesium, with none of the normal trace elements present.

NORWAY

Donald Keyhoe wrote about an interesting case from Norway in June 1952. A disc glowing with a bluish coloured light was seen to descend over an electric power plant. A few weeks later six Norwegian jet crews, flying over the Hinlopen Straits, reported that their radios were 'jamming'. Upon further investigation, they discovered a 125 feet diameter blue metal disc, wrecked in the snow below. Later, the authorities denied any such occurrence.

However, in 1955 Germany's *Stuttgarter Tageblatt* carried the following article regarding the 1952 wreckage, claimed to be a flying saucer, found on the Norwegian island of Spitzbergen.

During an instruction lesson for Air Force Officers, Colonel Gernod Darnbyl, Chairman of a Board of Inquiry, is reported to have said; "These UFO remains from Spitzbergen will prove of utmost importance. Some time ago a misunderstanding was caused by saying that the disc probably was of Soviet origin. It has – and we wish to state that emphatically – not been built in any country on Earth. The materials used in its construction are completely unknown to all experts having participated in the investigation.

"Since the event at Spitzbergen, Second Lieutenants Brobs and Tyllensen have been assigned as special observers of the Arctic regions, and report that flying discs have landed in the polar regions several times. I think that the Arctic is serving as a kind of air base for the unknowns, especially during snow storms when we are forced back to our bases."

Despite inferring that the extensive report would be released after discussions with the U.S. and British experts, it never was made public.

188

SWEDEN

Whilst Sweden recorded 'ghost planes' and other strange phenomena after World War II, the following incident, detailed by Ted Phillips, indicates either alien visitors, or our own prototypes were present, long before anyone knew of their existence.

In May 1946, Gosta Carlsson noticed a light in an open space of an Angelholm forest. When he went to investigate, he saw a domed disc, fifty-six feet in diameter and fifteen feet thick. It had oval windows, and two metal 'landing legs'. Underneath was a large oblong fin, which stretched from the centre to the edge, and a ladder reaching from a doorway to the ground. An eighteen feet long mast, with three antennae, was above the dome.

Gosta saw a normal looking man, wearing white, close-fitting coveralls, and other people who appeared to be repairing a window. When Gosta came closer, the man raised his hand, motioning him to stop.

Soon the craft made a whistling sound and ascended into the sky. Holes around the edge emanated light beams which burned the grass below, and left a forty feet diameter circular landing mark. (In some ways this seems reminiscent of the 1967 'Michalak' case in Canada.)

In 1987 Dan Johnson, a 41year-old truck driver, from Tingsryd, Sweden, was driving home in his car, at about one in the morning. He was astounded to see a huge craft, about 250feet wide and thirty feet high, hovering above the road. He raced home, grabbed his camera, and telephoned the police from a call-box on the way back to the site.

Suddenly he saw the object again, but this time it had landed on the road. He nearly crashed into it, and his car stalled. He was 'frozen with terror', especially when strange 'man-sized' aliens came out of the craft, approached his car, and opened the door.

They pulled Dan out. He was kicking and struggling – 'screaming like he had never screamed before.' A lorry, carrying a load of timber, caught the activity in its headlights, and the beings retreated to their machine.

The lorry driver also phoned the police, who arrived to find Dan collapsed and in such a state of gibbering terror, they took him to the mental health unit of the local hospital. He was found to be quite sane, and most probably telling the truth, as his story was corroborated by a second truck driver.

CANADA

Some very interesting cases occurred in the late 1960s, and no definitive answers have ever been given.

The first was on 20th May 1967, at Falcon Lake in Canada. Stephen Michalak was preparing to prospect at a quartz vein, near a marshy area and small stream. Just after midday there was a great commotion from some nearby geese, as if something had disturbed them. He looked up to see two strange objects descending from the sky.

They were oval disc-shapes, at a forty-five degree angle, with 'bumps' on them. They glowed red as they silently approached, and one suddenly stopped, mid-air, while the other landed on a large, flat rock, about 160 feet away. The disc in the air hovered for a short while, then rose and quickly flew back into the west where it disappeared behind some clouds. Michalak noticed, as it rose, its colour changed from red, to orange, and then grey, only reverting to orange as it reached the clouds.

He turned his attention to the craft on the ground nearby. It was also changing colour from red to grey, eventually resembling 'hot stainless steel' surrounded by a golden-hued glow. A brilliant purple light flooded out of the openings on the upper part of the object. It was so dazzling, he was glad he was wearing his welding goggles, which were part of his prospecting equipment.

He kept his distance for a while, content to make some sketches of what he was observing. After about half an hour there was a smell of sulphur, and he noticed waves of warm air radiating from the craft, accompanied by a hissing, whirring sound, similar to a fast electric motor.

A door opened on the side, and Michalak could see some lights inside. He walked over and hesitated until he heard two human sounding voices, one higher pitched than the other. By this time he was convinced this was some new experimental American craft, and walked closer.

He called out in several languages, asking if he could be of any help, but got no response. Eventually he looked through the opening, and saw a 'maze' of lights, running in horizontal and diagonal patterns on a 'panel', and another group of lights flashing in random sequence.

He stepped back outside, and suddenly three panels slid back over the opening, sealing it from further entry. He walked around, touching the seamless, highly polished smooth surface with his gloved hand, only to discover that his glove had burned and melted, as had his hat which brushed the side.

The craft suddenly shifted position, and Michalak found himself facing a grid-like exhaust vent which suddenly sprang to life, sending a blast of hot air onto his chest. His shirt and undergarment caught fire, and the pain caused him to tear them off before he felt a rush of air and looked up to see the object departing the same way as the first had.

He was in pain, nauseous and vomiting, and eventually made his way home, where his son took him to hospital.

Some officials and researchers tried to label this incident a hoax, but Canada's Chris Rutkowski conducted one of the most thorough and professional investigations I have ever read. He was convinced Michalak was telling the truth, and I tend to agree.

Only three months later, there was another incident in Texas Creek, Colorado. Some of the finer details were similar to the Michalak event. Kenneth Flack was driving home at about 11.20pm. He started to overtake two cars ahead, when his engine and headlights failed. The other vehicles were experiencing the same problem.

Everybody got out, and they all could see an unusual object between them and the Arkansas River. Flack, a sceptic until then, decided to investigate and walked closer. He could see it was 'egg-shaped', with three 'legs' supporting it on the ground. Unlike Michalak, he did not get too close, and was still approaching the craft when it rotated about a quarter of a turn. The back end raised up and there was a bright flash.

Flack came to a dead halt. He felt paralysed and unable to move, and could only stand and watch as the legs retracted and the object slowly and silently rose from the ground and headed north. Flack lost consciousness, and the other witnesses carried him back to the road, where they eventually revived him and took him home.

EAST GERMANY

After escaping from East Germany, along with his wife and six children, Oscar Linke, the former mayor of Gleimershausen, and his daughter made sworn statements to West Berlin intelligence officers. Although this incident occurred in approximately 1952, perhaps the authorities were concerned that the Russians had already developed some new flying contraption of military significance.

Oscar and eleven year-old Gabriella were going home when the tyre on his motorcycle blew out near Hasselbach. They were pushing the motorbike, and walking towards the town, when Gabriella spotted something on the ground, about 140 metres away. Oscar thought it might be a young deer, but when he drew near, he realised it was two men, stooping over something.

They were wearing some form of shiny metallic clothing, and one had a lamp on the front part of his body, which lit up at regular intervals. Oscar crept closer, and looked over a small fence to see a large object resting on the ground. He said it looked like a huge metal frying pan, about fourteen metres in diameter. There were two rows of holes on its periphery, and on the top was a black conical tower, about three metres high.

Oscar said; "At that moment, my daughter, who had remained a short distance behind, called me. The two men must have heard her voice because they immediately jumped on the conical tower and disappeared inside.

"Now, the side of the object, on which the holes had been opened, began to glitter. Its colour seemed green, but later turned to red. At the same time I heard a slight hum. While the brightness and hum increased, the conical tower began to slide down into the centre of the object, which then began to rise slowly from the ground and rotate like a top."

He thought the cylindrical plant (conical tower) had gone down from the top of the object, through the centre, and now appeared from its bottom, on the ground. The craft was surrounded by a ring of flames, and when it rose a few feet up, the 'cylinder' disappeared back into the centre and came back out the top.

"The rate of climb had now become greater. At the same time my daughter and I heard a whistling sound.....and the object rose to a horizontal position, turned towards a neighbouring town, and then, gaining altitude, it disappeared over the forests in the direction of Stockheim.

"I would have thought that both my daughter and I were dreaming if it were not for the following element involved. When the object had disappeared, I went to the place where it had been. I found a circular opening in the ground, and it was quite evident it was freshly dug. It was exactly the same shape as the conical tower."

Many other local people also related seeing the object, and a nearby shepherd had thought he was looking at a 'comet', moving away at a low altitude from where Oscar and Gabriella had been standing.

POLAND

I was hesitant to include this incident, due to the high strangeness of the report, however Polish investigators were very thorough, and have attested to the honesty and reliability of the witness, Jan Wolski, who was very religious, and did not drink alcohol. In 1978 he had no access to TV or radio, and rarely read newspapers. Psychologists and doctors from the University of Lodz were convinced he was telling the truth.

At about 7am on 10th May, 71 year-old Jan was travelling along the Emilcin road in his horse drawn wagon, when he saw two people walking in the same direction. When he drew alongside, they jumped up onto the cart, on either side of him. They were wearing tight fitting one-piece coveralls, their skin had a greenish hue, and their eyes were slanted like Orientals. Jan thought they must be foreigners, especially when they talked to each other in some weird language.

A short time later, they reached a clearing where there was a strange, rectangular vehicle near the trees and hovering close to the ground. Jan likened it to a 'bus' and said it had a slightly curved roof. His passengers alighted, and beckoned Jan to follow them.

When they walked across the clearing to the craft, a platform on 'cords' descended to the ground, and he and the one being stepped on it. They were lifted into a dark, rectangular room that contained a few small benches. Two similar entities were inside, and one motioned to Jan to undress, which he did, despite the cold weather outside.

The other being examined him with something that looked like 'two plates', and from Jan's description, seemed similar to a type of X-Ray device. The beings then started eating some form of food, which he declined when offered. They motioned for him to get dressed, and he left via the same descending platform.

Jan went back to his horse and cart, and raced back home to his family. Later his sons and neighbours went to the site. The craft had gone, but there were several unusual footprints in the mud. Investigators later located another witness, whose son had seen the strange craft flying low over their barn.

HUNGARY

On 16th August 1992, several residents of Sandorfalva, in the south of the country, were mystified by what they saw that night.

At 10pm, V. Karoly and his girlfriend spotted a luminous circle above their house. It was larger than a star or planet, and disappeared after a few minutes. About the same time, B. Joszef was taking his dog for a walk, when he saw a brilliant white light at the edge of the forest.

As he got closer, the dog ran away in fright. Joszef noticed six strange 'beings', all just under four feet tall, standing at the side of the trees. They had big white heads, angular shoulders, and were wearing tight fitting silvery 'costumes'. He could also see a grey domed object, about three metres high, with octagonal windows and a red flashing light on top. The 'creatures' were making gestures with their hands, and seemed to be communicating in 'cooing' tones. Joszef realised he was all alone with something unknown, and after a couple of minutes, raced home to get his brother.

Before they returned to the scene, another man in a horse and cart, drove even closer to the then luminous object, and witnessed it slowly taking off, and disappearing quickly into the sky. The horse seemed disturbed, not wanting to cross the area.

The brothers returned, but could only see traces of the object by the light of their lantern. The next day they found a four metre diameter circle, with three deep conical holes. Four metres away was another conical hole, which may have accounted for a separate red light Joszef had seen near the craft.

The following night, another witness, B. Mihaly, said he was in his courtyard when a bright light appeared overhead. It was dazzling, and resembled a strong searchlight. Mihaly reported feeling so dizzy he 'didn't know how or when he went back into his house'.

MADAGASCAR

Anne Griffin of IUFOPRA sent me the following details of an incident from the island of Madagascar.

In May 1967, a platoon from the French Foreign Legion was on a reconnaissance exercise. There was the officer-in-charge, four NCOs and twenty-three soldiers. At midday they stopped in a bush clearing for a lunch break.

They were startled to see a bright metallic object rapidly descending from the sky. It resembled a 'shining egg', and made a piercing, whistling sound as it fell with a 'falling leaf' motion. They calculated it as being twenty-three feet high and about twelve feet wide, at its widest part. There was a thump as it hit the ground.

The soldiers felt momentarily 'paralysed' before it immediately took off again, rising slowly into the sky, and disappearing at high speed. They checked their watches. It was now 3.15pm. Where had three hours gone? They didn't know. They could see three marks on the ground that looked like they had been made by some form of legs, and there was a ten foot crater, with a sort of vitrified ring of coloured crystals at the bottom.

Two days later they all complained of violent headaches, a sensation of constant 'beating' around their temples, and continual 'buzzing' in their ears. Their senior officers forbade them to discuss the matter with anyone.

JAPAN

On 23rd February 1975. Two eight year-old cousins, Masato Kono and Katsuhiro Yamahata, were returning home from roller skating, when they noticed two blue lights coming across the sky. One light flew off, but the other came closer. It was disc shaped, making strange clicking noises, and shining down an orange light.

They were frightened, and ran into a nearby cemetery, hiding behind a tombstone. Once the object had flown away, they continued their journey, only to see what appeared to be a fire in the vineyard adjoining their Kofu housing complex. They went to investigate, and realised it was the same stainless steel/silver disc-shaped object they had seen earlier.

It was about five metres in diameter and two metres high, with a rotating dome on the top. There was a translucent 'window', with black vertical frames, between the dome and the main body of the craft. They walked around the object, and Kono noticed what he thought were 'alien characters' written laterally beneath the windows.

A door opened with a 'bang' to the right of these 'characters', and a ramp was lowered to the ground. The boys stood motionless, and stared into the dark interior. They could see machines, with red, green and blue blinking lights, and a small being sitting with his hands on a 'control lever'.

Before they could regain their composure, another creature, wearing a silvery suit, came out. It was about four-and-a-half feet tall, with brown wrinkled skin. They could not distinguish any facial features except for two huge pointed ears. It was wearing brown gloves, with only four fingers, and was carrying an instrument which the children thought was a rifle.

They were about to run, but Yamahata felt something patting his shoulder, and could hear a 'squeaking' sound. He instinctively turned around, and came face-to-face with the alien. He fell to the ground in shock. Kono grabbed him by the hand and they both ran as fast as possible back to the apartment that their families shared.

Their mothers went outside, and saw 'a brilliant luminous body, about the same size as a dodge ball' pulsating regularly with beautiful colours, a distance away over the vineyard. It continued for about five minutes before fading and disappearing from view.

Later that night, concerned about their sons' distress and tears, the two fathers went to the vineyard, but the object, and strange occupants, had vanished. The next day their teacher, who felt the boys were telling the truth, accompanied them back to the vineyard, and noticed a depression where they claimed the saucer had landed.

There was some possible corroborating evidence. Two other, unrelated witnesses, also reported seeing luminous objects in the sky that night. An instructor, at the local Technical High School, took his students to the vineyard, where they measured the background radiation and other anomalies, which were higher than normal and indicated an unnatural origin.

SOUTH AFRICA

Rick Barr, in an article, detailed the following case, which occurred just five months later. On 31st July 1975, Danie van Graan was walking across his land, just outside the village of Loxton, when he thought he saw a vehicle belonging to some uranium hunters, who had been in the area. When he came closer, he realised it was a round object, with rounded windows and triangular lights. He could see four human looking beings inside.

They were all about one and a half metres tall, and looked like normal people with rather long faces. One appeared to be busy at some form of instrument panel, while the others were looking at Danie. He wanted to get closer, but a flap near one of the windows opened, and his face was hit with a streak of light, which caused his nose to bleed.

He withdrew to a safer distance, and watched the craft and its occupants for about half an hour, until it silently ascended and disappeared within seconds. A later examination of the landing site revealed five equidistance marks on the hard ground, which seemed to have been made by a heavy object.

RUSSIA

According to author and investigator, Paul Stonehill, Russia also had strange craft crashing on its soil. In his book *'Russia's Roswell and Other Amazing Cases from the Former Soviet Union'* he tells of the crash-landing of a spherical flying object, on a hill top at Dalnegorsk, a small mining town in south-eastern Russia on 29th January1986.

It was not large, apparently only about three metres in diameter, perfectly round with the appearance of burning stainless steel. It flew slowly and silently parallel to the ground before ascending and descending. It made an abrupt turn, before making a couple of 'jerking' movements and hitting the edge of the cliff. There was no explosion – just a 'powerful impact', which created a small fire on the site.

Apparently CIA documents indicate that there was great interest in the craft fragments which were recovered. Some displayed anti-gravitational properties, and others, when subjected to heat, indicated some elements 'disappearing' only to be replaced by others. The Tomsk experts stated; *'It is impossible for us – in the present day state of our technology – to manufacture this sort of thing.'*

Dr. Vysoky, a specialist in Chemistry, added; *'Without any doubt, this is the product of a very high technology, and such things as these are not natural, and are not of terrestrial origin.'*

Some scientists who disagreed, went on to speculate that they were spy probes from the West, but later suggested that UFOs, seen over the area the next year, were extraterrestrial!

Gordon Creighton also translated articles regarding a great metallic body, which was located three metres underground, when members of a collective farm in Tallin, Estonia, were digging a well. After some of the hull was prised away, the Russian military sent it away for analysis. Leading Soviet scientists apparently said they *'had no doubt whatever as to the extraterrestrial origin of the artefact.'*

Russian researcher, Anton Anfalov wrote several letters to his Western colleagues. He believed that humankind had to be alerted to the dangers of alien contact. He claimed that several alien craft had been captured by the Soviets, many were operational, and others back-engineered. They were taken on test flights by a select group of pilots. He also stated that since 1978 the Russians had mastered alien technology quite successfully.

He said that the first EBE to be studied was seized on January 21st 1959, after a UFO crash near Gdynia, Poland. There were apparently other crashes in the sixties, and on 17th February1979, another disc and its occupants crashed near the town of Zhigansk. Later that year, a further craft was found near Lihanova in Ural.

One very detailed report, written by Anton Anfalov and Philip Mantle, was published in VUFORS *Australian UFO Bulletin* in June 1998.

In late June, 1966, a geology expedition in Western Siberia, was woken by a loud noise, and saw a blinding bright globe explode in the sky. The trees around their camp site were on fire. As soon as it was daylight, they surveyed the devastation around them, and noticed a semi-circle of flashing lights through the trees.

Raised up, out of a nearby bog, was the streamlined hull of a charred and burnt object. It looked like 'two basins put together, with blinking lights around the rim'. A hatch was ajar, with dense smoke pouring out. Something dark, almost like a 'tentacle', was lying prone near the edge of the hatch.

The men felt sick, their radio and compass were malfunctioning, and fearing radiation they moved away from the area. That night they heard helicopters, and the next morning the object was gone. When they returned to Moscow a KGB officer told them it was a state secret, and they were to say nothing. Many of the expedition died early with some form of radiation illness.

Researchers found other witnesses. Local villagers who had seen and heard the fiery globe come crashing down out of the sky, were also warned not to say anything.

One man, Sergey Petrovich, had been a member of a military helicopter unit at the time. He recalled going to the site where they lifted the saucer out of the bog, and it was transported to some secret military aerodrome. He said the craft was eight to ten metres in diameter, with the coloured lights still flashing around the rim.

He looked into the dark, smoke filled interior, and like the geologists, also saw the dark-brown flipper-type thing leaning out of the hatch. The scientist who accompanied them carefully wrapped it in some kind of polyethylene, and told them to say nothing about it.

He did not know much more after he saw the cargo helicopter leaving with the disc suspended below. Later he heard rumours that there had been some bodies inside, and the whole incident was classified 'top secret'.

Anfalov alleged that before his death, Dr. Troitsky from the USSR Academy of Sciences, said that the Soviet government knew that the UFOs were extraterrestrial in origin, but concealed the truth from the public. People who spoke out were confined to mental institutions.

Dr Valery Uvarov, of the National Security Academy, St. Petersburg, wrote of an interesting event which occurred on 2nd November 1989.

Truck driver Oleg Kirzhakov, and his offsider Nikolai Baranchikov, were driving from Arkhangelsk to Moscow, when they found the road near Emtza railway station was undergoing repairs. They had to detour down a dirt road in order to reach their destination on time.

After rounding a bend in the road, they noticed a huge 'structure' on the right-hand side, which they initially thought was more construction/repair equipment. When they got within about eighty feet of the object they could see its metallic sheen in their headlights. The truck's motor stalled, and they coasted to a halt around the next bend.

Oleg got out to investigate, and Nikolai remained in the cabin to keep watch and observe. Every time Oleg tried to approach the object, he felt some invisible resistance in the air around him, making it difficult to walk. After some persistence he came close enough to stare at something he was sure was 'not of Earthly origin'.

Thirty feet in front of him was a huge disc, about 130 feet in diameter, with a dome-shaped top. Along the perimeter were some dark holes, and underneath he saw two structures, which he thought were supporting the craft. The far edge of the disc was slightly elevated, and resting on some birch trees, two of which were broken. Oleg could see no signs of life, or any doors or windows on the object, and thought something must have gone wrong. Was some assistance required?

As if an unseen intelligence had read his mind, a glimmering red dotted line appeared in front of him. It morphed into a small transparent screen, upon which several words were written in red. Oleg thought it was asking for 'burning fire', and returned to Nikolai in the truck to get some matches and a bottle of laboratory alcohol, which they used as an anti-freeze in the braking system.

(Although the 'screen' and messages were in front of Oleg at all times, apparently Nikolai couldn't see it. I have spoken to witnesses in Australia, who have also experienced the same type of 'message screen'. It may be inter-dimensional or telepathic.)

Oleg told Nikolai to remain in the truck, and he returned to the shoulder of the road where he gathered some dry leaves and set them on fire. Suddenly the 'resistance' in the air was gone. A passage appeared on the surface of the object. It extended into the interior, forming a corridor, at the end of which was a glimmering, bluish light.

A 'shaft' extended down from the object to the ground, and a black 'mass', which looked like a 'bag or sack', came out of the corridor, slid down the shaft, and took the box of matches. By this time Oleg had fallen into a ditch with terror, and Nikolai's frightened face was pressed against the windshield of the truck.

The 'thing' had returned to the craft by the time Oleg had climbed out of the ditch. He stood there in disbelief, trying to recover his senses, and decided to wait and see what would happen next.

There must have been some form of telepathy in play, because as soon as Oleg thought he would like to observe the disc more closely, the screen reappeared with an invitation for him to enter. He tentatively approached, and noticed several round openings, which he thought may be portholes. A narrow metallic tube came out, just above his head, and when he grabbed hold of it, he suddenly found himself just inside an opening above.

He walked down a corridor, which had oval shaped walls and ceiling. There were no doors, just a shimmering light about twenty feet along at the end. Upon reaching it, he found himself in a large hall, with a domed ceiling and a diameter of about sixty feet. It had a diffused light, and panels of flashing lights along some of the walls. There was a long, straight divan, and a circular crack around the central part of the hall. He thought it may be to allow it rotate, giving access to various controls.

He saw two motionless black 'masses', like the one he had seen outside. They began to move towards him, and he stood still, his mind full of questions. The screen was still in front of him, but the answers appeared in his head before he could read them on the screen.

He was very curious about everything around him, including an oval control panel, and geometric symbols on the upper surface of some lamps. Eventually he got around to asking who they were, and where were they from?

The dome in the hall started to dim, and like a planetarium, a star map appeared on the ceiling. One star began to pulsate and slowly descend, and he was told it was in his galaxy.

He had many more questions, and again the answers appeared in his head before they were on the screen. He learned this was a scout ship, which used electromagnetic fields to fly. They were studying our planet, which they needed as a 'springboard' to the future.

He noticed another two 'masses' had come into the hall, and understood it was time for him to leave. He left the same way as he had come in, and returned to the road. He looked back to see the tube and opening had disappeared. The outer rim and dome had started to silently rotate in opposite directions, and a luminescence surrounded the craft until it resembled a 'ball of light'.

It slowly began to rise, then accelerated and shot out of sight to the north east. By this time there were two other cars on the dirt road, and all the occupants, along with Nikolai, raced over to Oleg. They were full of questions, but he was so overcome and trembling that Nikolai had to drive the rest of the way.

This case is interesting because it does seem possible that Oleg was interacting with alien artificial intelligence during his experience. The 'dark masses' he encountered never seemed to equate to a 'live being'. By 1989 we were more adept at detecting any intrusions into our atmosphere by extraterrestrial craft, and the 'visitors' would certainly have the advanced technology to access our citizens this way.

The second factor in Oleg's testimony is his reference to the 'star map'. In the Betty and Barney Hill case, (See *The Alien Gene* pp172-4), Betty was also shown a 'star map' which depicted trade routes and other information. She recalled a three-dimensional hologram, which, despite being disputed by some experts, was later verified by the astronomy department of the Ohio State University.

Marjorie Fish, who did the majority of the analysis on Betty's recalled 'star map', was convinced it was genuine and accurate, even to the extent that it contained astronomical bodies which we had not yet documented. Respected scientist and ufologist, Stanton Friedman, wrote an in- depth review supporting Marjorie Fish's analysis. His extensive article can be found in the *MUFON UFO Journal* Oct/Nov 2009.

I have always been impressed with the research of Paul Stonehill, Dr. Uvarov and their colleagues. Unfortunately, other early amateur Russian ufologists had a habit of sensationalising some of the sighting reports, and making wild, unsubstantiated claims, and I am hesitant to document some of their reports.

In 1998 a documentary, *'The Secret KGB UFO Files'*, was broadcast in many countries around the world. It purported to depict the retrieval of a crashed disc, and subsequent autopsy of a dead alien, near Berezovsky in 1969. Was it true, or an elaborate hoax, perhaps State sponsored? I don't know, and maybe never will. There are a lot of convincing arguments from both sides of the debate.

While there were many genuine events, similar to those in the West during the 1960s, a lot of incidents were due to the Soviets testing their own missile warheads, which upon re-entry from low-trajectory orbits, appeared to be UFOs.

On 30/31 March 1993, the Russian satellite launch rocket, Cosmos 2238, came crashing back to earth over Ireland, Wales and the west coast of Britain. It generated a lot of excited UFO reports.

More reliable Soviet officials have confirmed that 'of course UFOs are real', and their country was just as anxious to learn the advanced alien technology.

In early 1996, an interesting article appeared in *People* Magazine. It claimed that the Russian newspapers *Trud* and *Rabochav Tribune* had quoted rumours that government salvage workers died mysteriously after being sent to unearth the wreckage of a strange craft,

Believed to be thousands of years old, the object was buried, at a thirty-five-degree angle in dense woods north of Tallinn. It was made of silvery heat resistant material, fifteen metres in diameter, and weighed about two hundred tonnes. Workers dug a three metre trench around the craft, and several died of a paralysing illness whilst taking water samples back to Moscow.

Scientist Nikolay Sochevanov said they couldn't drill through the hull of the craft, even though it appeared to be only two centimetres thick. Eventually a pneumatic pick-hammer and diamond saws managed to break off a piece, and scientists examining the sample claimed there was no doubt the UFO was of extraterrestrial origin.

There is, of course, the famous Tunguska incident, which occurred on 30th June 1908. At an International Congress in Frankfurt, which was sponsored by Michael Hesseman, several Russian investigators from a Soviet delegation, discussed their research into the large object which crashed, nearly a century earlier, in a remote area of Siberia. The damage to the surrounding landscape and wildlife was enormous.

Witnesses had claimed that very bright object had been seen at 8am. It was travelling from east to north, but before crashing and exploding, it had changed its trajectory in the sky, which made them doubt it was an asteroid or comet.

In the afternoon they saw a second object, travelling from east to west, near the crash scene, before it flew away. The second craft was huge, described as being approximately five hundred metres long and seventy metres wide.

Over the following years there were a large number of biological mutations in the area. Although most experts thought that the crash site resembled a large nuclear explosion, the level of radioactivity was far lower than average, and not what the scientists had expected.

They also noticed another strange effect, a type of minor 'time distortion' which affected both mechanical and electronic watches at the Tunguska site. The investigators thought that maybe there was some form of energy field which remained at the sites of UFO crashes.

Later, in 1953, Professor Liapunov suggested that we "abandon the concept of a meteorite, and term the object a 'cosmic ship' of extraterrestrial origin." At the same time, another scientist – Kasanzew – indicated his belief that 'inhabitants of another world came into the atmosphere of the Earth in 1908'.

More recently, several experts, including Dr. Felix Zeigel and Dr Alexal Zolotov, had accompanied researchers into the area on several occasions. Zolotov was also firmly convinced that this was a nuclear-like explosion caused by an alien spacecraft.

At the beginning of the 21st century another group of scientists visited the area, and claimed they found evidence that it had been part of a comet which had crashed all those years ago.

I guess we will never know!

CHINA

The Chinese have never really been forthcoming when it comes to disclosing UFO activity.

MUFON UFO Journal 2009, published an unconfirmed account from July 18th 1947, which is of particular interest due to the 'Roswell' incident the same month.

A farmer near Chengdu found the remains of a crashed disc, or unknown craft, in his field, and soon Professor Zeng Zhanhan, head of the Physics Department at the local university, was asked, along with other experts, to analyse and report on the object.

They declared the wreckage to be a UFO, of alien origin. Soon the police and military arrived, and insisted it was only a 'weather balloon'. The similarities to 'Roswell' cannot be ignored, especially when the researcher, Michael Cohen, noted that the US military were stationed at Chengdu at the time.

CHAPTER 11

THE MYSTERIES OF OUR NEAREST NEIGHBOURS

EXPLORING OUR SOLAR SYSTEM

Russia launched its Sputnik satellite in 1957, and our first manned space flight was by Yuri Gagarin in 1964. We have certainly expanded our ventures into the Solar System since then. America succeeded in landing Neil Armstrong on the Moon in 1969, and now, in the 21st Century, it is 'full speed ahead' for activity and planning.

In 1957, the US Air Force chief of staff, Thomas White, stated; "Whoever has the capability to control space will likewise possess the capability to exert control of the surface of the Earth."

In 1967, in anticipation of further ventures into the Solar System, the United Nations sponsored the *'Treaty on Principles Governing the Activities of States in the Exploration and Use of Outer Space, Including the Moon and Other Celestial Bodies.'*

In essence this agreement states that; *'the exploration and use of outer space shall be carried out for the benefit and in the interests of all countries and shall be for the province of all mankind. Outer space shall be free for exploration and use by all States. Outer space is not subject to national appropriation by claims of sovereignty, by means of use or occupation, or by any other means. States shall not place nuclear weapons or other weapons of mass destruction in orbit or on celestial bodies or station them in outer space in any other manner.*

'The Moon and other celestial bodies shall be used exclusively for peaceful purposes....and States shall avoid harmful contamination of space and celestial bodies. Astronauts shall be regarded as the envoys of mankind.'

A multitude of satellites now orbit our planet, and most countries are dependent upon them for military, industrial and communication purposes. Most citizens of developed countries unwittingly rely on them in their everyday lives.

Our jointly operated manned Space Station orbits the planet, and as of 2019, the European Union and nine other countries can independently launch spacecraft. Although in 1967 over one hundred nations, including the United States, signed the 'Outer Space Treaty', forbidding the militarisation of space, Russian and USA plans to create a 'Space Force' means this consensus is unlikely to continue.

The actual purpose of a 'Space Force' is debatable. Is it for defence against earthly or alien enemies? Perhaps both! In the 1960s many American and Russian satellites went missing. Others experienced interference with their electronic control systems. Russian probes to Venus and Mars mysteriously vanished, as did the US Explorer III and Syncom I. The strange behaviour and disappearances of our probes and satellites continued, and despite reports of UFO activity above the Earth, nobody would admit that perhaps our ventures into space were being stymied by the aliens.

Now, in the 21st century, multiple countries have satellites, many of which are integral to their defence systems. The entire international community is dependent upon the current array of nearly five thousand satellites currently orbiting the Earth. Without them they cannot function. It only stands to reason that, in time of conflict, one would try to disable enemy communication and other capabilities.

Many years ago, rocket scientist Werner Von Braun advised against the weaponisation of space, however it seems his warnings have 'fallen on deaf ears.'

21st century space observatories are becoming much more powerful, and our robotic probes have gone far and wide. Plans are coming to fruition to return to the Moon, and land manned vehicles on Mars, perhaps installing a permanent habitable base there. The planets and asteroids in the Solar System are rich in minerals and rare substances, and resource poor but technology savvy nations are anxious to avail themselves of these resources.

But how did we get this sophisticated technology, and is anyone else out there?

THE MOON

Very little is said these days about anomalies on the surface of the Moon. In his book 'Cosmic Top Secret' Jon King quotes NASA's former data and photographic documentation supervisor, Ken Johnston, who claimed his superiors erased film footage taken by the Apollo 14 astronauts. It showed structures of unnatural origin on the Moon, and also five or six lights in a crater on the far side. This corroborates Armstrong and Aldrin's alleged claims to have also seen a light on the rim of a nearby crater during their historic landing in 1969.

Jon King also wrote about retired NASA and McDonnell Douglas engineer, Marvin Czarnik, who was originally a sceptic. He and geologist Ronald Nicks resolved that some of the Moon anomalies could not be the result of natural geological processes.

This lends credence to a handwritten letter a teenage girl showed me in the mid-1970s. It came from her uncle, who worked at NASA. He was very excited as they had discovered large 'artificial' structures on the 'dark' side of the Moon. He commented that they rose so high, he wondered if they were the remains of what may have been an artificial biosphere. I believed the authenticity of the correspondence, however it was insufficient evidence for me to publicise this important information.

Over thirty years later, in 2010, the *MUFON JOURNAL* published the much awaited corroboration. Janice Curry wrote an article about well-known American researcher George Filer. One paragraph jumped out at me in a 'Eureka' moment. It matched the contents, down to the last detail, of that young girl's letter, all those years ago!

'Filer served as an intelligence analyst to Tactical Air Command Headquarters at Langley Air Force Base, which shared space with NASA's Apollo Moon Program. He passed through the NASA side of the base daily, and learned through his acquaintance with officers at NASA, that our satellites had discovered an alien base, almost a mile in size, on the back side of the Moon, that lunar orbiters had found detailed artificial structures, including huge, tall thin towers, spherical buildings, and what looked like radar dishes.'

A documentary, 'Aliens on the Moon: The Truth Exposed', aired in 2014, supposedly showed NASA photos, never seen before, of these artificial structures. Robert Kiviat, producer of the two-hour SyFy Channel show, told NBC News that there is no doubt these structures exist. He also claimed that Russian Space Agency lunar orbiter photos show a twenty-mile high 'spire' clearly sticking straight up from the Moon's surface, as well as a partially destroyed 'dome'.

Much as I tend to be sceptical of sensational documentaries, these details further corroborated that handwritten letter I was shown forty years ago. By the mid-nineties researchers were poring over the images captured by the US Navy's Clementine Probe, which had previously 'mapped' the Moon. Although it appears as a barren, heavily cratered landscape, the debate, over the anomalies, still rages. Are they geological formations or artificial structures? Why is this so important? Simply because if there are artefacts on the Moon, it stands to logic and reason that there may also be more on Mars.

A report I have yet to confirm states that Armstrong claimed the Aliens have a base there, and we were told in no uncertain terms to get off and stay off the Moon. Certainly Armstrong himself has never confirmed this.

In 2003, the late Stanton Friedman made this interesting observation; *"A question for which I have never had a satisfactory answer is why the USA didn't launch Apollo 18 and 19? The hardware was all built. The crews had been selected and trained. President Nixon said it was to save money. But almost all of the bills had already been paid. Yes, I am aware that some have suggested that the aliens secretly told us to stay off their moon......At best an idea in my grey basket.*

"So the big question is, do we Earthlings want to take dominion over the Solar System, or do we wish to continue to be a primitive society whose major activity is tribal warfare? I am certain that the lost astronauts had greater vision than that."

It has been nearly fifty years since any human has set foot on the Moon. One of the 'official' excuses given was that we could not reproduce the thermal protection coating used in the original missions. I personally don't believe this. In an interview with *'This Week'* magazine in 1959, Werner von Braun was advocating our space travel progress, and considered that the radiation from the Van Allen Belt could be managed, and should not prove an impediment.

I have often wondered as to the real reason there was such an interval in our Moon missions. What kept us away for so long? Only now, in the twenty-first century are we returning. Several countries are manning new probes, and planning and designing self-sufficient lunar bases. Why? Other than for military purposes, it is speculated that the mysterious element, Helium-3, could also be present and mined along with other valuable minerals and resources.

Certainly there appears to be a race by the major nations to establish their presence on the Moon, with some aiming to investigate the mysterious 'dark side' more thoroughly.

America's NASA and private corporation Bigelow Aerospace have already announced, in advance, plans to build a lunar base. It may only be coincidental, but CEO Robert Bigelow has held a fascination for UFOs and aliens since early childhood. He has spent millions of his own money on research projects, including The Bigelow Foundation and the National Institute for Discovery Science. A couple of years ago, while appearing on CBS's '60 *Minutes*', he reportedly said that he was absolutely convinced that aliens exist and that UFOs have visited Earth.

The 'competition' to return to the Moon is heating up, and there is already legal debate as to individual mining rights and resource ownership. The actual definition of the 1967 'Outer Space Treaty' is also coming into question.

In 1984 only thirteen nations ratified the *'Moon Agreement of 1979'*, which states that *'Neither the surface nor the subsurface, nor any part thereof or natural resources in place, shall become the property of any State, international intergovernmental or non-governmental entity or of any natural person.'* It sounds very good, but in fact is essentially meaningless as so few countries have agreed to abide by it.

MARS

Since we first gazed upwards into the heavens, Mars, a rugged planet with two moons – Phobos and Diemos - has always been a source of wonder and speculation for us earthlings.

In 1901, Harvard's Lowell Observatory recorded a seventy minute shaft of light from Mars. Although astronomers considered it to be an inexplicable phenomenon, the brilliant scientist Nikola Tesla was sure it was an intelligently directed communication from a civilisation on that planet. He experimented with various methods of communication with the Red Planet, and wrote an article *'Talking With the Planets'* which was published in *Collier's Weekly* in February 1901.

In July 1965, when the US Mariner 4, at an altitude of 5,600 miles, took the first close-up pictures of Mars, they were relatively primitive and only very few.

Even so, at the same time, an unidentified disc was seen in close proximity Tidbinbilla Tracking Station, which was receiving transmissions at the time.

Was someone watching us watching them? In 2015 *'National Geographic'* noted that since 1960 we had launched forty-three missions to Mars. Twenty-three had failed entirely, and another two were only partly successful. Some never made it out of Earth's atmosphere, others stopped communicating, crashed on Mars, or just flew past the planet.

'People' magazine, 19th September 1989, reported that Tass, the official Soviet newsagency, announced that just before their Phobos probe 'vanished', an unknown object had approached , and it subsequently lost contact with ground control. Soviet space authorities had refused to release its final photographs, and most experts do not believe it was struck by a small piece of rock that happened to be in the same orbit.

'Mars Observer' mysteriously disappeared just as it entered Martian orbit in 1994. Its final transmissions were 'very strange' and a massive gamma ray pulse was detected, coming from the northern hemisphere minutes before it vanished. In 1976, Vikings One and Two were the first to land, and recently, probes such as 'Curiosity, 'Opportunity' and 'Spirit Rover', have been more successful.

My friend, Rosemary Decker, also had a fascination with astronomy, especially the planet Mars.

ASTRONOMERS' EYESIGHT AND THE MYSTERIES OF MARS

By Rosemary Decker

For well over one hundred years there has been an on-going controversy about what has exactly been perceived on Mars. It began in 1877, when Giovani Schiaparelli, in Milan, Italy, sketched the earliest linear grid he named 'canali', meaning channels. Over his years of observations, he was able to add many more such lines, but the controversy regarding their existence began early on. (Schiaperelli never entered the argument)!

In that same year, Asaph Hall, at the U.S. Naval Observatory, discovered the two moonlets of Mars, but because they were soon found by other astronomers, they did not become controversial.

The two factors, most responsible for the sudden advances in the knowledge of Mars, were the improvement in telescopes and the unusually close approach of Mars to Earth in 1877. Since closet oppositions occur only at fifteen to seventeen year intervals, astronomers need to have patience. For a period of about three months, they must work with great concentration during the several weeks before, during and following the opposition.

At such times, it swings within about thirty-five million to thirty-nine million miles of Earth. Even that close, perceiving and recording fine details on Mars' surface is difficult, largely because air turbulence only occasionally ceases, just for a few seconds at a time, preventing the usual blurring of images.

William Sheehan, a psychiatrist and amateur astronomer, produced a book, 'Planets and Perception', which describes many of the factors involved in human perceptual abilities, especially at the telescope. As he points out, it is necessary to know <u>how</u> to look, as well as having good, clear eyesight.

Whether amateur or professional, most observers benefit greatly by some training in 'how to look' – which includes the awareness that there is a 'blind spot' on each eye, just where the optic nerve enters the retina. This necessitates looking a tiny bit away from the objective, and changing focus frequently. (Nature does a certain amount of focus-shifting automatically).

Giovani Schiaparelli, Director of the Milan Observatory, was noted for his unusually good vision during most of his career. He was very careful to cease relying on it when, in later years, his eyesight began to weaken. Several of his contemporaries were able to observe and sketch much of the linear grid and other surface features of Mars, very much as he saw and recorded them. (At that time, photography was out of the question). Some other astronomers, unable to see the fine markings, openly objected that since they were unable to see them, they could not be real.

This argument, used early on, has been perpetuated right up to the present. NASA's original declaration that the Mariner and Viking probes found no linear grid, further bolstered the notion.

When Percival Lowell learned, upon his return home from Japan in 1893, that Schiaparelli was hoping his Mars work would be continued by someone whose vision was still excellent, he got in touch with him. They became lifelong *friends, although they were able to work as colleagues only briefly, insofar as telescopic observations were concerned.*

Backing for the excellence of Percival Lowell's vision was supplied by his famous colleague Dr. Earl Slipher, who was a young astronomer at Lowell Observatory, worked well with Percival, and made his own contributions to the Mar's mappings. Lowell was taken prematurely, by a stroke, at sixty-one years of age. Earl, however, continued with excellent health and outstanding eyesight for almost another half a century. While he studied our whole planetary system, as had Lowell, his greatest interest, like Lowell's, was Mars.

Possibly the very best evidence of Lowell's excellent vision appeared in the biography by his brother Lawrence Lowell – 'Percival Lowell' (1935) – now long out of print. Few people today know that Lawrence quoted Boston's leading ophthalmologist, Dr Hasket Derby, as saying that Percival Lowell had the keenest eyesight of anyone whose eyes he had ever examined.

Earl Slipher is still honoured today for his many contributions to planetary knowledge, and most especially two that continue to be useful. One is the excellence of his countless photographs of Mars, some of which had not been surpassed by the end of the twentieth century. The other is his of composite photos, made by combining several photographs made in rapid succession of the desired image. The technique is still in wide use.

It was this composite technique that Lowell photographer, Ivan Dryer, used in 1960 to obtain Mars photos showing several of the major 'canals'. He sent one of the 'glossies' to 'Sky and Telescope' in 1987, which was reproduced in the June '87 issue, along with Dryer's accompanying letter. Even with the lithographic reproduction, four of the canal lines can be seen.

During his long career, Earl Slipher was given an honorary Doctor of Science degree by the University of Arizona, and an honorary LL.D by the college which is now the University of Northern Arizona.

When he directed the Lowell National Geographic International Mars Patrol in 1954 and '56 from a telescope in South Africa, he was passing seventy, and still not in need of the aid of glasses. He continued to work at Lowell, (with only slightly diminished vision, as he neared eighty), right up until the day before passing in 1964, his 82nd year.

During the Mars Patrol of 1954 and '56 when Mars made close approaches to Earth, Slipher and his team, working in the clear atmosphere of the mountain country near Bloemfontein, South Africa, announced success in obtaining a number of photos showing several of the larger 'canals', including one that was over fifteen hundred miles long! Only a few of those were reproduced, due to the extreme delicacy of the fine lines. Reproductions of the linear grid are extremely difficult to achieve, as details not lost in the emulsion are often lost in the printing process.

E.C. Slipher's personal interpretation of the 'canal' grid included the comment; "Sometimes one 'canal' will run right through another – something no sensible river would do."

Among other 20th century astronomers who perceived the 'canal' lines, and added to them at times, were A.E. Douglass, William Pickering and Dr. Clyde Tombaugh – all of them eminent astronomers.

Although NASA claimed that the Mariner IV photos showed no fine grid, some astronomers – notably Dr. Frank Salisbury and Dr. Clyde Tombaugh disagreed. Tombaugh said he had found 'canal' streaks and 'oases' spots in seven of the twenty-two Mariner photos. Salisbury showed copies of the Mariner films to NICAP, (National Investigations Committee on Aerial Phenomena), and these also revealed straight-line 'canals'.

Another keen-eyed astronomer, the telescope manufacturer John Mellish, predicted early on that the roundish 'oases' spots on the 'canal' grid would prove to be craters. He was correct in this, but his eyesight has not been credited – only lucky guesswork. It is possible that he was aided by an awareness that, since Mars is not far from the asteroid belt, much cratering would be likely.

Even Britain's 'Dean of Astronomers', Dr Patrick Moore, who had observed Mars over many years, and was a sceptic regarding the fine-line grid, at last one fine night, during a few lucky seconds, saw a whole disc of Mars suddenly netted with the fine pattern – 'like lace-work'.

The apparent contradictions in the data regarding the reality or not of the 'canal' lines, may not be as perplexing as they seem. In all fairness to NASA, it should be borne in mind that in obtaining images at such close range, the lengthy markings which appear as narrow, regular lines from vast distances, may be indistinct and irregular in close-up. A deliberate effort would have to be made to enhance such markings, and for whatever reasons, it appears not to have been.

While the general public has long been aware of the 'canal' controversy, there is another important observational mystery that is much less known. Many astronomers have noted it for over half a century. In fact Percival Lowell wrote of it in 'Mars and its Canals' in 1906.

This is the 'wave of darkening' which occurs every Martian spring, as the related polar cap begins to melt, and which travels equator-ward at the rate of about fifty miles per day, until by mid-spring it reaches the equator and slightly crosses it. The immense desert areas are little affected, but the darkish features, including the 'canals', undergo the change regularly with the seasons. The darkening is a greening of a rich blue-green typical of the far northern forests on Earth!

Before the invention of colour photography, many astronomers claimed that the green colour was not real – that visual fatigue caused the defensive reaction of seeing the colour opposite that of the vast reddish-ochre deserts, in the area adjacent to them. (This can occur.) Eventually photography proved the green hue to be real, but then two other explanations were offered. The first was that volcanism produced ash globe-wide seasonally which picked up the moisture?? The second suggested that mineral salts darkened as they absorbed the moisture. However, there is no such seasonal volcanism, nor do mineral salts turn green in spring and summer, golden to brown in fall, and grey in winter.

Astronomer Earl Slipher in 'Mars: The Photographic Story' stated that in 1957 and 1959, Sinton had identified C-H bands in the infra-red spectrum of Mars at 3.67, 3.53, and 3.43 microns as being due to organic compounds – 'the same kind of bands as are produced by vegetation....Repeated observations proved that these showed strongly in the spectrum of the dark regions, but were absent or weak in the desert regions.' Regarding this greening, NASA remains silent!

There are other observational puzzles on the 'Green and Red Planet', as exo-biologist Strughold called it, however the two covered here are the most outstanding. Fortunately, in 2003 there will occur one of Mars' closest approaches in over a century – a distance from Earth of only about thirty-four and a half million miles. Amateurs and professionals alike will be having a heyday, and they will be better equipped than ever to solve the Mars mysteries.

Rosemary wrote this article in 1999, and in 2004 she published her book '*35 Minutes to Mars*'. Her research had taken decades, and at that stage she revealed her contact with many astronomers and experts including Dr Slipher, the Lowell Observatory, Richard Hoagland and many other respected authorities.

It wasn't until Rosemary passed, in 2009, that I could reveal her secret involvement with the Mars research. She once described herself as 'a lifelong hobbyist of planetary astronomy', and had shared this interest with George Adamski long before his famous meeting with 'Orthon' in the desert.

For decades she had liaised with many astronomers, engineers and geologists, (some ex-NASA scientists), regarding anomalies on the Moon and Mars.

Many considered that the government was less than supportive of their activities, and would prefer the public to regard Mars as a barren, inhospitable planet. As early as 1958, William M. Stinton of the Lowell Observatory published a paper detailing spectroscopic evidence of vegetation on Mars.

A number of the astronomers/scientists started working on private projects, later forming the 'Team of Independent Mars Researchers'. Rosemary supported their later, sometimes clandestine activities, and in 1994 helped organise a small local conference-networking weekend for some of them.

On 26th July 1976, the Jet Propulsion Laboratory in California, received at set of photos taken by Viking Orbiter 1's thirty-fifth orbit of Mars. They showed unusual 'formations' on the surface of Mars' 'Cydonia' area. Were they artificial or natural? The rocky image of a 'face', ten times the height of the pyramid at Giza, was hotly disputed by the experts. Some insisted it was not a natural formation, whilst others argued that it was merely 'a trick of the light' when the photos were taken.

The claims that other photographs showed images of adjacent 'pyramid' type structures only increased the controversy. Mark Carlotto, a former image-computing analyst with TASC, and author of the book '*The Martian Enigmas*', claimed to have, along with Richard Hoagland, also found evidence of a polyhedral formation, resembling an 'enclosed structure which had lost its roof'.

Whilst Mars is a planet of huge mountains, valleys and craters, which could explain extreme geological formations, I was certainly intrigued regarding the 'Face', as well as other reported anomalies. Rosemary sent me a copy of 'The McDaniel Report' written by Professor Emeritus Stanley McDaniel in 1993.

It was subtitled; *'On the Failure of Executive Congressional and Scientific Responsibility in Investigating Possible Evidence of Artificial Structures on the Surface of Mars, and in Setting Mission Priorities for NASA's Mars Observor Spacecraft'.*

It is a very detailed, in depth analysis of our initial voyages to the Red Planet, and the AOC (Artificial Origin at Cydonia) hypothesis.

McDaniel states; *'Currently a new spacecraft, the Mars Observer, is about to enter Mars orbit and begin mapping the entire surface of Mars. The Mars Observer carries a camera capable of taking high-resolution photographs that would most certainly settle the question posed by the AOC hypothesis. But NASA's position, regarding the priority assigned to obtaining photographs of these controversial landforms, to be highly equivocal and leave open a clear possibility that the photographs may not be obtained, or if obtained, may not be released.....During the seventeen years since the controversial landforms were discovered, NASA has maintained steadfastly that there is "no credible evidence" that any of the landforms may be artificial.'*

He goes on to detail NASA's failure to analyse and evaluate the images to any acceptable scientific standards. He also accuses NASA of regularly distributing false and misleading statements about its evaluation of the 'Face' to members of Congress and to the public.

Carl Sagan, the renowned planetary scientist and sceptic, described NASA's dismissal of the face as 'unfortunate'. He believed it was worthy of further investigation.

Even among INUFOR's own researchers there was disagreement. Our astronomy consultant, Claire Williams of the Canberra Planetarium and Observatory, was publicly quoted as saying; "They've taken images from the Viking and enhanced them to such a degree that they are no longer reliable or credible."

Today most space programs have concentrated on planning explorations, and possible territorial claims on Mars. Future missions are planned by the US, Russia, Japan, Europe, and in all probability China. I have often wondered... why? Was there more to the AOC theory than they are telling us? Considering its vast distance from Earth, Mars would have little military significance to our own hostile nations. Could it relate to a perceived threat of alien incursions from outer space, or are they already there? Whilst there are apparently some very rare and valuable mineral and other resources on the planets, the cost of mining and transporting them back to Earth would be prohibitive.

It has been admitted that Mars has days, nights and seasons similar to ours, as well as an atmosphere, clouds and polar caps. There is even talk of creating an 'outpost colony' on Mars, however it is much colder, with less gravity and carbon dioxide rather than the oxygen we need for survival.

Perhaps those astronomers who refused to follow conventional thinking were correct, and the Red Planet is not so uninhabitable and desolate as previously portrayed!

Over the last few years, since several probes have landed on Mars, scientists are also cautiously admitting that 'small quantities of water flow intermittently on Mars'. In 1996/7 Dr. Gilbert Levin conceded that primitive 'life' may exist on Mars. Although the temperatures a couple of feet above the surface are sub-freezing, as the sun mounts the atmosphere immediately above the surface warms considerably. In 2015 NASA was more forthcoming about the findings of their Mars Reconnaissance Orbiter (MRO).

These days our scientists and astronomers have very powerful technology at their disposal, including the Hubble Telescope, Chandra X-ray Observatory, Spitzer Observatory, space stations and multiple missions into our Solar System and the Cosmos. However, they are dependent on government and private corporation funding to continue their research. Who knows who or what they have discovered out there? I don't think they are going to tell the general public!

In the *MUFON UFO Journal*, 2001, George Filer agreed with Arthur C. Clarke that new images of Mars clearly show, at the very least, patches of vegetation are moving and changing with the seasons on Mars.

Elon Musk, the founder of 'Spacex', has announced future plans to develop a base and colony on Mars, and in 2012 stated that his goal was to develop a space transport system that would enable humanity to become a multi-planet species. Lawyers have suggested that, under the 'Space Treaty', governments and corporations would have no legal claim to Martian land where a colony is established, but would retain property rights over all materials it launches into space.

Our own history tells us that 'Treaties' and International Law are often disregarded and flouted, especially when the stakes are high.

I cannot leave any discussions regarding the 'Red Planet' without addressing the recent assertions being made about the US or others having already founded a base/colony there. Personally, given our current technology, and in the absence of any proof, I don't believe this...maybe in the future. Perhaps the so-called witnesses have been taken there by 'people' other than humans. Who knows? I don't!

However, in the interests of presenting a balanced viewpoint, I will refer to an article in the *'Daily Mail – Australia'* 30th November 2014. It stated that in 1979, a former NASA employee, along with six other staff who were downloading live feed telemetry from the Viking Lander, saw two men in protective suits walking towards the probe. The problem with this claim is that it was made by telephone to American radio station 'Coast to Coast AM'. There is no way of confirming the witness's bona fides or evidence.

Rosmary's continued interest in the planet Mars seemed to be very personal, and continued for the rest of her life. I only wish she were still here to pore over and analyse the latest findings.

THE SUN

The Sun, the giver of life and centre of our Solar System, whilst fairly stable, can also cause havoc when it emits a solar flare, or coronal mass ejection. Sometimes they cause minimal damage, and are hardly noticed, but there are other occasions, in a roughly eleven year solar maximum cycle, when they can be quite serious. It depends upon whether they impact the Earth, or go harmlessly out into space.

In 1859 a massive 'super flare', the 'Carrington Event', caused a great deal of damage to North America. Today a similar solar eruption would be much more devastating and would create world-wide chaos.

It could take out power grids and communications across the planet, and leave cities without electricity for months. Everything from defence, commerce, emergency services and all facets of our everyday life would be affected. There is little we can do about this natural occurrence, however recent satellite technology has been designed to give a short warning – hopefully enough time to disconnect electrical grids, electronic devices and other orbiting space craft.

ASTEROIDS and COMETS

Astronomers around the world co-operate in locating and tracking the multitude of comets and asteroids in the Solar System. Due to the vastness of space, indeed even around our own Sun, only a small percent of the thousands of comets, some up to six miles across, have been detected.

Asteroids pose an even larger threat to our planet, and evidence of previous devastating impacts can be found in several places in the world. Scientists have warned that an asteroid of even a third of a kilometre diameter, would impact at such an enormous speed, that it would create an unbelievable crater, and trigger massive earthquakes and tidal waves. The billions of tons of dust and debris would plunge the Earth into a major 'Ice Age'.

Asteroids are also difficult to detect, and international co-operation, involving the major 'space-age' nations, has been undertaken. Several 'Near Earth Asteroid Tracking' task forces and projects were implemented, and consideration given to various alternatives and plans of action should the need arise.

WHAT ABOUT PLANET X AND OTHER STRANGE BODIES?

Since the days of the ancient Sumerians there have always been myths and legends about the mysterious Nibiru, or Planet X as it is referred to today.

Zecharia Sitchen certainly believed in its existence, and wrote; 'I prophecise the return of this planet, called Nibiru, at this time. The planet is inhabited by intelligent human beings like us, who will come and go between our planet and their planet.'

I don't agree with him. Any celestial body in the frigid regions of outer space would be unlikely to sustain life as we know it. But does Planet X really exist? Many people, including some astronomers think it does, and over the last few years there have been numerous efforts to locate previously unknown objects within or just outside our Solar System.

In 1821, forty years after the discovery of Uranus, the French astronomer Alexis Bouvard and others detected discrepancies in its orbit, and claimed there must be another planet out there. They were correct, and calculated the theoretical position of Neptune, which was finally located in 1846. But this still did not fully account for the distortion in Uranus's orbit. Astronomers thought they had solved the riddle in 1930, when Clyde Tombaugh discovered Pluto.

The later detection of planetoid Charon still did not solve the anomaly in the orbit of Uranus, and some scientists declared that there must be another body way out there, which has an elliptical orbit around the Sun.

This is still a slightly controversial subject, but what was laughed about, several decades ago, is now treated a lot more seriously. In 2012 *National Geographic* wrote about Rodney Gomes from Brazil's National Observatory, who had calculated that a planet four times the size of Earth was orbiting our Sun around the outer fringes of the Kuiper Belt.

Astronomers mostly discussed the possibility of another planet, but in the early eighties there was the occasional reference to a 'brown dwarf'. Astronomer and ufologist Allen Hynek wrote about this in 1983:

'Can the object be a planet? Or is it a brown dwarf – a star that didn't quite make it, a body not massive enough to produce the high internal temperatures necessary to ignite its nuclear furnace and thus shine like our sun? Or could it be a neutron star that has gravitationally collapsed into a densely packed , dark remnant of its former luminous self? ......Planet X, which would have to be relatively close by – between six and ten billion kilometres away to alter the orbits of Neptune and Uranus....A brown dwarf or neutron star – much more massive than a planet would be - and located perhaps seventy-five billion kilometres away. These theories have their critics.'

The reference to a 'brown dwarf' had me intrigued. In *'The Alien Gene'* I discussed 'Ruth', a young contactee from the 1930/40s. During her meeting with a humanoid 'leader', she recalled him telling her about a 'brown dwarf' near our Solar System, and the aliens' concern that we may use dangerous methods to deflect or interfere with it. Have the aliens really come to steer us through a difficult time in the Solar System, and help prevent us using dangerous technology which may have repercussions in the wider Cosmos? I don't know the answer to that question.

I also wrote about Patty's liaison with aliens in New Zealand. Her father, James, told me that he had sent his family to live in the mountains in Australia because he had been warned of a future natural cataclysm, rather than a war.

In 1983, after some scientists claimed that they had located 'Planet X', NASA launched the IRAS-Infrared Astronomical Satellite. We are still exploring the Kuiper Belt – containing millions of chunks of debris, left over from the formation of the Solar System. It is a vast junkyard of icy, rocky bodies stretching for billions of kilometres. We are now querying much of what we assumed, and the field of planetary science is now undergoing an intense period of readjustment and discovery.

Astronomers are constantly searching for comets and 'Near Earth Asteroids'. A 'brown dwarf' is notoriously difficult to detect, as it emits only one weak radiation in the infra-red, however scientists have even better heat-seeking telescopes with which to scan the skies.

Three larger objects to have been discovered are Sedna, which takes 10,500 years to orbit the Sun, and Xena and Quaoar, none of which have yet been designated planetary status. Other large bodies have also been identified and named, including the three hundred mile diameter 1996 TL66 and 2003 UB313, which some experts claim is 2,100 miles wide. In 2012 VP113 was discovered, and who knows what else may be out there?

Whilst I cannot comment on, or verify the accuracy of the information, the *'Twilight Zone'* in *Nexus Magazine* issues Feb/March and April/May 2007, make for some very interesting reading.

Where astronomy, and the Solar System in particular are concerned, not all scientists and astronomers are in agreement. Professor James McCanney disagrees with many of his peers regarding astrophysical tenets, and the lessons to be learned from ancient history. He once said; *'The history of this planet, as it is taught, is false.'* His views do not follow conventional thinking, and have caused controversy.

He wrote two books – *'Planet X, Comets and Earth Changes'* and *'Surviving Planet X's Passage'* – and was a firm supporter of the work of Velikovsky, Shoemaker and Dr Robert Harrington. Several years ago he realised authorities did not like him speaking out, and alluded to the fact that Harrington met an untimely death in 1993, after claiming to have discovered and plotted Planet X. He was also aware of Shoemaker's suspicious car accident in Australia, when all his files went missing.

After the IRAS infrared telescope went into orbit, many new findings and conclusions were released. On 30th January 1983, Ray Reynolds, an astronomer member of the Ames Research Centre told the *'New York Times'* that; *'Astronomers are so sure of the tenth planet that they think there is nothing left but to name it.'*

Several researchers, from different leading universities, have followed their own line of investigation. In the long history of our planet, there have been several inexplicable biological mass extinctions. They attributed these to possible comet or asteroid strikes, where the resulting debris cooled the atmosphere, and many of the creatures could not adapt in time to survive.

The problem was that these mass extinctions happened on a regular basis, with some deviation, over many millions of years, and comets and asteroids are not 'regular'. While the scientists have not reached and definitive explanation, they have not yet ruled out the 'Planet X' theory.

Carole Rutland, executive director of Columbus State University Space and Science Center, reportedly said: *"Scientists leaning towards the existence of Planet X argue that a larger planetary body in a highly elliptical orbit, may take seven to nine lifetimes to complete one orbit. Planet X could go undetected if it travels in a highly elliptical orbit at nearly right angles to the orbits of the nine known planets. This orbit could be so elongated that the unknown planet circles only every 700 to 1,000 years."*

Another astronomer commented that *'not all passings of Nibiru at perigee between Mars and Jupiter cause cataclysmic effects. Apparently it depends on whether the Earth is on the same side or the opposite side of the Sun, and therefore shielded to a degree.'*

CHAPTER TWELVE

SCIENTISTS, ASTRONAUTS and ASTRONOMERS

Our own highly skilled 'boffins' are the most qualified to analyse the unidentified craft seen all over the planet. Many of the scientists who contributed to our early space exploration were seconded from Europe at the end of World War II. They, of all people, would have been well aware of any technical breakthroughs made by the Germans, or later by the US, Canada or Britain.

Professor Hermann Oberth originally studied medicine, and began his professional career as a doctor for three years in a military hospital. He designed his first rocket in 1909, and completed a set of blueprints for space travel in 1923. Later in his career he was regarded as the 'Father of German Rocketry'.

In so far as his work in Germany was concerned, he pointed out that as early as the beginning of the century Dr. Ing Walter Lewetzow had developed a gravitational theory: "In Prague, then in Vienna, we were the first to develop, during the war, an instrument which really looks like a UFO. The V7 was a helicopter which had two wings, twenty-five metres in length, and at the ends were ram jets. At a distance the whole thing looks like a shining disc.

"Helmut Zhorowvsky in France is building machines similar to the V7, and there are also a number of reports that lead to the assumption that there are such machines. But they fly with much noise, and leave a contrail in the atmosphere. The UFOs do not!"

Dr Ernst Stuhlinger, who also worked at Peenemunde, quoted Oberth as saying that their true goal was not the launching of rockets, but travel through space and the exploration of the unknown out there.

Along with his former pupil, Werner von Braun, Oberth was instrumental in the US Moon missions. Von Braun said; "He has always been twenty to forty years ahead of us."

Oberth was quite outspoken in 1954. In one article he wrote; *It is my thesis that flying saucers are real, and that they are spaceships from another solar system. I think that they are possibly manned by intelligent 'observers', who are members of a race that may have been investigating our earth for centuries.'* He later went on to say he favoured the theory that the craft were 'flying by means of artificial fields of gravity – although UFOs may be something altogether different, something no-one has thought of heretofore'.

The same year, during a lecture, he disputed any suggestions that craft seen over the US and Europe were of Russian origin. If the Russians had such a valuable vehicle, they would not risk the Americans firing upon or capturing it. He pointed out that by 1945 Russia was, as a nation, quite exhausted and depleted, and had trouble getting back on its feet again. He then made an odd comment saying that 'they' had searched Russia at that time as thoroughly as they did Germany later on. If they had been working on 'high frequency things at Magnitogorsk', they would have seen it.

He reminded everyone that in 1942 only one of four rockets had been launched successfully at Peenmunde, and in 1944 only 80% of the V2s reached their target. In 1962 he was quoted as saying that; "Today we cannot produce machines that fly as UFOs do – they are not built by human beings."

In 1955 his career took an unusual turn, when he was commissioned by the West German government to conduct a three-year study into the UFO mystery, and in 1959 he completed his contract as head of the US Jupiter Space Program.

It was after that that Oberth felt able to speak more freely. He stated that the US Air Force was taking the so-called 'flying saucers' much more seriously than their public 'debunking' policy, and that their scientists were trying to duplicate the UFOs' propulsion system.

He was however, optimistic that although they didn't yet have the means to influence gravity, considerable success has been attained in this program, and he believed within five years, men would be able to travel to the Moon in craft propelled by electromagnetic means.

Whilst Oberth never said where or how he gained his advanced scientific knowledge and theories, he advocated peace and harmony with our fellow man and the environment - exactly the same message contactees had received from the 'Visitors'.

He once commented that: "(UFOs) are conceived and directed by intelligent beings. They probably do not originate in our Solar System." Years later he was quoted as saying; "We cannot take credit for our record advancement in certain scientific fields alone." When asked by whom, he replied; "People from other worlds."

In 1954, Arthur Joquel, a noted authority on rocketry and space travel, made the following statement; "For hundreds, or even thousands of years, observations and reports have been made regarding these objects. Accurate, well-trained, impartial witnesses have described them, using almost the same terms in all ages and times. There have been sufficient reports concerning these objects made by scientists, military personnel and trained civilians, to have removed any doubt as to their existence.

"No country on Earth could have built such vehicles hundreds of years ago. It would strain the ability of any country today to develop such flying objects, and to construct, test, and launch them, and furthermore keep their place of origin a secret. It seems more logical, under the circumstances, that flying discs have their place of origin somewhere in space, and visit the Earth for some reason or purpose."

Werner von Braun was more reticent, but in 1959 he told a representative of *Neues Europa*; "We find ourselves faced by powers which are far stronger than we had hitherto assumed, and whose base of operations is at present unknown to us. More I cannot say at present. We are now engaged in entering into closer contact with these powers, and in six to nine months' time, it may be possible to speak with more precision on the matter." Of course, he never did 'speak on the matter' again.

In the early 1970s I met the Australian scientist Sir Mark Oliphant, who said he regretted his contribution to the atom bomb. In the 1950s Oppenheimer, another eminent European scientist, was experiencing difficulties maintaining his 'top secret' classification. Oppenheimer had opposed the use and development of the hydrogen bomb. Unlike Teller, his opponent, he felt it was much more dangerous than the atom bomb. Author Donald Burleson thoroughly investigated the AEC hearings, and his dissertation can be found in *MUFON UFO JOURNAL* July 2005.

Burleson makes a convincing argument that Oppenheimer was directly involved in the UFO crash retrieval operations at Aztec, New Mexico, and possibly earlier at Roswell in 1947. It is interesting that a draft 'Oppenheimer – Einstein' document, discussing possible interactions between humankind and alien cultures, was prepared for, but never sent to the President. It is complex and detailed, and must have taken a long time to compile before it was ready for signing in June 1947.

NEXUS Magazine published this draft, which they claimed is available on the Majestic Documents website. I am going to reproduce parts of it here, as I consider it extremely important to know what these two eminent scientists thought five years after the 1942 Los Angeles event and weeks **before** the Roswell crash.

Relationships with Inhabitants of Celestial Bodies

'Relationships with extraterrestrial men present no basically new problem from the standpoint of international law, but the possibility of confronting intelligent beings that do not belong to the human race would bring up problems whose solution it is difficult to conceive.

In principle, there is no difficulty in accepting the possibility of coming to an understanding with them, and of establishing all kinds of relationships. The difficulty lies in trying to establish the principles on which these relationships should be based.

In the first place, it would be necessary to establish communication with them through some language or other, and afterwards, as a first condition for all intelligence, that they should have a psychology similar to that of men.'

They then address the possibility of extraterrestrial biological entities desiring to settle on, or colonise Earth, and consider the legal standing the United Nations would have in determining the issue.

Their thesis continues with a discussion about international law, and whether or not extraterrestrials may have colonies, in artificial environments, on other planets in the Solar System, perhaps to exploit their natural riches. They debate the possibility of a future cosmic international law, and anticipated complications. One situation alluded to was if another species was already present on, for example, the Moon, given our own legal principle of *res nullius,* who would have legal claim?

Another couple of pages urge restraint in our development of atomic warfare and hydrogen bombs, and future plans for space vehicles with nuclear warheads.

'And now to the final question of whether the presence of celestial astroplanes in our atmosphere is a direct result of our testing atomic weapons.

The presence of unidentified space craft flying in our atmosphere, (and possibly maintaining orbits about our planet), is accepted as de facto by our military....When artificial satellites and missiles find their place in space, we must consider the potential threat that unidentified space craft pose. One must consider the fact that misidentification of these space craft for an intercontinental missile, in a re-entry phase of flight, could lead to a nuclear war with horrible consequences.

Lastly, we should consider the possibility that our atmospheric tests of late could have influenced the arrival of celestial scrutiny. They could have been curious, or even alarmed by such activity, and rightly so.......

In conclusion it is our professional opinion, based on submitted data, that this situation is extremely perilous, and that measures must be taken to rectify a very serious problem is very apparent.

The submission, intended for the US President, was never signed and submitted, as the real controlling 'powers' did not want Einstein or Oppenheimer discussing this with the President. What is very significant is that either two of the world's most brilliant scientists were losing their minds, or much more likely – were telling the truth!

This brings me to another situation which could potentially confront government personnel, or even the general population, when encountering the occupants of UFOs. Herbert Prouty, MUFON's Director of Legal Affairs, wrote an in-depth analysis – *'Killing an Alien: The Legal Ramifications'* – in the April 1997 *MUFON UFO Journal*. Our laws recognise terrestrial aliens (foreigners from another country) as having legal status as a human being. What about 'Humanoids' from another planet? Would we differentiate their status from the 'Reptilians' or 'Greys'? This is a fascinating article, well worth a read, which covers many varied contingencies and possible repercussions.

Another important early scientist was Konstantin Tsiolkovskiy, who was born in 1837 and died in 1935, before World War II. He was a Polish immigrant to Russia, where he achieved fame as a great pioneering rocket expert.

As early as 1920 he already believed that the Earth was being observed by extraterrestrial civilisations, and pondered over why there hadn't been open contact. He once wrote; *'Intelligent beings are found in endless numbers. The spread of life from one Solar System to another, even from the Milky Way to other galaxies, is entirely possible....Certainly advanced extraterrestrials possess the means of interplanetary travel.'*

His opinions didn't necessarily encompass the thought that aliens would come with our best interests at heart. While he regarded them more as a colonising force, he felt they would be benevolent in accelerating the development of other societies.

Tsiolkovskiy hypothesised that advanced alien societies were already, unbeknown to us, monitoring and trying to influence mankind. He considered it necessary that we try to detect this, and suggested that although extraterrestrials were already present, they considered our civilisation was not ready for interstellar relations.

Other highly qualified military personnel have also spoken out over the years.

In 1949, Colonel MacLaughlin, a missile expert, said; "Many times I have seen flying discs following and overtaking missiles in flight at the experimental base at White Sands Proving Ground, New Mexico, where, as it is known, the first American atom bomb was detonated."

At a press conference on 16th January 1957, Admiral Delmer Fahrney, previously in charge of missiles, stated; "Reliable reports indicate there are objects coming into our atmosphere at very high speeds, and controlled by thinking intelligences."

Air Force Chief of Staff, George S. Brown, while speaking in Chicago said; "I don't know if this story has ever been told, but they plagued us in Vietnam during the war. We didn't call them UFOs. They could be seen only at night in certain places. They even triggered an air-sea battle in which an Australian destroyer was hit."

In November 1971, at a conference at the University of Arizona, several experts spoke out about their knowledge and opinions on UFO data and extraterrestrials. It was attended by many eminent scientists, including astronomer Dr. Allen Hynek, who had participated in the US government's 'Project Blue Book'. He said that UFOs were now a respectable subject for scientific study.

Canadian biophysicist Dr. John Munday said; "I certainly don't think all UFOs are from our own Earth. One thing that convinced me of their existence was a case I investigated in Chicago several years ago."

He went on to explain how a housewife, who opened her front door to watch a bright orange light, some distance away. Like many other witnesses, she suffered severe symptoms of ultraviolet radiation and possible high frequency energy.

Dr. Robert Creegan, a professor of philosophy, made the following comments during his presentation: "I'm convinced there is intelligent life in outer space. UFOs are not just illusions. Some reports show them to be controlled objects. To me, the most acceptable and realistic theory is the UFOs are controlled by intelligent beings from outer space."

He also pointed out the electro-magnetic effects which had been observed, including electrical failures and the stalling of automobiles, motorcycles and scooters, as well as tractors on farms.

Dr. Frank Salisbury, Head of the Dept. Of Plant Science at Utah State University shared an interesting opinion: "We don't know whether UFOs are controlled by space beings of intelligence – but it is a strong possibility and a theory which we must seriously consider. Then what kind of beings could they be? One possibility is that they could be virtual immortals. Certainly there are plant cells which have never died. These beings could be similar. It would help explain their survival for centuries or more if they were coming from other stars in our Milky Way, or even from other galaxies."

Dr. Emerson Shideler summed up the general consensus when he said; "I believe the evidence is quite clear that UFOs exist. The most probable explanation is that they are controlled by intelligence from another planet. There is a very real possibility that they are completely unlike our accepted ideas of normal life. I do not believe that they are any threat to us. But their impact on our notions of culture and religion would be tremendous if their visits could be proved."

Although the official government stance is to persistently avoid the extraterrestrial subject, their space scientists and defence strategists apparently do not share their reticence. In 2006 Drs. Taylor, Boan and Powell co-authored the book 'An Introduction to Planetary Defence', which specifically addresses the defence of Earth in the event of extraterrestrial invasion, and the means at our disposal to combat the aliens.

Ovni magazine quoted Latchezar Filipov, head of the Space Research Institute of the Bulgarian Academy of Sciences, as saying that "the aliens are here observing us, but unobservable by us for some reason. I feel that some kind of information is being taught."

He claimed they asked the aliens thirty questions about global problems, and received the answers in the form of pictograms in crop circles. His colleagues in Bulgaria were not impressed by his ideas, and despite Filipov's impressive credentials, wanted him to resign from the Institute.

Another interesting comment was reported to have come from Dimitry Medvedev, Russian Prime Minister from 2008 to 2012. He purportedly made several 'off the cuff' remarks, while the microphone was left on, following an interview with a journalist. He said that every incoming Russian leader was given two folders of information on extraterrestrials who came to earth and never left! He couldn't reveal how many of them are among us because it may cause panic. Was he serious or joking? We will never know!

Scientists who worked on secret prototypes, space exploration and armament projects often died prematurely, especially in the 1980s, in suspicious circumstances. BUFORA's *'UFO Times'* published a list of twenty-two fatalities, and the *'Hard Evidence'* magazine Jan-Feb 2004 provided more detail. Another author wrote an article *'The Curse of Marconi'* in which he related thirty suspicious deaths. I will leave the 'who, why, and how' of this to other investigators, more familiar with the circumstances.

ASTRONAUTS

Nearly all astronauts have scientific qualifications, and most were originally test pilots. It seems that, in the early days, they were much more willing to report 'bogeys' than their counterparts in later times. There has, however, been the ongoing problem of enthusiastic ufologists taking innocent comments and blowing them up beyond all proportion.

Gordon Cooper elaborated to this in a letter to the Granada Mission, which urged the United Nations to initiate a study into UFOs; *'Astronauts are very reluctant to even discuss UFOs due to the great number of people who have indiscriminately sold fake stories and forged documents abusing their names and reputations without hesitation.'*

Several astronauts have also become very spiritual since they ventured out into the cosmos, and this has, to a certain extent, affected their opinions.

My colleague Dr. Don Herbison-Evans wrote a fascinating article in 1969 about the opinions of our original space explorers.

('February 17th 1961 – Blast off for Russian launch of man and woman into space. For seven days, until February 24th, their conversations were recorded by tracking stations at Bochum, Upsala, Turin and Mendon. Something went wrong, and they were unable to return to Earth. On February 24th, each announced their physical condition to be good, but the lights had failed, and the air supply was almost gone.

'The woman's voice cut in; "I'll take it and hold it tight with my right hand. Look out of the peephole! I have it!"

'A second or two later the man said; "There is something! If we do not get out the world will never know about this." That was the last heard from the doomed pair.

'May 1963 – On his final orbit, Major Gordon Cooper radioed to Muchea in West Australia; "I am being approached by a greenish object moving east to west." This was contrary to the orbit of man-made satellites. It was seen and recorded by tracking gear in Perth Australia, and also by hundreds of technicians and newsmen'.)

(Cooper later elaborated, saying the object was similar to the ones he saw in 1951 - 'double-saucered lenticular'.) In his memoirs Gordon Cooper wrote about being a young second lieutenant flying an F-86 Sabrejet over West Germany in 1951. 'Bogies' were spotted, and the pilots scrambled to intercept. The metallic, silver saucer-shaped objects were higher than the planes' 45,000ft ceiling. They were out of reach, and tantalisingly moved slowly, and then faster, before stopping.

Cooper said; "We couldn't get close enough to form any idea of their size. For the next two or three days they came right over the base at regular intervals, but as far as I know, there was no official investigation."

He also tells of an incident in 1957 when, at Edwards Air Force Base, he was with two official cameramen who inadvertently filmed a smooth, metallic silver saucer, about thirty feet in diameter, which had flown silently overhead, hovered, extended some landing gear and set down about fifty yards away. When the photographers approached, it lifted up again, and after retracting its landing gear, and shot quickly back up into the sky.

The cameramen were told to process the film and photos, but not to make any copies or prints. They were then sent to Washington in the Base Commander's plane. I would suggest that it is possible this may have been one of our own earthly prototypes, we may never know.

When he testified before the United Nations, Cooper said that most astronauts are reluctant to discuss UFOs, but he believed extra-terrestrial vehicles and their crews were visiting this planet. He said that for many years he had lived with a secret which was imposed on all specialists in astronautics. He spoke of the thousands of witness and radar reports which, for fear of panic, no-one wanted to make public.

(Cooper, during his final years with NASA, worked with Mexican archaeologists investigating 5,000 year-old ancient ruins in that country. In his book *'A Leap of Faith'* he mentions records, which when translated, 'turned out to be mathematical formulas, used to this day for navigation, and accurate drawings of constellations, some of which would not be officially 'discovered' until the age of the modern telescope. This left me wondering: 'Why have celestial navigation signs if they weren't navigating celestially?')

Don Herbison-Evans went on to write; *'April 8th 1964 – on the launching of a Gemini spacecraft, carrying performance devices, it was joined on its first orbit by four UFOs – two up front and two behind. One orbit and they then vanished.*

'1967 – Gemini 7 – Frank Borman and James Lovell, on their second orbit, reported seeing a 'bogey'. (Space term for a UFO.)

'November 14th 1969, Charles Conrad, Apollo 12, spotted a bright UFO from the centre hatch window. On Sunday 16th the object was still with them, 170,000 miles deep in space. Houston controllers theorized that it was a spent stage of a Saturn V rocket (S84) which they had discarded after launch.

However, charts showed that the discarded rocket - the S84 - should have been about 2,500 nautical miles from Apollo 12 at that stage.'

There is still enormous controversy over our first manned landing on the Moon.

On 2nd January 1990, *'People'* magazine published an interview with Maurice Chatelain. The former head of NASA communications confirmed rumours that the Apollo 11 astronauts saw UFOs on the Moon's surface. He said Neil Armstrong, the first man to set foot on the Moon, saw two UFOs on the rim of the crater. (See *'Contact Down Under'*, re 'Moon slides'.)

"All Apollo and Gemini flights were followed - both at a distance, and sometimes quite closely – by space vehicles of extraterrestrial origin. Every time it occurred the astronauts informed Mission Control, who ordered absolute silence, and devised the codename – 'Santa Claus'."

I was already aware, when I read this article, that Australian and other ham radio operators, besides several excited Soviet astronauts, (who were 'rooting for them'), were monitoring the transmissions.

'People' then went on to say that documents from the Russian space program confirmed Chatelain's assertions.

'Moscow university professor Vlagyimir Azscizca says; "When Armstrong and Aldrin's landing manoeuvre was completed on the moon, they observed saucers were on the opposite side of the crater. Armstrong cried – "Damn, they're already here!" Azscizca claims Houston ordered the astronauts to stay on the Lunar Module until they had established that the UFOs had no hostile intentions."

In his book *'Above Top Secret'* Timothy Good said that Vladimir Azahzha, a physicist and mathematic professor, confirmed this and stated; "Neil Armstrong relayed the message to Mission Control that two large, mysterious objects were watching them after having landed near the moon module. But his message was never heard by the public – because NASA censored it."

Armstrong has never confirmed any of this, and we will probably never know the real truth about this incident. Another report states that it was Aldrin who saw the UFOs whilst they were in Moon orbit. Apparently he was scanning the surface with a 16mm camera, looking for a suitable landing spot. He noticed a light moving off from the Moon's surface towards the east. When the film was developed it showed two unidentified objects. Aldrin allegedly reported that they hovered together at first, manoeuvred sideways, and then both accelerated vertically until lost from view. One returned momentarily, a short distance away, before shooting off at tremendous speed.

Edgar Mitchell, who also 'walked on the Moon', later became a consultant for the TV series 'The X Files'. He is reported to have caused quite a sensation in the late nineties when he made the following comments at a UFO conference in the USA.

"The American government, and governments throughout the world, have thousands of files of UFO sightings which cannot be explained. As a scientist, it is logical to me that at least some of these have been witness to alien craft....

"The question of whether or not aliens are still visiting us is more complex. Such is our existing secret technology that what may look like an alien craft may well turn out to be a top-secret military plane. On the other hand the craft may be an alien spaceship. Personally, however, I'd say yes, it's quite possible we are still being visited."

His full speech is well worth reading, and can be found in 'Nexus' magazine, Dec.98/Jan.99.

Later, on July 25th 2008, the 'Daily Telegraph' July 25th 2008, also Edgar Mitchell as saying that the UFO phenomena was real. He was more outspoken than in earlier interviews, and claimed extra-terrestrials had paid repeated visits to our planet, but the encounters were kept secret by government agencies. He added that 'our technology was not as sophisticated as theirs, and had they been hostile we would be gone by now'.

NASA officials were always quick to dismiss the suggestion of a cover-up, but as early as 1974 the alien issue was being publicly discussed. A 'Special' was broadcast by the NBC 'Today' show on 12th April 1974. After a commercial break, Edwin Newman questioned Astronaut Brigadier General James McDivitt as to whether he thought we would ever have contact with extra-terrestrial life.

McDivitt believed 'they' were really around, but it may be a long time before we could communicate, but hoped it would eventually happen. He denied that an object seen, and filmed, during his Gemini 4 flight, on 4th June 1964, was an upper stage of a rocket or anything else from this Earth.

When asked about the various types of reported flying saucers and UFOs and the possibility of advanced propulsion systems he said; "Sure, fantastic types of propulsion systems, and other things. I don't think we are smart enough in the 1970s to really understand what's going to happen in 2300, or some other time like that, and these people could be way ahead of us."

According to an article in 'SAGA' magazine Dr. Garry Henderson, a top Space Research scientist with General Dynamics, stated that all American astronauts have seen UFOs, but have been told not to discuss their sightings with anyone.

"Conversations could be censured out of the transmissions between astronauts and ground control by the delayed tape technique, which allowed a lag of up to two or three minutes between Mission Control and the broadcasts into your homes. Actually, amateur ham radio operators, who operate on different frequencies, can pick up these censured pieces of dialogue."

Radio hams, probably the bane of NASA, claimed that they monitored exchanges between the space shuttle Discovery and Houston on 14th March 1989. One radio operator claimed to have made a tape recording of Col. John Blaha, in which he said; "Houston, this is Discovery. We still have the alien spacecraft under observation. We are continuing to lose power." Later, after his mission, Blaha denied that there were any UFOs.

Bob Oechsler, a former NASA mission controller, disagreed, and stated; "The fact is that aliens have tracked every mission that we and the Soviets have put into space." The National Aeronautics and Space Administration dismissed all these reports as 'nonsense'.

Astronaut Leroy Chiao was commander of the International Space Station from October 2004 to April 2005. He and a fellow cosmonaut took a 'space-walk' to install the navigational antenna. They were travelling at 17,000mph some two hundred and thirty miles above the Earth.

Suddenly Leroy saw a line of lights fly by at an even faster speed. He thought it to be 'awfully strange'. Although he didn't agree with the theory that it was the lights of fishing boats hundreds of miles below, he wouldn't say that it was a spacecraft as he was 'sceptical' of claims that we've been visited by aliens from another planet or dimension, although he didn't rule it out one hundred percent.

The Soviets were also experiencing strange 'anomalies'. On October 12th 1964, three Russian cosmonauts aboard Voskhod I reported they were surrounded by a formation of fast moving disc-shaped objects.

In 1979, Soviet cosmonaut Victor Afanasyev reported to Mission Control that an object was close to his capsule whilst en route to the Solyut-6 space station. He described it as being a metal structure, about forty metres long, with inner hulls. It followed them for half an orbit, during which time Afanasyev continually reported back to Mission Control.

"The object was narrow here and wider there, and inside there were openings. Some places had projections, like small wings. The object stayed very close to us. We photographed it, and our photos showed it to be twenty-three to twenty-eight metres away."

When Afanasyev returned to Earth, His cameras and film were confiscated, and he was told not to speak about the sighting. It was only after the collapse of the Soviet Union that he felt safe to speak out, and said; "It is still classified as a UFO because we have yet to identify the object."

Author Paul Stonehill spoke of Valery Burdakov, who had published over four hundred engineering science dissertations and patents. During his career, the professor had often communicated with cosmonauts, and knew of their UFO sightings. Following sixty years of studying the subject, he felt that three percent were real messages from extraterrestrial civilisations, and we should take notice of them.

Russia has always maintained a strict code of silence and secrecy regarding UFOs, especially in regards to its own astronauts. Investigators Philip Mantle and Paul Stonehill extensively researched this subject, and wrote an interesting article following an interview with cosmonaut Aleksei Leonov, who believed in ancient astronaut theories but denied space mission contact with UFOs. He criticised the very different opinions and statements of his fellow pilot/astronaut Marina Popovich.

In 1995, Russian researcher,Valery Uvarov, interviewed cosmonaut Aleksei Zolotov. His testimony was quite compelling; "Personally, I've seen UFOs in flight three times, and in connection with my research, which is carried out under laboratory conditions, I have visited three different locations where these objects have landed. One time, I even saw an alien, a humanoid – living , just like you. It's true, we didn't speak, only met at a glance, but I see his face even to this day."

Zolotov went on to describe his activities into UFO research, then made a quite amazing statement, which paralleled the views of several western astronauts and many investigators around the world:

"At our scientific laboratory at Tver State University, evidence was obtained confirming the existence of a Cosmic Intellect within the Universe, outside the consciousness of mankind, and from which we receive information on an intuitive level. This evidence has since been confirmed by the Tver Society of Scholars and the Laboratory of Bio-location under the Scientific Research of Geophysics.

"These are not simply words; there is laboratory research on this topic and scientific evidence obtained with the help of scientific experiments. Based on these results, which have been obtained by this laboratory, I can speak deliberately and confidently, with the unequivocal conclusions to this problem which we are now looking at – a Cosmic Intellect exists and we have proven it."

A few days after this interview, Aleksei Zolotov was found dead on the doorstep of his Tver home. He had been murdered.

Perhaps the final word should be given to Astronaut and Senator John Glenn, who made a guest appearance on the 'Frasier' TV show on 6th March 2001.

"Back in those glory days, I was very uncomfortable when they asked us to say things we didn't want to say, and deny other things. Some people asked, you know, were you alone out there? We never gave the real answer, and yet we see things out there, strange things, but we know what we saw out there. And we really couldn't say anything.

"The bosses were really afraid of this, they were afraid of the 'War of the Worlds' type stuff, and about panic in the streets. So we had to keep quiet. And now we only see these things in our nightmares or maybe in the movies, and some of them are pretty close to being the truth."

ASTRONOMERS

What about others, who are experts at deciphering what is seen in our skies and beyond? Astronomers have been peering through their telescopes for many centuries, fascinated by the cosmos and our own Solar System. Many recorded inexplicable anomalies, and I quote some of their reports from an article written by William Moser, then secretary of UFOIC in 1972.

His listing commenced in 1676, and included the famous Halley, who saw an object illuminating the sky for more than two hours on 6th March 1716, and noted similar sightings May 1677 and 31st July 1708.

June 17th 1777, Charles Messier, could not identify a number of dark, disc shaped spots in the sky.

Only a few years later, on 18th August 1783, Cavallo, a fellow of the Royal Society, saw a strange luminous object at Windsor Castle, and a scientist named Wilkins made reports of similar phenomena March 1718 in Oxford, and in both 1737 and 1742 in London.

French physicist Francis Arago claimed that objects moved across the Embrun sky, in military precision, on 7th September 1820. He mentioned that a number of other scientists had seen similar events.

On 11th May 1845, Capocci, a well known Italian astronomer, working at the Capodimonte Observatory Naples, saw a number of smallish size shining discs. Some were star shaped and others sported a tail-like appendage. In 1863, German astronomer, Waldner, saw similar objects, as did British astronomer Bird in 1867.

These are only a few of many reports, made long before mankind mastered the art of taking to the skies!

In more recent years, astronomers have been a little more reticent where the reporting of UFOs is concerned. Admittedly, they only view a very narrow portion of the sky at any one time. Further, they are subject to peer pressure and their ability to attract funding.

They have, however, on occasions, reported strange craft that they have observed, away from their observatories, as ordinary members of the public. In 1976, three astronomers saw an object outside the Monte Izane Astrophysical Observatory, at Galder in the Canary Islands. They watched it for several minutes, and described it as a brilliant sphere with a swirling centre, which approached the observatory before making a ninety degree turn and moving away at speed. A couple in a car also saw the same object as they rounded a curve in the road, and their car radio failed. It was spherical, transparent, and tall figures seemed to be inside. Several other eyewitnesses near Galdar reported seeing it for up to half an hour.

Soviet Astronomers, on several occasions, have watched UFOs through their telescopes. In the 1960s astronomers in Kazan tracked a crescent shaped object. They claimed it was over 1,000ft in diameter, and travelling at about 10,000mph at a height of between thirty to sixty-five miles. Another telescopic observation referred to a disc about three hundred feet in diameter surrounded by three star-like objects.

In October 1999, several scientists and astrophysicists watched and videotaped a large disc-shaped object which was overhead for several minutes. They had been attending a conference at the Shemakha Observatory at Baku, on the Caspian Sea. After studying the tape and other data, they were unanimous in concluding that the object could not be explained as any known atmospheric phenomenon, and was not of terrestrial origin.

Whilst it is acknowledged that there is obviously secret, advanced military and other technology covertly traversing our skies, scientists, pilots and others involved in the aerospace industry would be more expert in differentiating what is ours, and what is not.

CHAPTER THIRTEEN

MORE VISITORS 'DOWN UNDER'

<u>BETTY</u>

Born in 1946, Betty was raised in Bondi and had a traumatic childhood resulting in nervousness and learning disabilities. Betty, like her mother, is psychic and as a child 'saw' things. She suppressed these abilities for a long time, but now practises as a psychic medium – sensitive to audio, visual and touch. Ever since she was a child she can hear sounds – like 'frequencies'.

In 1964 she spent a year on a working holiday in New Zealand, and was employed at and living in a hotel at Waitomo Caves. Just after she had been out with a caving group she went to bed at 11pm Friday night. She wasn't ill, but stirred on Saturday afternoon, then did not wake or remember anything until Sun afternoon 4-5pm. Betty feels it odd that she has never forgotten this, despite her abilities later in life.

She often had strange dreams – like it was a 'medium' experience – looking through a 'veil' with the spirits on the other side, maybe in another dimension. In about 2006 she was living in Parramatta when she woke up in bed – she doesn't know why, but was fully awake and not dreaming. She saw a 'veil' – as if between two worlds – but this time it was opening and she could see what looked like a laboratory, with lab equipment that seemed to be 'floating molecules'. She was very frightened and kept thinking that 'aliens' would 'step through' or walk out and get her. She closed her eyes in fear and 'went out like a light' – not waking up until the next morning.

Whilst she has inter-dimensional connections, she always considered it on the spiritual side, but when in a writers' group suddenly had a compulsion to compose a story about UFOs. Betty had never attended any UFO meetings until a friend told her about a 'get-together' that I run. She felt an inexplicable compulsion to come, and later confided in me.

Betty felt that something she cannot consciously remember has happened to her, either in New Zealand or at some other time. She initially indicated that she would like me to arrange a regressive hypnosis session to find out, but then hesitated and retreated back into her protective shell. Often possible witnesses or contactees are torn between wanting to know or pretending nothing happened.

THERESA

Theresa has lived on the Central Coast since she was four, and did not have a happy childhood. Her father was violent to her mother and brother – but not to her. She received no love or affection from her mother.

Theresa started getting anxiety attacks when she was in her early teens at high school. She would dream of the 'eyes' of ETs, and paint numerous pictures of large, black luminous eyes in a window behind her. She said she always had to put several coats of paint on the 'eyes', to get the colour and luminosity 'just right'. Therese said 'words' in her head formed images which she would then draw and paint – but she could never put the 'eyes' in until the last minute.

Theresa meditates quite often, displays some telepathic and psychic abilities, and sometimes has very rare out of the body experiences.

Three or four months before she conceived her son Trevor, she was sitting alone on a beach, watching the stars twinkling in the sky. She was startled to see what appeared to be a giant walking through the waves towards her. She could suddenly taste 'salt', and was surprised that the closer the 'giant' got to the sand the 'smaller' it seemed to become.

Trevor's conception occurred due to an unexpected 'one night stand' with a work colleague. It was prompted by a strange, inexplicable attraction which evaporated after the encounter. (Other female abductees have also reported sudden sexual impulses, often resulting in a gifted child.)

Three months later, she was alone and pregnant. One night, at 3am, she was distraught, and praying for help, when she got a telephone call from Theo, an old school friend, who came over to comfort her. He married her shortly after, and Trevor is still not aware of his true paternity.

When Theresa gave birth to Trevor she obviously entered an 'altered state'. Witnesses said her eyes were open, but she didn't respond to anybody or any stimulus. It was like there was 'nobody home'.

Theresa said it was not anything she had 'willed', and was so real it did not seem like any conventional out-of-the-body experience. It was as if she had been 'sucked out of her body', and was floating in some kind of substance, with resistance – similar to, but not, water. She was being swiftly carried into a blue/black/purple universe – full of planets and stars which were expanding and stretching. There seemed to be a light, metallic vapour, and she could smell and taste something like 'crisp ozone'. She was enjoying the experience which was peaceful and calm, as if she was 'invisible' but 'connected to everything'.

Theresa felt no fear, and it seemed she was drifting for hours. Whilst the experience was 'overwhelming' when she returned to normal consciousness she wanted to go back.

Witnesses said that Theresa was actually in an 'altered state' for only about thirty seconds, and during that time all her vital signs were normal and stable. She had been in labour for twenty-four hours, and was exhausted. Eventually the doctors performed a 'forcep' delivery. During that time she had only been given a low dose of Pethidine.

Theresa and Theo had a second son, Neville, just over a year later, and several more children in the years to come, but Therese never experienced that same 'altered state'.

When Trevor was two, and Neville one, she suddenly experienced unremembered dreams, and developed an inexplicable intense fear that ETs were going to take her children. She would force herself to stay awake at night, sitting on the front porch, staring at the moon, and silently pleading; "Don't take my children – please don't take them!"

Eventually, she was so exhausted her concerned family took her to the doctor, who arbitrarily diagnosed Bi-Polar and prescribed medication.

Not long after that, when she was pregnant with her third child, her husband hired the film 'Signs'. After watching it, the same irrational fear for her children returned, and she was so scared they moved house to a spot more elevated, where she felt safer. They lived there for twelve years until they all suddenly started experiencing strange electrical vibrations. Native animals, and even the ants, were behaving in an unusual 'anxious' manner. They then moved to their current location, a remote property, further to the north, where all is peaceful and uneventful, except for the sightings of strange lights in the sky some miles away.

Therese has weaned herself off the tablets, and actually seems very sane and sensible. She has always felt an affinity with nature and the animals she has lived with the in bushland high above the Central Coast. While she 'senses' she had some form of contact in the past – she doesn't want to 'know', and refused any regressive hypnosis,

Her fear for her children, especially Trevor, always somewhere in the back of her mind, surfaced in 2016 when he came home from a camping trip, excited that he and his friend, Max, had spotted an unusual object and lights over the 'Wollemi', north-west of Sydney. This is a very rugged, uninhabited part of the National Park. Theresa, along with Trevor and Max, met me shortly after at their home on the Central Coast.

Trevor, who was in his early twenties, appeared to be of nervous disposition. He was highly intelligent, and apparently, with very little effort, topped his class in high school. He and Max, knew nothing about UFOs until they searched the internet after witnessing and photographing the strange lights they had seen in the sky.

It was early November when they went for an hour's walk into the bush. At sunset, around about 7.30pm, they were sitting on a rock above the river. The objects seemed to be in the 'Wollemi', north of the Grose Valley and behind Mt. Solitary, near Mt.Wilson.

The Wollemi National Park, which covers hundreds of square kilometres, is a vast wilderness of extensive swamps and virtual jungle amid rugged mountainous terrain. Much of the area is still unexplored, its mysteries known only to the local indigenous people. Trevor knew there were no roads or houses in this area, and wondered what on earth this object and lights could be.

For about three hours, until 11pm, he and Max watched a stationary glowing light coming up from a valley near the horizon – the actual source was out of sight. There also seemed to be a white light going across the horizon below the trees. While this light was always there it seemed to flash just before two separate lights – pulsating orange – came from behind the horizon – one to the left and one to the right. They did a 360 degree circle then slowly went back down to the stationary light behind the horizon. Trevor and Max never actually saw these lights touch the ground. Once in the air they would remain orange for a while, but before returning down, the object on the ground, would dim – flicker white and then turn red. The airborne lights would then appear to turn into two lights, one white and one red which would flash as if synchronising with the object in the valley.

At times they seemed to separate, and Trevor mentioned they were a small distance apart with what seemed to be a small disc between them. There was a strong wind but the objects did not seem to be affected by it. Lights would come up and go down – sometimes five or six at the same time – during the entire period they were watching.

They went back the next night, to the same spot at the same time, and stayed for about two hours, witnessing an identical phenomenon. It seemed that there were 'signals' - by means of red and white flashes between the object on the ground and those in the air. They had taken a torch with a red and white light and flashed it at the objects, which then flashed back in the same pattern. When the lights gave the appearance of coming closer they became a little apprehensive and turned off their torch, leaving soon after.

Around the same time, there had been other sightings over the Wollemi, which holds particular significance to the local indigenous people. Unfortunately Trevor's photos, taken with a mobile phone, were unable to be analysed to any meaningful extent.

(Other witnesses have told me of strange craft in this rough unexplored terrain, and some claim there is an extraterrestrial base hidden there. Perhaps, one day, more definitive evidence will surface.)

DANIEL

Late in the evening of 31st October, 2016, Daniel rang me in a slightly agitated state. He lived at Quakers Hill in Sydney, and was more concerned about the wellbeing of his family than himself.

It was Halloween, and at about 7pm he had taken his daughter 'trick or treating'. At 8.30pm they walked back up his street as his neighbour had carved some pumpkin heads that he had promised to light up with candles. It was a clear night as they were returning – just on the other side of the road from their own house.

His daughter Mandy pointed to the sky, and was so terrified she raced across the road and into the house to her mother. Daniel looked up. Directly overhead, at an altitude of two to three hundred feet, was a huge, silent, boomerang-shaped triangular object. It resembled two wings joined together with nothing in-between. It was at least three house blocks wide, two or three house blocks long, and was like a half transparent whitish glow.

Whilst also a little scared, for about twenty seconds Daniel tried to focus on the object. It was a very quiet street, but nobody else had seemed to notice it. The 'craft' was cruising slowly – about 100kph from the south towards, but to the west of Richmond.

Daniel went on to explain that approximately twenty years ago, in about 1996 he had seen unidentified flying objects on three different occasions.

1. He was driving with his wife at dusk, presumably in the western Sydney area, when they saw a bright white light for about five seconds. It was travelling at a medium, steady pace – high in the sky – when it suddenly went straight down vertically behind the mountains.

2. On lunch break in Parramatta/Blacktown area, he and his workmates watched two white 'chrome' orbs/discs at an altitude of about 2,000ft.

3. At Doonside he saw three bright orange lights, in a triangular formation in the sky. They then lined up behind each other, and after about four minutes one shot into space, to be followed by the second one two minutes later. The third light remained.

Daniel did not want any publicity, or further investigation. I think he just wanted to speak to someone who believed him, and get reassurance that his family was safe.

LETITIA

Letitia, who is in her sixties, first contacted me after I had given a talk to an interested group of people. She was born and raised in Somerset, UK – only moving to London for nursing training – and coming to Australia in her twenties. She is a now a palliative care registered nurse – working in an administrative position and writing a book of her own.

Letitia was an only child. Her mother had severe gynaecological problems, and for ten years was told she could never have children. Letitia has a conscious pre-birth memory of being told this, and agreeing to become her baby.

Her father was a motor mechanic – drafted into the army during WWII – and a POW in Germany for four years. His father was in WW1 in Africa, and her maternal Grandfather at Gallipoli.

She was not above average intelligence at school, but has psychic and prophetic abilities. Like many others, her conscious memories of any childhood experiences in the UK are vague. She recalls that when she was little she would hide under the bedclothes – scared something was coming to get her.

When Letitia was sixteen she was losing blood. The doctors told her she was pregnant and having a miscarriage. It didn't look like a 'normal' pregnancy – and furthermore she was certified a virgin, having not had any physical relations. It was very distressing that her family would not believe her.

In 1982, when she was twenty-two, she was travelling in a car with two male friends. They were going from Wales to Somerset. When very close to the Salisbury Plains they sighted a large silvery craft – very close and low. She has no way of knowing if there was any missing time.

Like many other female experiencers, she also had polycystic ovaries – and after having three children underwent an early hysterectomy. The doctors did vivisections on the cysts, and said they were like cutting a 'watermelon'. She also has an interest in genetics and recommended 'The Biology of the Leaf' by Dr. Bruce Lipton, who has been working on the human genome project.

She and her husband now live in the southern suburbs of Sydney. In 2012 the whole garden was lit up 'red' and the dog was going berserk. Afterwards, her car electrics were 'gone'.

Another time she was driving in Panania, with her three daughters in the back, when they saw a huge black triangular shape craft, the size of a football field. She experienced a very strange sensation, and this made her frightened for her girls.

Once, when in Dubbo, in western N.S.W. she saw a blue sphere in the sky. She cannot consciously recall any aliens – but recently felt drawn to the UFO subject – hence her going to a couple of lectures. Like many 'experiencers', she is having some 'flashbacks', but does not want any regressive hypnosis at present.

LORNA

In the late 1980s the people in Pheasant Creek, Victoria, were somewhat mystified and apprehensive about the strange objects in the sky above them.

It was 9.45pm on a warm October night in 1987 when 'Lorna' and her daughter-in-law were having a quiet after-dinner chat and drink. A bright light was shining through the window, and the dogs and sheep were 'running mad.' She rushed outside to see the whole yard was lit up.

"I nearly fainted," she said. "Hovering straight above me was the underside of a large, fluorescent blue disc. It was as large as a low-flying jet. There was absolutely no noise, and the pulsating lights were blinding. I was so terrified I couldn't move, then it silently took off. In the time it took me to say 'sh-i-t' it had disappeared over the horizon."

Lorna went back inside and told her daughter-in-law what had happened. She was still very shaken, and they both hoped that 'thing' wasn't hostile.

The same night, a woman reported a similar disc following her car in Broadford. Her account appeared in Melbourne newspapers, as were many other reports of unexplained lights that night. Lorna suffered headaches for the next fortnight. Although the neighbours were aware of what happened, she said nothing to the media. She was in business, and 'couldn't afford the ridicule.'

Only a few weeks later, 'Eddy' was driving down High St. to Wallan. It was about 9pm, and he had his wife and grandchildren with him. His wife and the kids were the first to spot the 'bloody massive' disc overhead, and right above the car. It was bright blue underneath, with a white/blue body 'flashing pink'.

First it was above the vehicle, then dropped back, catching up again and flying above them along the winding road. When they finally reached the left hand turn to Wallan, the grandfather pulled up, and finally got to see what had been following his car. He admitted that he thought he was going to have a heart attack, and was relieved to see it silently head due north in the direction of Broadford.

He got the family home safely, and although his wife and grandchildren were unaffected, he was so upset, he was sick for a couple of weeks, and wouldn't talk to anyone about it.

The following year, just after midnight on 30th June, Lorna was home in her bedroom, when the wireless and lights started 'playing up'. The dog ran under the bed and wouldn't come out. She could hear the sheep outside 'carrying-on', and the birds in the pine tree were screeching. Thinking it may be a fox, she went out into the yard, but couldn't hear anything.

Just to be on the safe side, she managed to get the sheep into the shed for the night, and was about to go back inside when she saw something approaching from the western sky. This time there were two objects, following each other. They were similar to the craft that had been seen previously, but this time higher in the sky.

They passed overhead and she could see they were slightly 'flattened' with a dome – a beautiful fluorescent blue underneath, bluish/white and a pinkish dome with a golden glow.

By this time the sheep were 'hysterical' and the birds going 'berserk'. She was stunned, and stood and watched the two craft going sedately across the sky and disappearing over the western horizon. The animals quietened down, and she went to bed.

"I couldn't sleep, because by this stage I was beginning to doubt my sanity!"

In 1989 another elderly lady saw a similar object which passed over her house at about 10pm, when she was outside, 'putting her car away'. She wouldn't have looked up except her ducks and animals started panicking. It had come from the direction of Hanging Rock, and disappeared over the horizon near Wallan.

One man was not quite so lucky. 'John' was driving from Romsey on a dark night, when his car radio started screeching. Then both the radio and his headlights 'died'. His car, the road and surrounding area were lit up by a 'tremendous light'. He looked out of the car window, and above him was an oval, massive blue/white pulsating 'thing'.

John was terrified, but kept driving, and the disc followed him along all the twists and bends in the road. He said it was huge, and flying low. By this time he was so traumatised his whole body felt like 'a blob of jelly'.

He finally spotted a farm house, with the lights on. He drew level, pulled up, and despite his portly build, ran and leapt the gate. He banged on the door, and when a woman answered, hysterically told her what had happened. She was less than sympathetic, and said she could see nothing in the sky, further, his car lights were on! She finalised by telling him to clear off, or she would 'set the dogs on him'. John drove home, still badly shaken, but glad his mysterious pursuer had gone.

In all these cases, they were the same, or very similar objects, with multiple witnesses who didn't want any publicity. I have my doubts, due to the behaviour of the craft, that they would be any of our own prototypes. It would cost the career of any test pilot who behaved in this way.

VERA

Forty year-old Vera contacted me in October 2017. Like many experiencers, she was more concerned for the wellbeing of her children than herself. She just wanted to talk to someone who would believe her and the strange events which had been occurring since she was a young child.

Her grandfather was Scottish, and had fought in the First World War. Her mother left Scotland to marry her Australian father, but the union was not a happy one. He left when Vera was small, and subsequently died when she was twenty.

Her mother, who raised Vera alone, noticed odd behaviour from her child at a very young age. She frequently walked and talked in her sleep, and used to get recurring bad dreams, which involved dark shadows and huge insects. Vera recounted the ceiling and floor sliding away from under her. She was somewhere else –super high – and scared to look up.

One night, when Vera was six, her mother found her staring out the window, saying she couldn't sleep and was waiting for someone or something. Later, when she was about fourteen, her mother heard Vera shouting for help in the middle of the night. She was trapped under the fitted sheet on her bed! She was on top of the sheet earlier, and couldn't have put herself there. How did it happen?

Vera and her mother lived in Sydney, and Vera attended North Sydney Girls' High School, where she did very well. They did not have the money for her to go to university.

Vera commented that she cannot go to bed at night without the light and the TV on, something her first partner couldn't understand or live with. I did not tell Vera, but I have heard this from many other experiencers.

Vera now lives outside a country town near the mid-north coast of New South Wales. Her house is surrounded by fields and bush. For some time she has noticed two round purple bruises, about half the size of a five cent piece, which periodically appear on the underside of her left arm. They are inexplicable, and last for about two weeks. Her doctor, whose name she gave me, is also at a loss.

Sometimes she goes to bed at night, and suddenly wakes up at four or five in the morning to find herself on the lounge in another room.

She has two sons and a daughter, all of whom are very intelligent. They talk about 'seeing things in the sky', and one seems very 'intuitive', knowing things before they happen.

In November 2016 they all saw a huge blue light in the sky. It moved to the left, hovered for five minutes, then took off fast towards the coast.

RAYMOND

Raymond was another person, who contacted me, and whilst he tried to recall events from his childhood, was nonetheless scared of what he may discover. When he was five, he used to see 'little elves' at the bottom of his bed. By the time he was nine, he had an irrational fear that aliens were going to come and 'get' him.

In the early 1980s, when about sixteen years old, he was living in Sydney, on a twenty-five-acre farm at Luddenham, half way between the then active RAAF Bases at Penrith and Richmond. One clear, twilight night, he was alone, up on the dam for about thirty minutes, when he saw a light to the right and behind the dam.

It was whitish - about half the size of the moon, silent and unconventional, and as it came closer it seemed to expand. It stopped and hovered. It is not really known if he had any missing time, however he described a 'telepathic feeling'. After hovering, the object landed behind a hill, which it lit up. Later it 'took off' at an exceptional speed.

Raymond, who is now a respected scientist, has developed an interest in UFOs, and wanted to know if he has any 'hidden memories'. He is still considering hypnosis.

___

BARBARA ENGLAND

In 1981 Barbara England was just sixteen years old when she worked as a jillaroo on a property near Young on the Australian 'Riverina'. The elderly owner and his wife claimed they 'couldn't deal with' a recent alien 'encounter'. Barbara didn't quite understand what they meant, until one night she went for a drive with her brother and a couple of friends.

It was about 7.30pm, and a large silent disc, dark underneath with flashing multicoloured lights above, hovered over their sedan car. The vehicle came to a halt, and the headlights went out. They got out of the car and Barbara reached up and tried to touch it. The craft moved away and they watched for a couple of minutes as it came down on the cattle grid, then took off and 'whooshed' off into the sky.

When Barbara was twenty her father died. She moved to the city, and was living in a fifth floor flat in the beachside suburb of Cronulla. One clear night, in the summer of 1985, she was on the balcony, looking out over the sea, when a massive unseen force knocked her over. She must have been unconscious for a while, but has vague flashbacks of two entities picking her up and then dropping her.

When she 'came to' her neighbours took her to hospital. She had concussion, one eardrum was blown out, her kidneys were bruised, and she required sutures in her back. At first everyone wondered if it were some invisible abnormal weather event, but the Department of Meteorology said there were no bad conditions that night.

She went on a working holiday to Europe, and by July 1995 had returned to Sydney and moved into a flat in Penshurst. One night she opened the sliding door to the balcony and another invisible force hit her in the chest. She fell backwards and suffered concussion and bruised elbows.

In 1985, after the first experience, she inexplicably stopped menstruating for twelve months, and then suffered very heavy periods. The same thing happened in July 1995. Doctors have no explanation, however they found problems with her fallopian tubes and ovaries, a common complaint with other female abductees.

Barbara has a professional career, and managed to gain a position back in the country, moving to Mudgee a few years later. She has seen a couple of other discs in the sky since then, and is very concerned that each time she heard a 'buzzing' noise and an unrecognised male voice telling her to 'get out of there'. She feels, whatever the explanation, they are 'bad entities'.

I wondered about any generational aspect to all of this. Barbara said she sometimes has psychic abilities, as did her grandmother. Both her father and grandfather were officers in the army during the World Wars. Only one memory really puzzled her.

When she was eight she was confronted by a large black snake in the middle of the paddock. Her father was some distance away, but she felt an 'energy' wrapped around her, and the snake backed off. Her father came over and said; "The Universe is looking after you." It was only after his death that she started having unpleasant experiences, and I wondered if this was relevant.

KYLE

Sometimes the connection and corroboration between UFO sightings can be quite uncanny. A friend from Blackheath, in the Blue Mountains, knew of my interest in UFOs, and told me of a classic flying saucer she had seen travel over her house when she lived in Blacktown in 1971.

Recently she rang me to tell about a rather 'eerie' event when she saw her sixty-four year-old neighbour, Kyle, walking along the road with a strange figure which suddenly 'dematerialized into thin air'. She asked him about it, and when they both realised they had seen the same UFO, hovering over the forest three months before, he agreed to ring me and lodge a report.

We got chatting, and I was astounded when Kyle started talking about his friend in Cowra, who had collected many thousands of technical and scientific books. I immediately recognised a case I had discussed in *'Contact Down Under'* where four university students had suffered several hours of missing time whilst returning from a technical survey near Wauchope in NSW.

One witness subsequently died, one went to Darwin, and the third fled the area for Canberra after being harassed. It was mainly the fourth, to whom I gave the pseudonym, 'Roy', that I had worked with documenting the case. Since their strange possible encounter, Roy and his family had several other UFO experiences, and he had succumbed to an overwhelming compulsion to purchase and store, (safely inland), every technical and scientific book he could get his hands on.

Kyle gave me 'Roy's' real name, and it didn't take me long to realise that Kyle was the fourth student who was in that car in the 1960s. He had long since returned from Darwin, and led an almost hermit existence in his house in Blackheath.

Kyle talked about other 'findings' during his studies in the Northern Territory and out west. One day he tripped over a rock, and noticed there were others, in a definite geometric placing. There were also many hieroglyphs there, and he wondered about their relevance to the Egyptian glyphs at Kariong, on the NSW Central Coast. (See *'Contact Down Under'.*)

Kyle's life experiences differed from those of Roy, in the fact that his family had several instances of generational alien interaction on his mother's side of the family. He also had vague memories, dreams and psychic abilities going back to his childhood. The incident in the 1960s at Wauchope was not his first or last experience of missing time, and I wondered if he was actually the main target of that encounter.

Kyle was highly intelligent, as were the rest of his family. The alien experiences, and apparent genetic interference had taken an emotional toll, and I decided not to take the investigation any further. I did, however, realise that since the 1960s, all four of those young men had, like many other experiencers, moved away from the coast and settled on a much higher elevation.

One of INUFOR's investigators, Dudley Robb, inspired confidence in some of the more timid experiencers, and here is one of the reports he sent for us to publish.

FROM THE PAST

An Investigation by Dudley Robb.

When a Hobart girl saw a small landed UFO take off vertically in the Spring of 1945, other sightings and strange events followed.

The lady – 'L.G.' – who now lives on Sydney's North Shore district, was eight years-old at the time, and living at Derwent Park, about four miles from Hobart, Tasmania. The date was approximately fixed as 'a few weeks after the atom bombs were dropped on Japan'. L.G. remembers her teacher describing that profound event, and her first sighting followed a few weeks later.

It was mid-afternoon and she was home, playing in her back garden, which blended into an orchard. She glanced across, and could see something in the orchard. It looked like an illuminated, shiny spinning top, about the size of a football, and curious to learn more, she walked over.

It was stationary, on its pointed end, and glowed with a silvery light. When she reached a distance of about ten foot from the thing, it suddenly took off vertically into the blue and quickly disappeared. A few minutes later she saw several dull metallic-gray objects, motionless in the sky.

She went inside to contemplate what she had just witnessed, but said nothing at the time, because she was in a sole-parent family and it wouldn't have been considered important.

Between the ages of eight and eleven, she remembers periods of missing time. Typically, when coming home from school, she would sit at the edge of a pond, to relax for a short while. It would be a bright, sunny afternoon one minute, and then suddenly she would notice it was much darker, and late in the evening. Upon returning home, she would be punished for returning late. Only she, herself, realised it wasn't her fault, and couldn't understand the time lapses.

By the time Dudley interviewed the witness, she was already in her sixties, and wary of regressive hypnosis, which I don't encourage unless requested. Along with his report, Dudley made these interesting comments;

'Continually more evidence surfaces around the world to show that the so-called 'modern' wave of UFO sightings and related events didn't suddenly start in 1947 with Kenneth Arnold's famous report. There is probably a multitude of 'sleeper' cases going back into past generations, involving these strange sightings, associated abductions, missing time and so on! The world simply needs more UFO investigators to uncover all the facts surrounding what appears to be a massive operation of the UFO phenomenon interacting with human beings.'

CHAPTER FOURTEEN

AUSTRALIAN and OTHER RESEARCHERS

Australia and Britain have many first-rate UFO Researchers, each with their own experiences and excellent investigations. I only intend to mention a few here, but there are many more who do not get the recognition that they deserve.

GLENNYS MACKAY

One valued colleague of INUFOR is Glennys MacKay, who founded the Queensland UFO Network in the early 1980s. Here she assisted people suffering trauma from memories of alien contact. and provided a forum for people to share their interests and experiences,

Glennys was later the Queensland Director of MUFON followed by ten years as their Australasian Director. In the late 1990s she co-ordinated and hosted two Australian International UFO Symposiums in Brisbane, providing the opportunity for international scientists and researchers to liaise and exchange information.

Glennys also participated in our 1997 INUFOR-MUFON- UFOR NSW Joint UFO Seminar, and included the following thoughts during her presentation:

WE ARE NOT ALONE

'Over the past two years I have worked, against all odds, to bring people together to share updated information, from many countries, about the UFO phenomena. There are powers who do not wish this information to be given out to the people. This negative power, that seems to be sweeping our planet at the present time, has made me realise more and more, the importance of raising the level of consciousness of this planet to awaken within, the knowledge that 'WE ARE NOT ALONE'.

'For the last few centuries human beings have tended to regard themselves as the only highly evolved form of intelligent life in the universe. Many developments in recent years have challenged and undermined this view.

'Too frequently, across the world, people from all walks of life are turning to the skies and reporting strange objects. Many have detailed close encounters

with an alien form that seems very foreign to our belief of what people should look like.

'Over the past ten years I have been directed to go to various places, where, along with my husband and other people, we have had encounters with craft and beings who have shown themselves to us. Although much has been written about 'grey aliens', our encounters have been with people who look like us, only taller and very intelligent. We have communicated, both verbally and telepathically. One wonders if there is an almighty cover-up in regards to these people who are walking among us. Where do they come from?

'In all the years of my having communicated with them, they have expressed the importance of the people of this Earth getting back to finding our own spirituality and learning to love one another. We must save this planet from greed and destruction, and from the powers that seem hell bent on destroying what our Creator gave us. We must always remember we are the caretakers of this Earth.

'Regardless of what we are told – 'we are not alone'. If only we could all live in peace and harmony, regardless of race, colour or creed, this spiritual journey that we have begun is a never ending journey. Let us continue to find that inner peace, then we can create a domino effect throughout the Universe.'

Glennys is quite reticent about her own experiences, but told me of a couple of instances from the past. Both she, and her family, have reported unusual events, including being followed by craft when driving down isolated roads. She has lived in both Australia and New Zealand, and like many other witnesses has seen normal looking 'humans' suddenly vanish into thin air.

As a child Glennys lived on a farm in Tasmania. She recalls a blond haired 'friend' who used to come and play with her, and tell her stories about Snow White and Alice in Wonderland. Glennys remembered being taken on a trip to a place she was told was 'Never Never Land.'

In 1964, when on a car trip, she was followed home by a strange craft, experienced some 'missing time' and recalls aliens in grey body suits with knobbly 'claw' fingers. After she was married Glennys lived on a farm in Greytown NZ, and they saw UFOs hovering close and near to the house. When in Masterton, a UFO landed in their back paddock. She also had sightings, one in particular near Wellington, at the same time Quenton Fogarty and the entire crew of his plane photographed strange lights in the sky.

When in New Zealand, and in contact with Bruce Cathie, Glennys was told she had cancer of the larynx. Six days after another encounter, the cancer was gone and she got her voice back.

Glennys has also spent time in Hawaii, the United States and South America. In September 1991, while in a plane above Arizona, she saw a round, disc-shaped UFO being pursued by five Stealth fighters. Other witnesses in the plane also witnessed the encounter.

In 1993, whilst in Hawaii, she and a film crew had been taken to a remote valley. They were told by a 'Navy guy' that they must leave no later than 4pm, but they forgot the time and missed the deadline. At 4.30pm it looked like part of the mountainside was 'falling away. There was some shaking and an entrance opened, from which a craft with a green ray emerged and flew off.

Another night, with other witnesses, at about 11.40pm, near a Chinese cemetery, she saw two very tall 'Nordic' aliens. One was a woman who ran towards a nearby alien type craft.

Glennys has also reported other encounters with UFOs and tall, intelligent beings who look like us. These events often took place with her husband and others present. Her communication with the visitors has been mostly telepathic, and she also, like many other experiencers, has received warnings about coming earth changes.

During our 1997 Conference, Glennys detailed a few of the more inexplicable events which had occurred in Queensland's vast, sparsely populated outback.

Over the past few months she had been liaising with several farmers, who worked on an open-cut mining site in the North-Western district of the State. It was dusk, and five of them were travelling through an isolated area about forty minutes away from Bileola.

When they spotted a UFO in the sky, their reactions were markedly different. Andy, who made the report to Glennys, was amused at the response of the other men. Only one wanted to turn back and investigate further. Another, normally a rough, tough individual, put his hands over his eyes, and his companion said,

"Just keep going and don't slacken your foot off the accelerator!" The fourth, a very religious fellow, stared straight ahead; "I didn't see a thing!"

On another occasion, it was dark, about 8.45pm, and having been rostered on the night shift, they were driving to work. Andy was travelling with three other people, in the same area, when a very tall person, in a silver suit, stepped out on the side of the road.

It wasn't Andy's first experience. In about 1994, while working the 'drag-line' he got the distinct feeling someone was watching him. It was 4.45am, but he wouldn't put it past his supervisor to be checking up on them. He turned the bucket from right to left, at a very fast speed, thinking 'that would fix him for spying on us'!

When he looked around, it was not the boss, but two average sized people dressed in silver body suits. They turned away and about five minutes later a UFO took off at great speed and disappeared. At the time there were four other men on the site, who also witnessed this.

On a station, about three hours drive from Bileola, the owners have had many disturbances in regards to their cattle. One evening Maurice put nineteen young yearlings in a holding paddock. The next day a truck was coming to pick them up. He came back in the early morning to find they had been mutilated, a few more than others. Some were dead and quite a number had to be destroyed. While some neighbours claimed they had seen an animal resembling the now extinct Tasmanian Tiger, it was unlikely to have done this much damage.

Another station, up in the Gulf of Carpentaria, had also reported quite a few sightings and landings. More recently, a Kiwi stockman had arrived at the homestead to tell them that they had left the lights on in the stockyard. When the owner told him that there were no lights up there, the stockman insisted he take a look for himself.

There, by the stockyards, was a long object with a huge spotlight on top and several coloured lights flickering around the bottom area. It was hovering, not much higher than a 75ft windmill on the property. When they shone a torch at this round disc, it immediately disappeared and reappeared several yards away.

Over the next hour, they played games with this object, and every time they shone the torch on the disc, it would repeat the behaviour. In late October 1996, the local Aboriginals had up and left, saying that the 'little people were back'.

During the mustering in November 1996, eight head of cattle got away from the herd. When the jillaroo and aboriginal stockman were sent to bring them back, a 'cloud' seemed to come down and block off the view of the station hands. Next thing they were entirely hidden by this strange mist. Within minutes the jillaroo and stockman came bounding out of the cloud. They looked pretty grim and frightened. When the mist lifted the cattle had gone.

Round circles have been found on this same station, and the stock will not go near them. Large crevices had recently been discovered on the property. They were about eighteen inches across, and stretched for many miles. Were they caused by an earthquake or some underground activity?

ALAN CRADDOCK

Before one can claim what the witness saw was truly an unidentified object, all possible conventional explanations must be ruled out. At INUFOR we were blessed to have an expert on board. Alan Craddock, a private pilot, and now retired Air Traffic Controller at one of Australia's busiest airports, is always available to analyse the reports we receive, and give his expert advice.

After we had disappointed many witnesses, who truly believed they had seen a UFO, he wrote the following article for our 'INUFOR Digest'.

UFO or IFO

What you see is not always what you get.

Thanks to today's technology, not too much happens under, on or above our planet which does not attract some form of human scrutiny.

As a species, we are fascinated with discovering why certain phenomena occur. By virtue of the latest innovative advances, we have become accustomed to getting those answers almost immediately.

Take, for instance, the quantum leap in the field of aviation. It was barely a fledgling industry ninety years ago, and is now one of the most important fields affecting our everyday lives. The advent of the flying machine has outstripped everything else in the way of transport, and will continue to do so as long as there is a demand to move vast amounts of people around the planet.

The fascination flying holds for humanity has not waned since the heady days of air races and world record flights. In fact, it has increased tenfold by becoming the more accepted way of personnel transport. Chances are that most people will fly at least once in their lives. For many it is quite normal, whether for business or pleasure, to traverse the skies from one side of the planet to the other.

Due to the enormous amount of traffic in the sky, at any one moment, modern radar is so sophisticated that it can pinpoint an aircraft to within a few centimetres. Not much escapes this all-seeing eye. It has the ability to bring an aircraft into touchdown at an aerodrome, and place the wheels on the runway at an exact point. All the pilot has to do is sit back and monitor this modern miracle.

Humans have a basic 'need to know', and this curiosity drives us to find bigger and better methods to guard our skies securely. In fact, it has been stated that there is not one place on the planet that is not covered by some form of radar.

For the most part, people going about their everyday lives take a lot for granted, and give little thought to the three hundred people in an 'aluminium tube' flying high overhead at a speed of several hundred miles per hour. Late at night, whilst out walking, we see a group of lights in the sky and assume that it is just another aircraft going somewhere. That is, until it either manoeuvres in a way to which we are not accustomed, or at a speed we assume is impossible.

In very low light conditions, most people's eyes seek out any form of light and movement. It is a natural, automatic reaction that aids us to position ourselves to counter any potential threat. We are creatures that are stimulated by light.

During normal everyday hours, our eyes can be tricked into seeing what is not really there. We all have the ability to recognise familiar shapes in the clouds, and invariably feel comfortable in the knowledge that not too much out of the ordinary is going on around us.

Some people have a heightened curiosity, or a special interest in aircraft or objects seen in the sky. Chances are they will have seen a proportionally higher number of unusual phenomena than the average person, who may only gaze up to the sky when resting on the lawn or watching an air-show. Most amateur *astronomers will admit to seeing something in the sky that they couldn't or wouldn't explain away.*

Aircraft recognition, in our particular field of interest, is of paramount importance. Not only can a very basic lack of understanding of aircraft and their systems cause confusion with lay people, it can lead to some pretty wild claims by the witness in question.

Although the 'Concorde' is known to many people, it still causes confusion with certain groups in the community, especially those intolerant to the noise it makes. Having dealt with several complaints concerning this aircraft, I was amazed to hear stories embellished to a point beyond all reason.

Another current problem stems from so many varied aircraft that the average 'Joe Public' has a hard time identifying them all. Even the media often cannot differentiate between a Boeing 767, an Airbus or a DC10. I have even seen footage run to show several aircraft, from a two engine B767 to a tri-motored DC10 in the same story about only one plane. It stems from a basic lack of knowledge.

With the new generation of aircraft flying higher and faster, in particular the fighter planes which frequent most skies, we all have difficulty keeping up with the new shapes which the military trial to keep an edge over their competitors. The more complex the shapes, the more fantastic the tale told.

This is not belittling the people who genuinely see something out of the ordinary, and through interest note every single detail including every marking on the craft. I am trying to point out that some people are more observant and trustworthy than others.

So who is expected to know the answers to at least some of the questions raised when a witness comes forward with a story about an unknown aerial vehicle? We, the trained ufologists – that's who! We had better be accurate, so as not to malign away information or damage a person's credibility through our own misinterpretation of the evidence provided.

The best way to cover most of these options is to gather at least the most basic details of the sighting and correlate it to known factors of height, speed and size. Verification with radar reports, other eye witnesses, and physical traces (such as falling debris or ground markings). One must also check the known performance of civil aircraft usually seen in the area.

Most aircraft perform as we expect them to, but given some unorthodox weather conditions, you can set up a scenario for a very confused witness. I think that almost everyone would have seen the effect landing lights can produce, from say a Boeing 747, travelling in split level stratus cloud. From a ground observer's point of view, without the aircraft being observed, the clouds seem to light up and perform amazing manoeuvres, especially when scattered clouds block out the light at regular intervals. Another phenomenon is the fact that we can see lights and condensation trails from an incredible distance.

We can frequently visually track from Sydney traffic departing Melbourne. When they reach the top of their climb, ranging from twenty seven thousand to thirty three thousand feet, given the right temperatures and light conditions they leave tell-tale vapour trails. This usually occurs at dusk in late autumn, with the sun providing adequate backlight for this phenomenon.

Another case in question is early morning, before sunrise, when traffic from Los Angeles, tracking on one of the many corridors into and over Sydney, can be seen as far away as three hundred nautical miles. Little more than a starlike object, it is at first hard to differentiate between a plane and a star.

Now, having talked about known IFOs, radar has the uncanny ability to pick up bands of ionised air, which cause what are known as 'Angels', 'Spooks', 'Caspers' and a whole load of other silly names. Frequently these anomalies can, and do, cause some concern to air traffic controllers, who double and triple check all the airspace that they are looking after. For instance, I recently witnessed several of these radar returns track over Sydney, heading south, then turn in a northerly direction and track over Gosford.

They maintained a steady seventy knots all the way, which excluded birds as the possible culprits, (unless they were jet-powered pelicans)! Flying in a tight formation of three, these were represented on the radar screen as small crosses, leaving what are known as 'past position marks'. (Radar can plot where you have been and where you are going).

They would frequently drop from the screen and reappear, in this instance always in the same formation. Activation of the low level filters on the radar had no effect, and subsequently these anomalies disappeared into the ether. These were genuine UFOs because they could not be identified. It is quite possible they were some type of natural phenomena, but after due consideration, I could find no logical explanation.

As can be seen, any number of variations in temperature, lighting conditions, atmospheric ionisation, cloud formations, meteors, satellites and bolides can cause us to misrepresent what we are actually seeing. This fact alone still allows Ufology to be perceived by the general public as a group of fringe dwellers – perhaps not to the extent that it once was.

Ours has to be an exact science, one which provides absolute proof to get our message across, with very little margin for error in our estimations. The recent upsurge in military, commercial and private pilotless drones has made the task increasingly difficult. We have to be able to provide countless possibilities before arriving at the truth. This is not always easy, especially when confronted with confused, and at times, scared witnesses.

The implementation of new technology, including the 'Advanced Australian Air Transport Systems', gave us an even better chance of answering all the questions that kept cropping up every week.

I recommend that all investigators practice aircraft recognition, and keep abreast of all the new developments in the aviation industry, the military in particular. With reports of large 'black triangles', other strange craft and sonic booms frequenting our skies, who knows just what is being tested at the moment? One thing is for sure, people are probably seeing the next generation of 'Star Wars' toys, or if not, alien technology that is so fantastic it makes our stealth technology look like an 'Air-fix' kit.

There are some simple 'rules of thumb' in aircraft recognition:

If you are sitting in an aeroplane, facing the front, the left wing will have a red navigation light on it, and the right wing will have a green coloured light. The tail will have a white light and a red rotating beacon. Several strobes may be used as well, to illuminate the aircraft whilst in flight.

Landing lights can be seen, on average, for one hundred to two hundred nautical miles, (given the right conditions and height), and even further in an inversion. Jet exhaust, such as long flames, is usually only seen on military aircraft. High by-pass engines, fitted to modern airliners, do not normally produce a visible light from the exhaust, however there are some exceptions, such as the Concorde on take-off.

Aircraft can effect what they call 'Shadow', which is a rare occurrence in some light conditions. If the aircraft is travelling at a high altitude, with the sun low and behind, it blocks the light in front of it, in some cases up to twenty miles ahead. This leaves a corridor, or shadow, which can confuse some people.

Most aircraft, even military ones, usually take a fair amount of time to traverse the skies, depending upon altitude. They stick fairly rigorously to set airways, especially over built up airways, so they should not suddenly divert from their path.

Finally, check all known flight corridors for regular traffic flow patterns. These are available from any good aviation shop at your local airport, and are known as IFR (Instrumental Flight Rules) and VFR (Visual Flight Rules) Maps. They are a wealth of information concerning known traffic points – a little confusing until you learn to read them – but a must for the serious ufologist.

Alan always respected the confidentiality required in his profession, and never divulged anything he saw or heard as an air traffic controller. He did however have one personal experience when driving his aunt down the NSW South Coast.

They suddenly heard a pounding noise on the roof of the car, which at first he thought was the roof racks coming loose. He couldn't see anything amiss, and noticed the cool night air had become oppressively hot. There was a strange odour outside.

His aunt was becoming nervous, so they got underway, only to have the same thing happen a few kilometres further on. The area seemed unusually illuminated, but his headlights were only on low beam. Suddenly two lights appeared over the road ahead. Instantly they veered left at a ninety degree angle, and shot off over the side of the road, leaving a red vapour trail.

Alan slammed on the brakes, and looked to where the strange object had gone. There was no road – just a fence and thick line of eucalyptus trees bordering the beach. When they reached their destination, a short distance away, friends told them they had seen lights in the sky, and helicopters chasing several 'orbs'.

A similar incident, which I discussed in *'Contact Down Under'* occurred on a nearby stretch of road in May 1993. A retired airman and his family were driving along the highway in the early hours of the morning, when they saw what appeared to be a large truck, with bright flashing lights, coming towards them.

They pulled over to the side, and a large airborne metallic object, as wide as the road, and about fifty feet long, shot sideways and disappeared inland, at incredible speed, over the rough bush terrain.

USA

ROSEMARY DECKER and MILLEN LE POER TRENCH

American researcher, Rosemary Decker, was a very dear buddy of mine for several decades. She was also a friend of Millen Le Poer Trench, whom I got to know after she quietly moved to Australia, many years ago. In my book *'The Alien Gene'* I discuss Rosemary's work and both public and private persona at some length.

An academic in her own right, Rosemary was a valued independent researcher and colleague, affiliated with INUFOR, and many other organisations. Over the years she contributed several articles to our magazine *'The INUFOR Digest'*. I would like to share one of them now.

RENMINISCENCES OF GEORGE ADAMSKI

By Rosemary Decker

Adamski was the first alleged contactee I ever investigated over a long period of time. He was also the most-often visited and enjoyed.

It began after the memorable 'Desert Encounter', with his several witnesses, on November 20th 1952. It was fairly easy to make the visits to his place, as I lived only an hour's drive from the locale, Palomar Gardens, which was at the three thousand foot level of Palomar Mountain.

He had already begun to hold an informal 'Open House' on nearly all Saturdays and Sundays, and the mountainside yard was pleasant most of the year. Anywhere from a dozen to forty or fifty people would come to discuss their UFO sightings with each other and with George. He replied to questions good-naturedly, or simply related his own experiences and philosophized. George thoroughly enjoyed being heard!

Occasionally, guests would report their own close encounters. Very few of them ever publicised their own contacts. I learned early on that the vast majority of these early contacts were never made public. (Neither were the later ones.) Most of the contactees I became acquainted with found ways to express appreciation by doing something to benefit our troubled planet.

Many careers were switched; - writers changed their themes – holistic healing was explored – and teachers at all levels, up to university, broadened their scope – not only among those pioneers who still remain with us, but among contacted and abducted people today.

Because of the atmosphere of inquiry and learning at Palomar Gardens, many visitors were able to form lasting friendships with other enquirers. Early on I met two married couples who were already friends, and we all kept in close touch for many years. There were occasions when some of us met eminent people, such as Desmond Leslie, (the Irish researcher who co-authored 'Flying Saucers have Landed'). He could combine serious business with a barrel of fun.

The couples I'd become very fond of – the Markers and Richardsons – had for some time been driving up from San Diego on weekends, to lend Adamski a hand with building and repair projects. The building needed improved plumbing, work on the well, and a variety of projects to make it adequate for visitors as well as for Adamski and his staff. On the morning of November 21, 1952, the couples drove up together, expecting the fellows to be put to work, as usual.........

There was nothing usual about the place! George, Lucy, Alice and everyone were talking excitedly of the Desert Encounter from the previous day. George seemed unable to complete a sentence, interrupting himself every few seconds. The others weren't doing much better. Harold and Dick checked the car that carried Adamski's 'scope and photographic equipment across the desert, and found all the tyres to be badly cut. They went forth and bought a new set.

Over a period of many months I was able to separately interview all but one of the six witnesses to the "Encounter'. They had needed to use binoculars from where they stood, along the road, about half a mile from the site.

By the time I had become certain of the reality of that 'Encounter', in addition to the spacecraft photographs Adamski had succeeded in taking earlier, I had been climbing up to the busy little center for many months. I continued to come, as did many others, because of the expanding knowledge, and further friendships, including that of Adamski himself. It was a delightful period, with lots of sharing, and a few rigid opinions based on prejudice or wishful thinking.

Among those whose lives I followed closely was George Hunt Williamson, the young anthropologist who had made plaster casts of the 'Visitor's' footprints on the day of the 'Desert Encounter'. He made several expeditions into dangerous South American jungles in his search for ancient clues. Each time he and companion John McCoy returned to the States, he arranged lectures at many towns and cities to raise interest in the ancient 'space connection', and raise funds for further explorations.

One evening several friends and I were attending a talk he was giving at the Recreation Center in Vista, California. It was January 11th 1958. Those of us who lingered a bit, to speak with Williamson after the presentation, experienced the treat of a lifetime.

McCoy came trotting into the auditorium with the remark; "George, they're flying again!"

Promptly George led us out the doors into the large patio, where a sizable crowd had already gathered – some folks from the lecture and others were teenagers from the Saturday dance. Over our heads, silhouetted against the stars, was an immense 'mother ship', which at the moment was still hovering. The details of this magnificent display were well reported in the January 16th issue of the 'Vista Press'.

Curiously, although the varied display lasted over an hour, and had already occurred in almost exact replication at the five previous recent Williamson lectures, it seems to have never had any other publicity than what the 'Vista Press' gave it. It simply disappeared from history, except for the times I have been able to share it during presentations at UFO conferences.

On one such occasion, in February 1989, I learned from fellow speaker, Bill Hamilton, that he too had witnessed one of the successive displays in December, 1957 and January, 1958. Checking with him recently, he told me that he had been at the El Monte lecture a week before the Vista one.

Regarding Adamski's early photos of spacecraft, (before the 'Desert Encounter'), I was remarkably fortunate to learn of their authenticity quite easily. I'd seen two or three of them in reprint, displayed on a counter in the little cafe near Palomar Gardens, in February, 1952.

Previous to moving up on Palomar's slopes, Adamski, his staff, and some of his students, had an acreage in Valley Center, not far below. It was adjacent to my Uncle Bill's ranch. I asked Bill if he knew anything about Adamski's spacecraft photos and he said that George had shared them with him and Francis, one by one, as he had been able to take them over quite a long period.

He had let Bill see the negatives. Bill himself had previously observed three craft, in a silent triangular formation against the night sky. At the time 1949/50 he was working as an engineer in Saudi Arabia.

Because of Adamski's hobby of stargazing, his students had given him two telescopes. There was a large one in a 'housing', and a six-incher that was manoeuvrable enough to be carried about and set up anywhere convenient. In the summer of 1956, when I knew the planet Mars was in an unusually close approach to Earth, (about thirty five million miles), I asked George if I might come up one evening and have a look through the six-incher.

He kindly arranged for one evening, and I brought a friend with me. We had the thrill of seeing the face of the planet for the first time in our lives. When I asked about a possible 'bug' on the lens, George checked and began to chuckle.

"Look at the shape of it. Recognise the Syrtis Major?" Well, yes, I'd seen that famous dark area on Mars maps, but had to look carefully to discern it on an image no larger than a dime.

Mars rotates on its axis in almost the same time that Earth does. 'Martians' do get an extra thirty seven minutes in their day/night cycle, often a cause for joking among us hurried and harried Earth-folk.

In relating to Adamski, we all found him to be genuinely kind, and deeply concerned with the problems the human race was creating, both for themselves and the planet. It is important that all honest researchers of that era keep this in mind, because unfortunately his 'Achilles Heel' was an immense ego, which grew alarmingly as time went on, and his fame spread.

As friends and colleagues who had visited and worked with him, for years, we became worried about his well-being. Eventually we were impelled to withdraw our support.

Increasingly he contradicted many of his own statements. He offended and alarmed co-workers both at home and overseas. He resented any counselling attempts by those close to him, and began doing things his Space friends had discouraged, because he passed their advice onto his students and the public from time to time in his newsletters. I think it unwise and unkind to dwell on the mistakes he made during that period.

One item I shall mention, because it might prove helpful to someone. He was told that using self-hypnosis in an attempt to reach extra-terrestrials would be dangerous to the person involved. When a staff member learned he had discarded this admonition, and asked why, his reply was that he had grown so powerful he could protect himself against any negative influences!

In all fairness, it should be remembered that Adamski was not the only early space pioneer to undergo stresses greater than they could handle. Williamson and several others experienced similar difficulties, and the world was all too quick to forget the fine work they had done, and condemned them – completely.

Because all this troubled me, I asked Dan Fry, (who had maintained a stable course), if he understood the situation. He replied with one of the finest bits of counsel ever given me.

"You simply cannot know the intensity of the pressures, exerted from many sources, on the lives of contactees unless you have walked in their shoes – as I have. Without condoning their blunders, be compassionate and patient. We are not in a position to judge them. Always keep in mind their basic purpose - to assist and enlighten – and support them in that."

Certainly Adamski was under very heavy stress at that period, with a deep fear of undercover agencies of various kinds. Although he invited some members of 'officialdom' to meet with him in the D.C. area in early 1965, it was not easy.

Only weeks after his joyous filming of a little scout-craft at Silver Springs, he was stricken with a heart attack which ended his Earth life. Whatever his errors, his 'upstairs friends' surely understood the difficulties he increasingly lived under, and brought the gift of reassurance. In briefly visiting him and the Rodeffers in Silver Spring at the end of February, 1965, they were probably aware that his time left on Earth was very short. The film footage obtained was validated by experts later. I, and I am sure some others, have always been grateful for that last contact, after a long lapse, and for the Rodeffers' hospitality to George.

While there were some hoaxes and fantasized adventures, which gave all the alleged contactees a bad reputation, many UFO researchers not only fail to recognise the reality of any genuine contacts made during that early phase, they fail to take note that in many places, world-wide, friendly open contacts with extra-terrestrials and ultra-terrestrials continue to occur.

The whole UFO scenario unfolds in orderly, phase-to-phase progression. Undoubtedly the unfoldment will continue as long as there is hope that Earth humanity will get a glimmer of its cosmic heritage, and 'Take the necessary step upward on the long ladder of its liberation' while there is still time.

Rosemary often talked of the many people she met during her forty-odd years of UFO research. The individuals' lives varied across a wide spectrum; Scientists, engineers, a secretary, musicians, homemakers, Naval Officers, a NASA employee, and even other UFO researchers.

"Very few of these folks ever publicised their personal experiences. They had jobs to protect, as well as family and friends. Because many of those I met early on have passed away, it makes it easier for me to record their experiences now, although in some instances I still use a pseudonym.

"Their experiences covered over half a century, the earliest having occurred in 1930, the latest in the 1990s. Three continents were involved – North America, Europe and Australia."

WALES

MARGARET FRY

During my twenty-five year membership of BUFORA, I became good friends with Margaret Fry, a very ethical researcher who operated out of North Wales for many years.

When Margaret sent me the details of several cases, for publication in the 'INUFOR Digest', she also made some insightful observations:

'As Roger Hilton, my friend and long time partner in ufology, says; - most people who seriously investigate the abduction mystery desperately try to find alternative, natural explanations. They find solace in the known sciences and psychology.

'Abductees are instinctively aware of the reality of their experiences, so they find these answers destructive and unacceptable. As a result they turn to the occult, channelling and spiritualists. Believe me, these groups of people get far more people turning to them, than us, the down-to-earth so called scientifically orientated UFO investigators.

'If we really want to understand this phenomenon we should be aware of this trend and realise we have to listen more, and co-operate and combine to meet the needs of abductees. There are sceptics who are advancing the theory that hallucinatory 'contact' experiences are activated in the percipient's brain by electrical impulses.

'They consider that earth bound geological processes create a luminous phenomena, which in turn release an electromagnetic effect to the temporal lobe structure of the witness's brain. This causes them to 'believe they see extraterrestrial craft'.

'In the first instance, a great number of people, all over the world, have seen actual 'nuts and bolts' craft in the sky. These include aircraft pilots, who are responsible people, carrying the lives of hundreds in their capable hands. To suggest that their brains are being temporarily affected by electromagnetic fields is truly arrogant. Sometimes entire airline crews report these sightings. They are highly trained people, yet these crackpots are implying that they are in an hallucinatory condition, with no objective reality or control of themselves, let alone their trusting passengers!

'Why not just accept that this is a technology way in advance, hundreds of years ahead of us, that at present we have no explanation for given our present scientific knowledge?'

ERNIE AND GWYLIM

MYNYDD HIRAETHOG MOORS – CLWD - NORTH WALES – 1966

Investigated by Margaret Fry

The road from Cerrigydrudion to Ruthin is the B5105. At Cerrigydrudion, a lonely, small village at the tail end of Denbigh Moor, the road forks to the right, and you wind up to a lonely pub called 'The Crops Keys'. From here you fork off again along narrow country roads which eventually lead to a small hamlet in the centre of the Hiraethog Moors. This is where Ernie spent his childhood, and it is not very far from *'Worlds End'*, a very isolated area where there is a vast underground military base.

When Ernie was a young lad of sixteen, he worked at R.Ellis & Sons in Ruthin, and every evening he would walk the five miles home. It was his habit to call into the off-licence at The Bridge Hotel in Bontuchel. He would buy a packet of five Woodbine cigarettes every evening before continuing his homeward walk. There was a clock there, and this particular evening he noted the time was 7.05pm.

From there he passed the small Bontuchel Saw Mill, and within ten minutes reached a beautiful five mile stretch of secluded road. It is situated on the high grounds of the moors, and eventually leads to the hamlet of Cyssylliog. The road wends its way through a narrow valley with forests on one, sometimes both sides, at the bottom of which a river runs.

Ernie was approaching a small bridge. At the side of the road was a low hawthorn hedge, with a small tree on the other side. Suddenly, over the trees, a small 'Adamski' type craft came over the forested area into the valley. As it approached it was swaying gently from side to side, like a falling leaf.

He experienced a sudden rush of fear, and ran to the centre of the road, looking wildly about for some means of escape. At that time of year there was very little traffic, except for the occasional fellow villager or local farmer.

To his immense relief, he heard a truck approaching down the road. He flagged it down and immediately jumped in. After he caught his breath, he turned to the driver. It was an acquaintance, Gwylim, who drove his truck around the area, and possibly lived in the town of Denbigh. Ernie knew he had a wife working as a nurse at Denbigh hospital, but other than that, didn't even know his surname.

Ernie's finger was shaking as he pointed out the craft that was approaching, and had now positioned itself right over the bonnet of the vehicle. They both yelled in terror.

The next thing that either were aware of, was that they were miles past Cyssylliog, and near the cross roads of the A525/A5104. It was now pitch dark, as there were no road lights in that remote area. (It is of interest that, some years later, in 1979, another man was abducted off his motor bike at this very same spot.)

They were both tired and afraid. Gwylim turned his truck around and they went back to Ernie's hamlet of Gyffylliog. Ernie thought it may have been as late as 1am when his anxious mother met them at the door. Why was her son so late back from work? Ernie and Gwylim had lost several hours and didn't really stop to consider it at the time.

During the 1960s and 1970s many other locals had reported paranormal experiences around the bridge on that narrow road. The road is flat, straight and well maintained with very little traffic. In 1965 a driver inexplicably shot off the road into a tree. A lorry landed in a hedge at the same spot, and other vehicles have frequently gone off the road, or their engines cut out for no apparent reason.

Ernie's own sister-in-law had seen a strange figure there. His nephew, Ron, was driving his small Mini along that same stretch one evening, when his lights cut out, and a big figure on a horse passed him by. He was so afraid, he abandoned his car, and raced all the way home to the village.

A month later, Ernie had a red rash from head to toe, which blistered, itched and was painful. He visited the Doctor, who gave him some soothing ointment. For the next year the rash came and went – appearing in the spring, disappearing in summer and reappearing in autumn/winter. He was left with a brown mark on his side, towards his back, which he did not have before. For a while after he felt as if he had a 'stone' just under the skin of his lip. This eventually went.

For the first few years, Ernie did not follow the normal pattern of most people who feel they are abductees. Although he knew he had lost some hours of time, he never had any subsequent nightmares, and hardly considered the matter. He was still living amongst friends and acquaintances, who just accepted that something strange had happened. Many others had experienced paranormal events at the same spot.

In the following years he got a job in a hospital as an ambulance officer, and his attitude changed to not wanting to discuss the matter at all. Unemployment was particularly high in Wales, and he didn't want his boss thinking he was unsuitable for his position.

Later, he had another close sighting of a UFO, and conscious memories came back to him of being taken into this small Adamski-like craft. He vaguely recalled the smell of burning rubber, and seeing beings similar to humans, but with grey skins. They were about his height – six foot. He thought they gave him the usual type of medical examination, and conversed with him telepathically.

In about 1985, while driving the ambulance, Ernie suffered a serious road accident and got early retirement from work. He had time to reflect on what happened that night so many years ago. Unlike most people, it was just a burning curiosity, rather than any deep-seated fear.

In 1987 Welsh investigator Margaret Fry met Ernie, and found his case extremely interesting. Some of her various Welsh friends had known him since school days. They considered him to be a very sane and sincere person, and Margaret feels the same in the following years after she got to know him.

She, and her friend, local researcher Margaret Hainge-Llloyd, taped his interview and visited the spot near the bridge. Unfortunately, they could not locate Gwylim. By that time he would have been well into his fifties, and had moved on long ago.

CHAPTER FIFTEEN

UNDER AND OVER THE SEA

It is logical to assume that the safest place to remain undetected on this planet would be under our vast oceans. Having said that, it must be remembered that most of the major powers on earth monitor 'the deep' for unwanted intrusions by enemy submarines. Some coastal coal mines and similar facilities have shafts and tunnels extending for miles beneath the adjoining sea. I am sure our technicians and engineers have at least explored the possibility of constructing deep-ocean facilities. It is more than possible that undersea bases, be they earthly or extraterrestrial in origin, do exist –underwater and out of sight.

In the words of George Wild; *'The average depth of the seas and oceans is two miles. Man has barely begun to explore this untapped continent, whilst vast resources are poured into the exploration of space and Star Wars technology, (in some peoples' view to keep unwelcome visitors out.) Yet here is a vast area in all probability already occupied by non-residents of this planet. So let us continue with our study and hopefully unearth more clues to these most mystifying of events.'*

Since he wrote these words, in the late 1980s, our military and scientists have much more sophisticated technology to monitor our oceans, some of which has been accused of endangering marine life. While we are now able to detect any intrusions much more easily, I have yet to hear of any 'flying submarines', although I am sure the boffins have probably devised one!

In *'Contact Down Under'* I discuss how craft enter and fly out of the waters around the Solomon Islands, however this phenomenon is not restricted to the South Pacific, or even this century.

For hundreds of years, mariners have claimed that besides 'craft' in the sky, mysterious lights and objects, often silver in colour, have followed their ships, sometimes above the surface, and sometimes below.

Ivan Sanderson wrote about a case in 1825, when a US naval ship, off the coast of Hawaii, witnessed a large, round luminous body rising up from the water. It was red in colour, and illuminated the decks of the boat before shooting straight up into the clouds.

In 1887, the British vessel 'Siberian' was sailing near Cape Race in Newfoundland, when the crew saw a giant, glowing round object rise out of the sea. It reached a height of fifty feet, and moved slowly towards their ship, before quickly disappearing into the sky.

In 1945 fourteen crew members of the US Army Transport Ship, the *Delarof*, near the Arctic Aleutian island of Adak, were startled to see an object emerge from the sea. It approached and circled around the ship, before flying away to the south, and vanishing in three flashes of light. On the opposite Pole, at the Antarctic, similar incidents have occurred. (See *'The Alien Gene'*).

In the summer of 1954, the Netherland's government ship, the *Groote Beer*, was eighty miles off New York when a flat, grey 'moon-like' disc rose from the depths, and began to surface. The captain and crew watched as the lower half of this strange object brightened, and they could see what looked like lights along its rim. Suddenly it ascended above the water, and soared upwards into the sky, until it was lost from view.

Four years later, in September 1958, 18 year-old navy machine operator Chester Grusinski was on board the aircraft carrier USS Franklin D. Roosevelt, which was cruising off Guantanamo Bay. Some excited colleagues were rushing up on deck from the engine room, and he followed them.

It was a dark night, and they could clearly see a cigar shaped object, belching flames, closing in on the ship. They could see non-human figures watching them through the strange craft's portholes. The 'Roosevelt's' engines shut down, and did not start again until the 'saucer' took off at tremendous speed and 'vanished'. Older crew-members told Chester this had happened three times before in 1952, 1953 and 1956.

He said that their ship was transporting thermonuclear bombs at the time, and the next day a team of special investigators came on board, and said if they told anyone, even their families, about the saucers, they would be court-martialled.

There has always been activity off the coast of Central America, and Puerto Ricans insist there is an alien undersea base nearby. Late at night, on 11th November 2001, three witnesses, including a policeman, saw a black disc rise out of the sea on the north coast of Puerto Rico. It had pulsating red and orange lights, and affected the headlights, radio and engine of a nearby car. Once above the water, the craft flashed its lights, then headed north and straight up and into the sky – out of sight within fifteen seconds.

On the night of 1st August 1962, French fishermen, from the Mediterranean port of Le Brusc, were out in their boats when they spotted a huge metallic craft on the surface, about three hundred metres away. It didn't look like a submarine, and while they were debating the matter, the water next to it became disturbed.

A dozen 'frogmen' emerged from the sea and climbed aboard the strange vessel. They ignored the friendly shouts of the fishermen, but before the last one entered the craft he turned and raised his right arm in a 'salute'. Suddenly the object lifted off the surface of the water.

As it hovered above of the waves, red and green lights started flashing around the rim. The strange craft revolved from left to right, glowing with an orange light before making a graceful arc up into the sky and disappearing within seconds.

In 1978 some fishermen on the nearby Adriatic Coast refused to go to sea without naval protection. On 9th November, Nello de Valento, captain of a naval patrol boat, saw, along with his two crew members, a brilliant red light emerge from the sea and fly rapidly away. During this time all radio communication was disrupted.

On 4th August 1967, Dr. Yepez was fishing in the Gulf of Venezuela when he felt vibrations, and the sea began to 'boil and bubble' in a circle. A six metre diameter flat 'globe' emerged from the water, and hovered just above the surface. It was bluish-grey in colour, with a 'revolving section and triangular windows'. It slowly ascended in an arc, then shot upwards into the sky.

South America has often been a 'hot-spot' for unidentified craft. Many of the locals from the Argentinean Gulf of San Matias claim there is an underwater base located there.

On the morning of 27th June 1970, several witnesses in Brazil, on the coast of Rio de Janeiro, saw a disc-shaped craft floating on the water. It was about eighteen feet in diameter, with a transparent dome on top. Two small, thickset men, dressed in shining coveralls were seen doing something on the top of the object. Everyone was curious, and watched for about thirty minutes. Suddenly the two 'men' were back inside the dome, and the vessel skimmed across the water for about one hundred yards, then rose into the air and flew off.

Strange craft were also seen to rise from the water, on the other side of the world in Australia. One morning, just before sunrise in December 1978, a policeman and two friends were in a boat, just off Rockingham, headed for Rottnest Island.

Without warning a twelve metre area of water, not far from the boat, began to light up. He said; "Whatever was down there began to surface – and as it did, the water foamed and hissed. A grey-black object then emerged. It resembled two saucers, joined at the lip, with a green glow at the base. It rose silently from the water, hovered for several seconds, then took off for the north-east at incredible speed."

New Zealand's *'Xenolog'* Magazine published an extract from the *'Sunday News'* on 31st July 1977. One fisherman, in his boat five miles to the east of the Great Barrier Reef, described a glowing silver disc which 'jumped from the sea' and sped into the sky at an incredible speed. He said it scared the hell out of him, and asked the journalist not to put his name in the paper or people would think he was 'a bit nuts'.

There was a second report from a Tairus motel owner, who was also fishing about six miles off the Great Barrier Reef, when he and a friend saw, and photographed, a silvery object which quickly emerged from the water, moved towards their boat, and then shot away extremely fast.

In the early morning, about dawn on the 10th March 1993, an amateur photographer was standing at Ochre Point, Maslin Beach, in South Australia. Way out to sea, he noticed a swirl of white foam, and a grey object, which he initially thought was the conning tower of a submarine. It suddenly rose out of the water and started to rise in altitude as it moved towards the shore. When it came closer, the witness noticed it had three legs projecting below, and quickly took a couple of photos.

The craft was rotating slowly, and retracted the legs into the body. He noticed a second, smaller craft, approaching from the north, and as it neared the first object, he took another picture. The smaller object positioned itself below the larger one, and moved into a 'cavity' which was under the base. The witness noted that the bigger craft had three large lights underneath, and more lights in the 'cavity'. Once the manoeuvre was complete, the craft rose straight up and vanished.

The photographs were later authenticated and published. This entire incident bore many similarities to a report from Brooklyn, north of Sydney, four years later in 1997. (See *'Contact Down Under'* pp37/39)

This was not the first report from South Australia. In January 1959, a retired pilot was walking along the beach at Port Gawler, South Australia. His wife and daughter were by his side, and they all stopped to admire the sunset and watch what they thought was a periscope or silhouetted dome coming out of the sea. Was it a submarine? They were still debating whether it may have been the Russians when the object came up above the water.

It rose to a considerable height, moved silently towards them and hovered. It was spherical and a shiny silver colour, like 'polished aluminium'. Underneath was 'a curtain of white like some form of propulsion.' An identical object came in from the south and stopped next to the other craft, before both flew off, one accelerating to at least three thousand miles per hour.

In August, 1970, a group of Russian hydrologists were aboard a boat, doing research on Kronotsky Lake, situated in an inter-mountain depression in the Kamchatka region.

About a kilometre away they noticed a dome of rising water, from which a fifty metre, grey-coloured oval object emerged. It rose to an altitude of a few hundred metres, and hovered, motionless. The stunned scientists watched for a couple of minutes, then realised their boat's motor had stopped working. As they started to row, the object rapidly sped off and disappeared. As soon as it had vanished their motor began working again.

Over the years, many incidents have occurred in the North Atlantic and Arctic regions. My British colleague, Tony Dodd, researched some of these before his untimely death a short while later.

The first major event was Operation Aeneid, which commenced in September 1970 and ran until March 1971. It followed several sightings of UFOs, and was purportedly a joint Anglo-American 'exercise', which also involved Norwegian and Icelandic forces.

There were many reported encounters during the six month period, and most included larger objects accompanied by smaller glass balls. Strange craft were observed from the ground and on radar. Military planes were scrambled in futile pursuits - a couple crashed, and all suffered equipment and communication failures. There has been no information released as to the identity or origin of these unknown intruders.

In late 1992, Russian divers in the Gulf of Finland came across an enormous 'submarine' which suddenly shot up out of the sea and into the sky. On 20th December 1992, three UFOs were seen descending into the sea off the east coast of Iceland. Three days later, an Icelandic Coast Guard Vessel and two gunboats were stationed off Langeness, where UFOs had been seen entering the water.

Within a short time they were joined by American and NATO warships. (Another colleague, said his brother who was a submarine captain, was also ordered back on duty that Christmas Eve.) It was veiled in secrecy, and publicly called a 'military exercise'.

This 'exercise' continued for some months, and was joined by vessels from the Russian Navy. Eventually, both American and Russian troops landed at Tiksi in Siberia. The entire operation was top secret, but it was logical to assume it involved repelling the strange objects invading the ocean and sky above.

It was during these operations that the top secret stealth barge the 'Sea Shadow' was utilised specifically for hunting UFOs and other underwater anomalies, bases and activities.

On 19th February 1996, a terrified Icelandic fishing crew reported seeing a gigantic sphere hovering in the air, not far from their boats. It slowly moved away, then descended and disappeared into the sea. Later, six large, silent, blue fluorescent 'tubes' were hovering nearby in the air. Two months later there was a great deal of naval activity and some sort of 'battle' in the area, and all fishing and civilian vessels were ordered to leave.

This activity in the 1990s indicates that the unidentified craft did not originate from any of the countries involved in the 'hunt'. These 'world powers' were probably the only ones remotely capable of engineering such craft, so it is most likely that their 'quarry' was not of earthly origin.

On 19th January 1997, there was a large number of UFO related events over the sea off the south coast of Iceland, and the next day airliners were delayed at Keflavik airport due to UFOs flying in civilian corridors.

South American researchers, Liliana Flotta and Eduardo Grosso, of the ONIFE group, wrote a fascinating article about, Orlando Ferraudi who is now over eighty years old.

In 1956, Orlando, then only eighteen, was fishing at a remote spot on the northern shore of Buenos Aires in Argentina. A strange man came up and took him by the arm, mentally asking him to come with him. Orlando 'lost his will', and couldn't refuse this 'person's' commands.

The man was over six feet tall, with an athletic build, white skin, blond cropped hair and amber eyes. He was wearing a yellow/orange one piece suit which gave off small 'sparks', and Orlando realised that this fellow was not terrestrial.

He was 'receiving' assurances to stay calm, they were going on a journey, and no harm would befall him. Orlando saw a huge dark shadow coming from the river, and an object, about seventy metres in diameter, and shaped like a soup bowl, was close to the bank. A ramp appeared, and his companion and another being helped him to walk across and into the craft.

He entered a small domed room, where there was a young Argentinean girl, Elena, who had also been taken from her home. A tall blond woman, obviously also an extraterrestrial, gave Orlando a change of clothes, and performed some decontamination processes.

All communication was still telepathic, but he and Elena were told that they were going into space, but to avoid detection would go underwater to the Bay of San Borombon, to the coast of Uruguay, and finally cross over to Africa from where they would leave our atmosphere.

Orlando gave investigators a detailed description of the disc's interior, and controls, which needed to be manned by a minimum of nine beings. He also explained some of the alien technology, which I am sure would have been of great interest to our own military and scientists.

He watched as they passed the Earth and Moon, and soon their captors told them they would be returning, at an incredible speed. This time they plunged into the Caribbean, and soon saw a transparent underwater structure, which must have covered five or six hectares of the ocean floor. They also spotted several other craft, and were told it was a 'maintenance station'.

They entered the facility via a 'sort of tunnel', and once there, subjected to medical examinations. Later they were given back their clothes, and told that 'work' had been done on their pineal glands. This would enable the beings to more easily telepathically contact them in the future.

Orlando was full of questions, many of which they answered. They also explained the need for secrecy regarding their base; "We must take these precautions so that we can avoid being regarded as invaders or conquerors. We want your people to get used to us slowly, to see us just like anybody else, because we are not strangers in this part of the Universe."

They also demonstrated a fearful weapon. A small hand-held device, which when activated totally disintegrated the target. He was given a stern warning for humans of Earth; "We want you to know that this power will be brought to bear against you, much to our regret, if you jeopardise interstellar harmony."

He didn't know how, but next the thing he remembered was waking up at sunrise from the same place he had been taken. Six hours were missing from his life, but the complex technology he could describe added credence to his report.

Military and commercial vessels at sea also have trained observers, and in modern times advanced technical equipment to identify everything in the surrounding area.

On 26th February 1942, at the height of World War II, many of the crew on the ship 'Tromp' witnessed a large aluminium disc. It was first spotted with binoculars by the officer on watch. It approached at speed, and then circled at an estimated altitude of 4-5,000ft. Without warning, after three or four hours, it veered off very fast and disappeared from sight.

What about actual reports of what may exist beneath the sea? Occasionally there are reports of strange craft entering the water. When one considers our vast oceans, it only stands to reason that possibly more of our own prototypes and alien craft have crashed into, and disappeared beneath, the waves.

In late February 1963, a British RAN frigate, on exercise in the North Atlantic, detected an unidentified craft on its radar. It was solid, over 100 feet in diameter, and flying at 35,000 feet. When jet planes were sent to intercept, it plummeted, at speed straight into the sea. The ship's sonar then tracked the object zigzagging onwards and downwards into the depths, when it soon evaded any further sonar detection.

In 1978 a US Federal government officer told of how, sometime before, workers on *Pacesetter II*, a Shell Oil Company rig, were drilling 90 miles off the New Jersey coast, when they struck metal 600 feet down. They brought a fifty feet diameter object, covered in barnacles, to the surface. It had a central area on top, with small rectangular appendages all around.

The informant, plus three Shell officials and a physicist, arrived by helicopter, to examine the unusual retrieval. Once it was cleaned up, it displayed its original shine, and the dumbfounded physicist could not identify the metal – it wasn't steel. The rig workers were enlisted to help dismantle the vehicle, so that the experts could better examine the equipment inside.

The physicist could not figure out the propulsion system, and thought one piece of equipment was an 'anti-gravity machine', but it was not radioactive. He dated the craft as being 600 years old.

Another helicopter arrived, and five CIA agents insisted they were taking possession of the object, which they would load onto their own boat as soon as it arrived. An argument broke out between them and the Shell executives, who insisted on claiming their legal salvage rights.

The physicist continued retrieving panel boards from the craft's 'control room', and commented that he'd never seen equipment like that before. He and the rig's mechanic brought a few smaller items on deck, including a small tube.

They pointed it at the water, and pressed a red button on the end. A thin white ray shot out with a blinding flash, and travelled about a mile before petering out. Next, they got a small 'control box', pointed it at the craft, and pushed the button. A 'conning tower' panel slid open, and a three feet metal rod emerged. They manipulated it skywards, and pressed a second button. An electrical bolt, like lightning, shot skywards and punched a hole in the clouds, 10,000 feet above.

By the time they had collected more small gadgets, and thought better of testing them out, the CIA ship arrived, and confiscated everything!

As Ben Rich said; "Some are ours, some are theirs, and some are hand-me-downs." There is no way of ever knowing which category this craft belonged to!

CHAPTER SIXTEEN

MORE GENERATIONAL CASES

In my book *'The Alien Gene'* I examined many cases where several generations of one particular family have experienced alien encounters and interference. This can cause enormous trauma and confusion for the affected contactees, many of whom are reluctant to divulge any details.

JOCELYN FRAZER

Like many other experiencers I have worked with, Jocelyn was born in Britain, where her male ancestors served in the military.

Jocelyn's father was a highly intelligent man, who served in the British RAF as an aircraft mechanic, and later in the merchant navy. After migrating with his family to Australia, in 1968, he worked as a civilian aircraft engineer, before taking his skills on to a position in a power production plant.

I asked Jocelyn if her father had ever discussed aliens or UFOs, and her reply was interesting; "My father, who was an atheist and highly sceptical, only mentioned one possible incident from when he was ten years-old. He recalled something being present in his room, and pressing him down on the bed.

"When we discussed this a while ago, I thought he would jump at my explanation of 'sleep paralysis'. Instead he became adamant that something had been present in the room, and only left when he 'screamed blue murder', and adults came running."

Jocelyn's mother was also quite brilliant, and after graduating from London University worked both in a laboratory and as a science teacher.

When Jocelyn was ten, her mother became mentally distraught, and was fearful that someone was going to steal her children, Jocelyn in particular. At one time she was worried that people would come over the roof to kidnap her. When Jocelyn asked her if someone was overhead in a helicopter, her mother suddenly 'clammed-up'. She suspects that her mother had experienced some form of UFO or alien encounter in the past.

One interesting family 'generational' anomaly is a scar on the top of Jocelyn's right foot. Her mother had an identical scar – same appearance and location - as has her daughter Sonia. She is sure it was not there when Sonia was born, and medical colleagues have assured her that scars are not an inherited feature of three generations.

Like many other female experiencers, Jocelyn only reached out to contact me after she became concerned for the well-being of Sonia. She confessed as to once sharing her mother's irrational fear about aliens taking her own daughter.

Sonia (who is now thirteen) has always been physically healthy, and was exceptionally intelligent from an early age. When she was young, Jocelyn only allowed her to watch ABC type 'kids shows' on television, usually with animal characters – certainly nothing 'creepy' or any mention of 'aliens'. She was very unsettled when the following conversation occurred.

'When my daughter was four, and had just started kindergarten, she suddenly announced from the back seat of the car; "Mum, there are good aliens and bad aliens. You see those lights - (pointing to a particular shaped street light) – I like to think they are the space ships of the good aliens, and they can use these to win against the bad aliens." I responded by asking her what the spaceships of the bad aliens looked like, and she shrugged and said she didn't know.'

Jocelyn convinced herself that Sonia must have got this idea from something she picked up at kindergarten, but she naturally still felt uneasy. Like most of the third generation children, Sonia was very articulate and bright, even as a young child. She had always been creative, thinking outside the box, and enjoyed art and music. Whilst she can be a bit dreamy, and highly imaginative, Sonia has already displayed psychic abilities.

Jocelyn's own earliest childhood memory of an unusual event was not long after the family arrived in Australia. They were living in a rental home on a bush block. Her father strode over to the couch, lay down, and appeared to instantly fall asleep. His head was on Jocelyn's rag doll, and she tried to pull it out from under him. The doll's hair became damaged by the time Jocelyn dragged it out, but her mother just stood staring out the window, 'in a very unsettling way.'

"Don't worry about the doll," she said. "They are coming now."

Jocelyn remembers going across to her mother's side, and telling her that her younger sister was asleep on the floor. Instead of picking her up, her mother kept silently staring out of the window. She recalls a massively bright white light appearing and expanding to 'a huge level of brightness' in front of the window, but cannot remember anything after that.

'Later, I asked my mother why she thought Dad fell asleep on the couch so quickly, and showed her my damaged doll. She said I must have dreamt this happened. In retrospect, I think she truthfully believed this to be the case, and her memory of preceding events had somehow been erased.'

A year later, when Jocelyn was five or six, her grandmother became ill, and she returned to London with her mother and sister for a period of time. She has a vivid memory of attending a childcare centre with her sister. She cannot exactly recall travelling to or from that place, just what happened whilst there.

Jocelyn's report of this incident, and her mother's reaction, is interesting.

'The teacher was a young-looking woman, with light skin and fair hair. There were boys and girls involved in all sorts of activities, which seemed to be organised around the room. I was overwhelmed by the degree of noise and frenetic activity. I noticed a cubby, the like of which I have never seen since. It resembled a small cottage made of some hard moulded plastic. I convinced my four year-old sister to go in with me, and bolted the door shut. I was tense as the noise outside was still very loud.

'Soon I heard the other kids saying 'knock, knock', and asking to be let in. I was replying; 'You cannot come in,' but not in words.

'I did state verbally to my sister; "They are knocking, but don't let them in." She looked baffled, and said that no-one was knocking. At that point I heard the teacher, as clearly as if she was standing next to me stating; "Jocelyn, it is nice to share with the other children, you should let them in the house."

Again, my sister obviously did not hear this, and protested when I told her we had to get out.... The teacher got everybody to hold hands, and soon we were moving in unison and weaving spiral patterns. It was as if we were all connected mentally, quietly working together. I found this peaceful and enjoyable, and almost regretted the arrival of my mother to take us home. I remember the teacher saying, "We will see you next time."

Jocelyn doesn't actually remember leaving the place, and later asked her mother not to send them there again. She was bewildered when her sister said the other children made no noise at all, and no one spoke, except once when the teacher held her hand.

'*Mum looked genuinely confused. She stated she had no idea what we were both talking about, and that we had gone to no such place, cutting short any disagreement between my sister and myself. I believe all communication in this place was happening telepathically, and that for whatever reason, my sister was not able to tune into this form of communication, at this time at least.*'

Jocelyn's next memory was much more disturbing. After her grandmother died, they returned to Australia. When she was about seven she noticed a vaginal discharge, and her mother took her to the doctor – but it was not the surgery or doctor she normally attended, and she doesn't remember travelling there.

They were met by a different fair-haired woman, who showed them into a room with a metallic floor and walls. This 'surgery' was very spacious, with an arch but no actual door. The 'doctor' wore a white gown and mask, so Jocelyn is unable to describe his face.

Jocelyn was made to undress, and assisted onto a metallic table. She noticed what looked like several metallic surgical instruments, but the doctor produced a large syringe, with a very long needle. She was asked to remain very still, and slowly and carefully he inserted it into the general area of her urethra. She cannot remember what else was done, but the doctor said to her; "You are very special to us Jocelyn." She did not know why.

Back in the 'reception' area Jocelyn, her mother and the fair-haired woman were joined by a tall man wearing what seemed to be a long white robe. He had long dark hair and a beard, and she recalled him lifting her up as she hugged him around the neck. She also remembered that after this she lay on his lap, and listened to his low resonant singing before she drifted off to sleep.

Later, Jocelyn wanted to ask her mother further questions about the weird nature of this visit to the doctor. Much to her incredulity her mother had no memory of them going to the doctor, or of Jocelyn having an infection.

Like many other experiencers, by the time she was fifteen Jocelyn had become a vegetarian, and developed an interest in animal welfare, ecology and peace and justice issues.

For many years after that Jocelyn's life was mostly uneventful, but during her late twenties to thirties, she began to experience inexplicable 'missing time' episodes. She would go for what she thought was a short drive into the country, and arrive home, to an angry and frantic partner, hours later than expected.

On most occasions she has no recall of what happened, but has partial memory of one instance when she was in her early thirties. She was working as a nurse at the time, and decided to visit her parents on her day off. She arrived at about 9am, planning to stay until at least mid-afternoon.

Suddenly, about thirty minutes later, for some reason she could not comprehend, she felt an urgent need to leave. She got into her car, and followed a strange compulsion to drive to a lookout in an isolated area.

'I recall parking and going up a small flight of stairs to the lookout. Once there I saw another car pull up, and a family get out. I remember communicating telepathically with someone that there were other people present. A reply came that they would soon be gone. Sure enough, they got back in their car and left.

'My next actual recollection is driving down the freeway to Melbourne. I got home about 7pm. I entered the house to a very angry husband. He wanted to know where I had been, as he had rung my mother, the police and every major hospital. I honestly did not know, and made up some excuse. I felt angst ridden, confused and just wanted to shut the whole incident down and get on with life, which eventually happened – until the next time!'

Jocelyn was not always aware of her 'missing' episodes. In 1999 she was the overnight nurse in charge of an elderly residential facility. Occasionally she would see a tall, thin shadowy entity. It seemed to be watching her, often for considerable periods of time. She told herself that she must be suffering from sleep deprivation due to the night duty. She nearly lost her composure when one of the residents asked her about the tall, thin man, and gave her an accurate description. One night another resident told Jocelyn that she was 'physically' missing from the facility for several hours, but she cannot recall being anywhere else.

Strange things were also happening in Jocelyn's home. The radio would turn itself on in the middle of the night, often fluctuating the volume from soft to ear splitting levels. Electronic toys would self activate at odd hours. This frightened Jocelyn so much she bundled them up and gave them to a charity shop.

On the health side, Jocelyn was quite well, with only one disturbing issue. While she did not give birth to Sonia, her only daughter, until she was forty, from her early twenties she suffered from persistent lactation, which could be quite embarrassing. Despite a medical investigation, the doctor's could offer no explanation for this occurrence.

In 2010, when Jocelyn was in her early forties, she began to hear strange 'frequency' noises, and also developed a disturbing 'precognition' on a couple of occasions. Just like many other experiencers, she sensed 'some impending cataclysmic event'. At that stage she was unaware of other abductees' reports, and thought she may be losing her sanity. She felt an inexplicable fear, started stocking-up on non-perishable provisions, and is still considering moving inland to higher ground.

In 2017 Jocelyn had a disturbing experience which caused her to re-evaluate her past memories, many of which she had dismissed or pushed to the back of her mind.

'With echoes of my father suddenly falling asleep on the couch all those years ago, one night my husband suddenly announced he was off to bed. I was surprised at both the suddenness of the decision, as well as by the fact he was heading to bed so early. He tends to be a night owl, and often retires after me.

'I lay down to relax on the couch, and must have drifted off to sleep. My mind was dwelling on earlier mundane household events that evening, when suddenly I fully woke up. There was a profound level of silence. I couldn't hear the heater fan or the clock ticking.

'I was not able to determine whether I was dressed or not, but I was totally immobilized, in a state of paralysis. I didn't feel afraid, or in any state of panic, and somehow this scenario had the feel of some well-worn routine. I tried mental communication, reaching out with my mind and asking who was there, but got no response. I could not open my eyes, and at one stage felt pressure on my brain, and a jerking on my neck.

'I finally awoke at about 3am, and took myself off to bed, convinced I must have experienced some form of sleep paralysis combined with lucid dreaming. The next day I noticed a small stinging sensation on my left forearm, and

noticed a smear of blood and small puncture wound. There was a small track mark with a slightly palpable donut shape object at the end.

'Three days later, when I was sitting on my daughter's bed, to tuck her up for the night, I noticed an identical object in the same spot on her left forearm. There was no puncture wound scar, so I wondered if it had been there for some time. I was even more concerned when, a few months later, at a family get-together I noticed an identical thing on my father's arm. I surreptitiously checked my husband's arm and could not see one.'

Jocelyn had always ignored her periods of 'missing time', and didn't consciously associate it with any problem until it caused ongoing difficulties within her own family. Finally, something else happened which prompted her to contact me in 2018.

She sometimes had vivid dreams, which she always considered to be just that – dreams. During one of these episodes there were grey type 'beings' and also tall blond men. They all wore greyish/blue jumpsuits with the same insignia. She was astounded when Sonia was testing out some new school highlighters, and started absent-mindedly drawing an identical insignia on the scrap paper.

Jocelyn is a sane, no nonsense medical professional. She does not know what occurred during her 'forgotten' experiences, and while she cannot discount some form of alien involvement, is just as prepared to entertain the thought of earthly mind-experimentation or something else she has not yet considered.

LEONARD

Leonard's father, who was born in 1930, had an English mother, (born in Chile), and an American Indian father, who was part of the Hopi Nation. When Leonard's father was nine, he was a sickly child, and rather a burden to the tribe.

One day he was alone, and started walking until he came to an old oak tree. He sat under it for ages until two tall beautiful people came up. The man and woman were both blond, and at first he thought they were Germans.

He felt a hand on his shoulder, and they said; "Come with us, we will heal you."

His father didn't feel scared, and followed them to a 'spaceship', which looked like a traditional 'saucer' on three legs. He followed them up a ramp, and once inside, it took off at a fast speed. He could see through the walls and the Earth was disappearing behind them.

He was reasonably sure that Mars was their destination. The craft orbited then went down into a tunnel below the surface. When he alighted, he was greeted by normal people, wearing three different types of military uniforms. They all spoke English, and he assumed some were from the US and Britain, and was unsure about the third. There were also other different alien races present.

His father couldn't see this base from above, but once inside he could see the sky through the roof. It was similar to a one-way mirror. The rooms were like compartments, and the floor glass. He was healed of his disease, and remembered having blood on his ears and nose. When they brought him back to Earth and his family, the visitors told him they would come back for him much later in life.

He migrated to Australia, and got married. Leonard was born in 1960, and became a mechanical engineer in his early adult years.

When he was in his twenties, Leonard met his first wife, and during that time he saw more than one unusual object. On each occasion, it was as if the surrounding area was in a 'cocoon'. There was no noise or wind. Once he called out, and his brother-in-law, David, thinking he was hurt, rushed outside and saw the craft. Leonard commented that David had been a very aggressive man in the past. Since that incident his personality had changed. He became much more positive, and seemed like a different person.

After his first marriage broke down, Leonard moved to the isolation of the country, and purchased a property thirty-five kilometres north of Tamworth in NSW. It was situated in a valley surrounded by hills, and the cliffs were rich in quartz and granite. He became self-sufficient, and enjoyed 'stone-making', often designing his own hydro-electric machines.

Late one dark night he looked out of the window, and saw some bright orange/yellow lights approach in the sky above, and thought it was a plane that might crash. He turned on all the lights and his torch so that it could safely land.

When he walked outside he realised it wasn't a plane. He saw two craft, which were slowly moving, side by side. They came overhead and hovered, and Leonard felt intense love, and the 'feeling' that 'we are all a part of everything.' After he mentally communicated that they could use his property if they wished, they landed.

For several years after that, many craft came, sometimes four or five at a time. He never once recalls ever seeing the occupants, but seemed to have a telepathic connection with them. The saucers themselves were of varying sizes. Most had a clear dome and were a dark, smooth, seamless aluminium on the underside.

Leonard returned to Sydney, and met his second wife Henrietta in the strangest of circumstances. He was just visiting his friend's cousin. He had never met these people before, but he walked into the lounge room and saw a woman he instantly recognised. In 1996, when he was still in the valley, he had what he thought was a dream.

He and Henrietta had both been in a 'park', surrounded by a white glow. Wherever they were, they were sitting back-to-back, and could only see each other's profile. All he could remember was one of them saying; "Don't forget me."

Before he could regain his composure, Henrietta jumped up and stared at him. "You're the Indian with the very long hair!" She recalled having exactly the same 'dream'.

So.....what about Henrietta's family? Her mother, who migrated to Australia in 1954, came from England. Her maternal grandfather had fought in the War, and often mentioned seeing strange lights in the sky.

Henrietta's father was from Austria, and had also come to Australia in the 1950s. In the early years he worked behind the counter of a shop/garage in the NSW country town of Hay.

One day two very tall men came in. They were both fair skinned and in their thirties. They were wearing hats and tan suits, which looked brand new, and he thought their car was an old Buick, gold in colour. He cannot remember anything else until he reappeared behind the counter one week later. He had been missing, without a trace, for a week, and the police and emergency services had been searching for him.

When Henrietta's parents married, they desperately wanted children, but she had several 'false' pregnancies where the babies just 'disappeared'. Eventually, in 1977, Henrietta was born premature, and lucky to survive.

In 2004, six weeks before Henrietta and Leonard married, they were driving back to Sydney with a friend. They were towing a trailer they had borrowed to help Henrietta move, and stopped at Singleton to get petrol. They checked the receipt later - it was just after midnight.

Back on the road, they saw a huge orange ball of light. At first Leonard thought it was the headlights of a goods train, but it was moving to the side and behind the car. They had a cat in a carry basket, and it was 'going crazy'. Despite covering the carrier with a blanket, 'Pussy' has never been the same since.

Everything seemed 'fuzzy' for two or three minutes, and suddenly they saw the Newcastle/Sydney sign on the Pacific Highway. It was 4.20am – where had four hours gone? They took the roundabout to the Freeway, and a short while later, a lady called out from a passing car; "You've got no wheels!" They stopped and got out. Two wheels, the nuts and all fittings were missing off the trailer.

Leonard and Henrietta moved to Werrington, and had two daughters. The youngest walked at nine months, and by the time she was one, could put her blocks in alphabetical order. Like other gifted children, she could read and write by the age of four. She would mumble or sing to herself, and yet rarely spoke. Leonard wondered if she was telepathic.

Late one night, in early 2016, Leonard took the dog for a walk in the local park. He saw a strange object through the trees, and although he thought he was only there for a few minutes, he 'lost' over two hours. Later that year he was diagnosed with incurable cancer. His young daughter put her hands on him and said; 'You'll be here a long time Daddy." Later X-rays showed the cancer had gone!

The older girl was not quite so bright, but very clever. In January 2018, she drew pictures of her family under an apparent saucer. When asked about it she said that she had seen 'lights' two weeks ago.

Leonard and Henrietta's case had an exceptionally interesting generational aspect to it. There was possible long-term alien interaction on both sides of the family.

BRIONY CARTER

Briony, who was born in 1943, is the mother of seven children, thirty grandchildren, and eight great grandchildren. She is of French, Irish and Scottish descent, with royalty and military connections on the French family tree. Briony is an incredible woman, and it took a great deal of courage for her to come forward with her experiences.

She married young, and by the time she was in her early twenties she had her first four children in four-and-a-half years. Her husband, who was Spanish, was very superstitious, and believed that all his male offspring would be cursed. Her four daughters are healthy, but her sons all had disabilities or psychological issues.

Briony also has RH Negative blood, and all her kids had health problems. She was taken to several different hospitals, including one major Sydney facility, where the students joked that she must be an alien. They kept asking if she had another partner – she didn't – as the last two children had different blood.

Briony's sister, Jeannie, is also affected by the 'alien' presence. Her sons (Briony's nephews) have had strange experiences, and one was abducted in South Australia, along with his girlfriend and her mother.

In the 1980s Jeannie was living in a rainforest property at Coffs Harbour, on the northern coast of NSW. Jeannie was away, and in order to check on the animals, Briony and her husband were calling in, on their way home from Queensland.

They arrived at Jeannie's 'farm', and were astounded when they entered the large 'accommodation' shed, which was the living quarters while a new house was being built. Briony's nephews had drawn pictures of spaceships all around the walls.

Later that night they heard the dogs howling, and her husband went out to see what was wrong. He didn't return for two hours, and couldn't recall where he had been, but insisted on taking Briony by the hand and leading her outside.

There was a huge craft, surrounded by coloured lights, on the ground. For some reason they just looked at it then went back inside.

Briony asked her sister if anything similar had happened. Jeannie said others in the area had seen and heard strange things. Some time before a woman had vanished, leaving her baby in the back of her car. She came back nearly five days later – obviously 'taken' – but no memory of what had happened.

A few years later, Briony was pregnant and staying with her sister in the new house at Coffs Harbour. There were no curtains on the windows, and she suddenly woke up to find herself in something that resembled an operating theatre. Everything was hazy, and all she could make out were grey 'shadows', and something being done to her nose. Later a little blood was trickling out of her nostrils, and it has happened again from time to time. (In the 1960s she often felt she was being 'watched', and remembers 'dreams' of being under big, bright overhead lights, like an operating theatre.)

When she was in her forties, Briony and her first husband were no longer together, and she put herself through university, later embarking on a career working with refugees and the disabled. She had remarried, but did not have any more successful pregnancies. Two ended in miscarriages, and the third baby was 'taken'. Doctors found both the foetus and her ovaries were 'gone', and could offer no explanation.

Briony has prayed for any of her offspring who have been ill. One son was expected to die soon after birth, but miraculously recovered, as did another daughter. Two granddaughters have been cured of cancer. She is very reticent to talk about more than one 'near-death' experience, nor about encountering a 'god-like' figure, and promising to be good if her child survived.

Briony is now a deeply spiritual person, and has certainly devoted her life to helping others. Colleagues reported that she once came out of a deep meditation saying; "We are a gentle race." It is to her credit that she does not want any publicity, or participation in abduction support or similar groups, a decision I respect.

CHAPTER SEVENTEEN

ABDUCTIONS, IMPLANTS, MEMORY LOSS, HYPNOSIS and the GREYS.

One disturbing aspect of the abduction scenario is that of young girls being taken and often sexually examined, or worse ova taken, from a very young age. As a researcher I keep these cases, which do not involve human sexual abuse, strictly confidential. The victims often have damaged fallopian tubes or ovaries before the onset of puberty.

IMPLANTS

In *'The Alien Gene'*, I devoted a whole chapter to 'Implants and Microchips'. In so far as the purpose of 'alien implants' is concerned, their purpose and how they work is still a matter of speculation.

When Dr. Roger Leir removed implants from several healthy patients, all of whom alleged alien abduction, he was left with many unanswered questions. These objects varied greatly in appearance and composition. They fell within three different categories – metallic, non-metallic and biological. Some had detectable electromagnetic field emanations while still in the body, and some had isotopic ratios demonstrating a non-terrestrial origin.

Besides wanting to know the origin of this technology, its purpose and how it operated, in 2002 he also made the following comment; 'How is the metallic structure produced, and can it be duplicated within the state of our own nanotechnology?'

As early as 1944 a group of academics at Princeton University, and others, were researching neurological communication and control. In 1973 Sweden legislated to implant prisoners, and some ten years later nursing home patients. This was supposedly for 'tracking' purposes, although there were claims that the technology could also alter peoples' moods and behaviour.

We have come a long way since these primitive 'implants' were mainly used for tracking purposes. These days all manner of 'chips' incorporate sophisticated microscopic technology. Where did we get it from?

Tiny silicon radio frequency identity chips, inserted under the skin of the hand, are activated when they come within a couple of inches of a 'reader'. This enables the wearer to open doors, activate computers, and access all manner of modern gadgets and information.

In 1998 scientists, at the Danish University of Technology, created a chip, where a single hydrogen atom, jumping back and forth, could generate the binary code which is the basis of digital information used by computers.

The same year, electrodes had been implanted into the brains of disabled people so that they could control a computer by the power of thought. An American scientist at the Emory University in Atlanta, Georgia, received a grant for continued research into an implant which could communicate the recipient's thoughts into a computer. In this 'Brave New World' many other boffins have envisioned various brain implants which connect to artificial intelligence.

These particular devices were covered with chemicals to encourage nerve growth, so that the person's own nerve cells would grow into the implant and connect with the tiny electrodes inside.

One disturbing innovation from 1999 is the 'Digital Angel' which is smaller than a grain of rice, and can be implanted into the body. Powered electromechanically by muscle movements, it can send and receive data from satellite technology.

In 2006, *Nexus* magazine reported on the 'Braingate Chip'. Measuring only two square millimetres, it is implanted onto the surface of the brain, and extends a hundred thin platinum-tipped electrodes down into the cortex. Each is only one millimetre long and ninety microns at the base. These can also pick up the brain's electrical signals, which are transmitted to the computer.

British Telecom Laboratories were also devising a memory chip which could take data from the eye to store on a computer. Over twenty years ago the Washington Naval Research Lab and other scientists were developing Hippocampal Neuron Patterning, which involves growing live neurons (from the brain) on computer chips.

Today, livestock and other animal implants can be injected. They are the size of a grain of rice, and contain a microchip and tiny antenna. Some human chips are only 0.5mm or smaller. New nanotechnology chips are so minuscule that it requires a microscope to see them, and scientists are quite excited about the innovation of 'neural dust'.

Scientists are developing biological materials, such as molecules of guanosine, (a building block of RNA), to behave like tiny transistors. Many of these innovations would be totally undetectable. In 2006, New Zealand scientist Graemme Brown claimed to have invented a computer chip made of DNA molecules. It is designed to be swallowed in tablet form, and can track various genetic defects and illnesses. (A very informative article about the use of medical chips and implants can be found in the *'Nexus'* magazine June-July 2003.)

Other scientists have developed a method called 'sonogenetics', which involves injecting micro-bubbles into the bloodstream. Once they are distributed throughout the body, they can activate selected organs and any other tissue by use of ultrasonic waves.

Many contactees have described a 'telepathic' communication with the 'Visitors', and today some scientists are seriously researching the ability of computers to read 'individual brainwave fingerprints', and to transmit super-micro radiofrequencies.

We know that implants removed from abductees can differ in origin, appearance and most probably purpose. In his book, *'Earth – An Alien Enterprise'*, Timothy Good describes an alien implant, known as an 'ania', used to induce telepathic abilities in human beings. (I would suggest they are more powerful than this. Many researchers think they may be responsible for the 'compulsive' behaviour some 'experiencers' exhibit, such as suddenly going to a particular location.)

The 'ania' was jet black, of a polyhedron shape, and once inserted, usually behind the ear, it dissolved into thousands of very small biological robots which were dispersed into the body. Unlike the more traditional implants, this made it very difficult to detect with normal X-rays.

I have often pondered as to why, given advanced alien devices, many abductees have implants similar to those manufactured on Earth. Perhaps they were a 'red herring', which we were meant to locate, without considering a further search for the undetectable technology.

Budd Hopkins, who worked with many experiencers, once said of alien implants: "There is a sort of assumption we make that these things will be monitoring or transmitting devices. But they may have different functions than anything we can possibly imagine. And when it comes to non-human or ET technology, we have to assume there will be implant qualities that we can neither measure nor detect."

Stanton Friedman echoed similar thoughts: "If we can manufacture these devices less than 75 years into the electronic age and the development of tiny microcircuits, imagine what aliens could do with thousands of millions of years of development time We do not know what purposes, benign or nefarious, the aliens have in mind."

The world's population are gradually accepting the implementation of sim-cards and all forms of miniature digital and nanotechnology in their everyday lives. There is a lot of evidence that we have already devised chips that can tie into the brain's neural network, giving the person who regulates the chip the ability to control the thoughts and actions of the recipient. In the future, there is the danger that, one day, we could all find ourselves being manipulated by our own government or even a covert alien intelligence.

MEMORY LOSS

Many UFO experiencers have lapses of memory and total recall from the time of their UFO or alien experience. Sometimes it can be that the witness's own mind is blocking recall of a traumatic experience. However, it is also well known that the 'visitors' can cause this amnesia. Most security organisations around the world have certainly desired to employ this useful ability in their own clandestine activities.

THOSE PESKY RUSSIANS

Following a trip back home to Britain in 1976, I had spent some time with UFO colleagues, including Betty Woods, the secretary of BUFORA. (The British UFO Research Association.) She encouraged me to write an article for the BUFORA Journal, and I submitted my rather amateurish attempt, which they published in 1981.

AMNESIA IN CLOSE ENCOUNTER CASE WITNESSES

For many years ufologists have constantly been plagued by the recurring problems of contactee witnesses suffering a complete lapse of memory regarding their experiences. This particular facet of investigations has created many difficulties for the genuine investigator, who wants to present a credible and accurate report, but must resort to subjecting the witness to hypnosis in order to gain the necessary data regarding the sighting and/or encounter.

All too frequently, information gained in this manner is disputed and ridiculed by the media and authorities, who are sceptical of the ability of any intelligence to erase a particular event from a person's conscious memory. If the conscious memory is erased, why not the subconscious also?

Not only is the authenticity of the event queried, but fear of psychic connotations cause the investigation to be disregarded. If it were realised that it is within even our primitive human technology to perform exactly the same feat, perhaps more credence would be given to this category of report.

Some years ago, scientists had established that DNA molecules form the genetic memory of our species. That initial discovery stimulated further interest and experiments into the storing process of individual memories and experiences, by means of RNA – Ribonucleic acids.

Scientists soon determined that there is a definite differentiation between our long and short term memory. Although everything we see, hear, feel, sense and think is recorded as a molecule cipher, in the form of protein structures in our cells, we cannot normally recall the majority of these experiences at a later date. New information is retained only fleetingly by a change in the structure of the RNA. It has to be 'recopied' on to more stable protein molecules in the course of the next few hours to become or remain in lasting memory.

Just as a violent concussion of the brain can prevent the transference of a fresh experience from the short to the long term memory, it was discovered that the same result could be achieved by an injection of puromycin directly after an experience. The puromycin prevented the synthesis of protein in the ribosomes, so that the animo acids did not form into protein molecules as instructed by the RNA.

In short, if we are able, by means of a simple injection, to prevent a person from storing a new experience in their long term memory, surely a more advanced intelligence or society should be able to achieve the same result by much more subtle and refined means.

The final proof, offered to us by the scientific community, that our witnesses may well be genuine, are the experiments that demonstrate that long forgotten details can be recalled by electronically stimulating certain sections of the brain, and that often hypnosis can obtain the same results.

Therefore, in the light of current knowledge, it is advantageous not only to investigate these particular cases with an open mind, but to pay attention to the finer details of the witness recall under hypnosis, in order to determine what methods are being utilised to prevent the normal memory storage process.

When I look back on this article, written about forty years ago, I realise that science has come a long way since then. I didn't think much of it until about a year later, in 1982, when I received a letter from Betty; "I thought you might like to see the interest your article has aroused in the USSR," she wrote. "I sent him a spare copy of the Bulletin as he requests."

She had enclosed the original Russian 'postcard', dated 31-7-82, which was addressed to me at Betty's BUFORA address.

'Dear Mrs McGhee,

I would greatly appreciate receiving a reprint or Xerox copy, of your articles on amnesia and the biological basis of memory, and Nigel Watson's pre-1947 UFO bulletin, published in: BUFORA bulletin, 1981, No.2. (or the whole issue if you have by chance a spare copy).

Many thanks:

It was signed by someone at a Post Office Box address in Novosibirsk USSR. But wait – why did it have a postmark from Chelsea in London?

These were still the days of spies and counter-intelligence, something I did not want to get mixed up in. I had a couple of contacts who were 'in-the-know', and passed the card on to them. A few weeks later they got back to me. The Novosibirsk PO Box did indeed belong to the KGB. Perhaps the Russians wanted to know how to block people's memories?

They would certainly know more about it than little me! I decided I wanted no part of the espionage game, and never responded to the invitation.

HYPNOSIS

Someone who is genuinely recollecting and reliving a past event, usually experiences the emotions they felt at the time. One subject, who suspected she had interacted with aliens, surprised the hypnotherapist and researcher when she suddenly burst out laughing during her memory recall.

Local authorities, near her US hometown of Jefferson City, had been perplexed as to the cause of a thirty feet deep hole in the ground. It was perfectly round and twenty feet in diameter. It was obvious something large, round and heavy had been there overnight.

The witness told of being led back to the craft, with a being on either side. Suddenly they released her and rushed back to their ship, which was slowly sinking into the ground. The aliens had made the mistake of landing on top of a Missouri sinkhole, which was giving way under the weight of their craft!

The use of regression hypnosis by UFO abduction investigators is highly contentious, and has multiple flaws. It has created more controversy than any other aspect of research. In 1982 the British UFO Research Association adopted a Code of Practise and in 1988 voted to impose a five year moratorium on any form of regression. Later they ratified and extended this policy permanently, and wisely preferred to rely on consciously recalled memory.

In the USA the American Board of Hypnotherapy has a strict Code of Professional Ethics, as do most Australian qualified hypnotherapists and psychologists. I have, however, heard of questionable techniques being used by less than responsible practitioners who are more interested in obtaining every last detail of an encounter, rather than the well-being of the witness, who can be re-traumatised when memories come flooding back.

There are so many pitfalls in 'missing time' investigations, and it is best left to qualified experts. Even then, multiple factors including emotional   stress, mental stability, false memories and religious indoctrination come into play. First and foremost, witnesses need respect, dignity, confidentiality and emotional support. The investigator must proceed with caution and patience. In many cases ideally there should already be physical and corroborating evidence, and the experiencer only has 'gaps' in an otherwise detailed recall.

ARE THE 'GREYS' BIOLOGICAL ROBOTS?

Given the apparent alien ability to master artificial intelligence on an undetectable level, there is a strong possibility that at least some of the 'greys' are very advanced biological robots. Their clone-like physical structure – large heads, big eyes, lack of reproductive organs and skinny limbs and bodies may lend some credence to this theory.

Many contactees have proffered this suggestion, and describe how these creatures seem to have a 'group mind'. They cannot 'think outside of the square' if something does not go as planned, and apparently most do not show any form of emotion.

Already we, on Earth, have manufactured primitive 'human looking' and other robots. An advanced alien society could invent efficient biological machines which can perform complex tasks and store, process and transmit intelligent thoughts. Since extraterrestrials have not exactly been welcomed by humans, perhaps the use of expendable artificial 'workers', is a preferable alternative.

MUFON UFO Journal July 2000, contains an interesting article by George Filer. It concerned a British man, Bill Eatock, who had been abducted from his car, and later, under hypnosis, recalled the event.

'......as I had been driving along the whole lock stock and barrel went up in the air. The car, everything went up into a ship, a spaceship! And after the 'greys' did certain various 'checks' on my person, they put me down in exactly the same position.

'There were non-human looking creatures, a lot of them. What I remember most about it was that there was a human looking being who was very tall, about forty-five/fifty, with grey hair, powerful, very well built, a very healthy looking person. He had total control over the 'greys'. He was the boss.

'He came to me after the creatures had examined me and spoke to me in perfect English. Clear, concise, inflection-free English. I saw that there were a lot more human beings as well. There was a girl next to me, a young girl, who said she came from Parbold/Dalton, or somewhere near there. She was terrified, and in a very fearful state.'

Often there appears to be a normal 'human-type' extraterrestrial being in charge, and this lends more credence to the theory that perhaps the Greys are very advanced biological robots. There is, however, cause for concern. Many experts have warned against artificial intelligence becoming smarter than their creators!

Some contactees have reported that the 'Greys' were overly interested in human 'emotions'. Even more disturbing is the distinct possibility that artificial intelligence is capable of 'cloning' and creating its own 'test tube' humans!

CHAPTER EIGHTEEN

INTO THE PARANORMAL

As a young researcher, I used to concentrate purely on 'nuts and bolts' evidence, and it took me some years to realise that the paranormal aspect of ufology was a serious component, closely intertwined with the craft and occupants themselves.

One such case involved Jaques Drabier, who was a Free French Air Force fighter pilot in 1944. He was flying a P-47 Thunderbolt when three unidentified craft intercepted his plane, and projected a green beam of 'energy' at him. It enveloped the plane entirely. He thought this was responsible for his subsequent recurring visions where he was in command of a 'starship'.

In 1963 he began having more strange visions, and he recorded them in drawings and paintings. He also developed medium abilities, and many of his psychic abilities proved accurate. He recommenced his career as a pilot in 1968, and had further sightings in Simi Valley and Death Valley, California.

MIRANDA VELLA

Miranda was born in 1985. She suffers from a profound hearing loss, and has a Cochlear implant which was fitted at Prince Alfred Hospital when she was six or seven years old. Only the outside part has ever been changed.

Miranda's case had much in common with other experiencers. Due to her hearing loss she can lip-read and speak coherently, but any regressive hypnosis is not a practical option.

Miranda feels connected to nature, the earth and animals. Whilst she is athletic, competing in several sports, she has an allergy to chemicals. She has ESP abilities, and knows what people are going to say before they actually speak.

Miranda is very intelligent, and like many other witnesses I have interviewed, when she was in kindergarten some people came and gave her IQ tests, which apparently showed genius level. She went on to a government selective primary school, but did not attend the comparable specialised secondary education when offered, merely attending the local high school. She went on to gain her Bachelor's Degree at University

Miranda was born in Sydney, and lived in the Penrith area of the western suburbs. In 1996, twelve year-old Miranda was going to bed when she saw a flash of red – like an explosion in the sky. Afterwards she recalls seeing a 'ghost train' going past her window. The next day she told her mother, who believed her, and claimed that she herself had seen 'things' in Werrington. Her mother rang a UFO hotline who said there was nothing astronomical to account for it, and no other sightings had been reported. About two months later her mother said there had been 'something' on the roof, flashing red lights.

In 2002 Miranda was eighteen years-old and her younger sister, (who had good hearing), was eight. They had simultaneous 'twin dreams/nightmares' and visions.

In about 2006 she, and her whole family, felt a 'need' to get out of Sydney and to a 'higher elevation' in the mountains – (common with several experiencers). They moved to Springwood and bought a house 'down the hill from the road', on the edge of the bush. It had been built in the 1980s by two doctors she thinks were 'Flying Doctors', who worked in third world countries.

There were more strange happenings after they moved to the mountains. One night, when taking their dogs out for a last visit to the back garden, there was a brilliant flash and the whole backyard lit up with a blue light. Miranda thinks it only lasted for a few seconds – but is a bit vague on the timing. She says she 'was in shock' and when she went inside the DVD she had on the TV was 'frozen' with a sort of 'crackling' across the screen.

Her mother said she had seen, on at least five different occasions over a period of time, 'blue flashes' in the bush, which lit up the backyard. (I have received reports from several other witnesses – not connected – who have had their backyard lit by a blue light just prior to an experience) Miranda hinted that there were more possible 'similar experiences' but didn't elaborate.

Miranda's family still continue to experience inexplicable events. It seems the phenomena are associated with the people themselves, rather than the area where they are living.

When the TV is switched off at the power point, it will suddenly turn itself on and take the volume up to the highest level. The doorbell, which has no batteries in it, will ring in the middle of the night. This has happened a few times, but they are too scared to go down to the door at three in the morning. Miranda also displays some kinetic ability – when she sits under a LED light, it starts to flicker. She seems to affect technology, causing static, and gets mild to medium electric shocks when she touches door handles or the top of the car. (I have interviewed other witnesses experiencing the same phenomena).

In 2009 Miranda fell asleep on a plane trip to Perth, and dreamed she was back home and walking into a room – and mother said at the same time she heard her. Her sister claimed not only to hearing her – she actually saw her!

The paranormal activity increased in 2016. One night, early in the year, when Miranda was on the Gold Coast, her mother and sister were home at Springwood. Suddenly they thought they heard a knocking on the window and someone simultaneously walking outside the door. They both 'froze'. Was it a 'break-in'? They could see nothing, and huddled together, listening to a sound of thumping – like heavy footsteps in the hall – not normal- then a 'scratching' on the walls – silence – then a loud sound like something 'shaking'.

Miranda's grandmother had passed away in 2013. They had saved her 'toy cat', which was packed in a chest, with blankets on the top, in the master bedroom. In 2016, two weeks before the anniversary of her death, Miranda had gone downstairs to use the en-suite toilet in the master bedroom – opposite the lounge room. She closed the toilet door but when she came out the bedroom door was shut. She felt a bit uncomfortable, and when her parents came down the open door was shut again. Then they saw the 'toy cat' on the lounge in the opposite room – but the chest, still in the bedroom, was shut with the blankets still on top.

One night, in September 2016, they looked out the back to see what appeared to be a fire in the bush behind the property. Miranda said there were three lights in a triangular formation flashing orange and red. If they were on an object it would have been fairly large. Due to the darkness and terrain, she couldn't tell if it were on the ground or in the air – suddenly it was 'gone' - and she thought it/they must have 'put the fire out' before the Brigade arrived!

Miranda and I had mutual friends, and had known each other for some time, but it was only in late 2016 that she decided to confide in me. I had no explanation for the unusual sightings and happenings in the past, and decided to further investigate both the physical and paranormal aspects of the case. Several so-called 'experts' in all things 'ghostly' were unwilling to go to the house, and this was not my particular area of knowledge.

Miranda herself has weird dreams, often about another part of the world. They seemed more *real* rather than a dream. Often they relate to incidents before they happen, which she then sees later in the media. Miranda's mother has precognition of disasters which happen to normal people. She says her mother talks about 'alien' things and shares 'secrets', that they don't tell her, with her sister. Miranda's younger sister supposedly 'sleepwalked' and was found elsewhere in the house without any memory or knowledge of how she got there.

I wondered if any of her female relatives suffered the tale-tale physical problems so common with contactees. Sure enough, Miranda, and her mother's sister and daughter have ovarian cysts on the RHS, as have many abductees when ova have been 'taken'. Miranda has other 'women's problems' which are consistent. It is not known if any other female relatives have similar complaints.

I thought to myself; "Is this another generational case with the possibility – to be ascertained - of contact, abduction or even human or paranormal interference?

CLOSE ENCOUNTERS OF THE FIFTH KIND?

Some years ago, I received a most interesting letter from 'L.K.', along with some intriguing art work. We corresponded for some time, and his sensitive pictures of an alien being so impressed me, that I included one on page 228 of *'Contact Down Under'*.

Here is what he wrote: *'In 1971, I was an inmate at the Washington State Penitentiary in Walla Walla, Washington. Every night, around 7.30 or so, I would go to sit in a chair in front of the Resident Government Office, and use my imagination (visualisation exercise) to picture a 'CRAFT' landing on the large concrete area between the big prison yard, laundry and maximum security building.*

After doing this for a while, I would go to my cell and lay on my bunk to do another exercise. I did this at the same time each night. I would visualise a conical beam of white light extending from my brow chakra, reaching endlessly into space. On this beam of light I would 'send' a telepathic message; "Interplanetary Brothers – Please Communicate".

This message was sent by seven breaths, then I did seven breaths of silence. No pictures or words in my mind, just listening, then repeat this message again for seven breaths. I did this message back and forth until I fell asleep. This continued for about thirteen days, the same routine. On the fourteenth night, I am not sure what happened. I was pre-occupied and forgot to do my nightly exercise.

The next day, I was told that several tower guards, and some of the inmates, had witnessed a 'ball of fire', high in the sky, stop right over the big yard at high altitude. It was seen there for more than a minute, then accelerated north at a high rate of speed, disappearing quickly.

That night I continued my exercises, and quite abruptly, I was standing inside the wall of the big yard, in my Astral body, facing the centre of the yard. I was looking up at one particular star in the night sky, when it exploded into a brilliant flash of white light.

Sitting in the grass, about seventy-five feet away, was a smooth shining craft, about one hundred feet across and about twenty-five feet high, in the centre. It looked like a Chinese wok turned upside down. I walked, without fear, right up to and onto the hull. It seemed to be made of metal that shined like liquid mercury, with brilliant, swirling colours all over, like petroleum in a mud puddle. It was then that I noticed I was bare footed and the hull of the craft was fairly warm, and it 'tickled' or sort of stung my feet, like a mild electrical charge.

I walked onto this wing, about thirty feet or so, and a door just appeared from nowhere. There were no seams to be seen anywhere. The door was about four to five feet long and about two and a half feet wide. It had rounded corners and the hull appeared to be about nine inches thick. I was quite emotionally relaxed, ducking a little, as I stepped down about three steps into the craft.

The first thing I noticed upon entering, was that half of the circular room on the left side of the room was blocked off by what seemed to be a glass wall with heavy thick swirling grey-brown smoke. The thing was, there was no glass wall, just swirling smoke. I felt that it was being blocked from me on purpose.

To my right, immediately inside the door, was a semi-circular couch (red) attached to the wall, on which sat two beings. They just sat there, smiling, not greeting me in any way.

The ceiling seemed to be a gray colour and covered with some sort of material that looked like carpet, with a thin texture like burlap. There were various shapes under this material. The ceiling was about ten inches above my head. When I sat down between these two beings, the ceiling was still ten inches above my head. It seemed to raise and lower in accordance to where a person was, so as to be convenient to reach whatever the objects were attached there.

First I want to describe the two beings. They both looked like identical twins, about seventeen years-old, yet I 'knew' they were easily more than two hundred years-old. If they were to stand, their bodies were in perfect proportion to their height. They were slender in build, wearing a sort of one-piece jump suit of a light cocoa brown. There was no visible hair on them, except on their heads, which was as thin as a new born baby's, and transparent gold in colour. Their heads seemed to be a little big for their bodies, but it was the height and width of their foreheads. Their eyes were a silver blue/pale blue/grey with aqua/turquoise streaks or specks in the iris, which was larger than ours. Their teeth were very white and small, having more than humans. Their skin was the colour like honey, smooth and soft looking, just like a baby.

They were so fantastically beautiful in physical appearance. I thought to myself that they are more beautiful than any female I ever saw on this planet. This thought got a reaction from them, and they giggled like a couple of school girls. Especially when I thought; "If their men look this beautiful, I can't imagine what their females look like." They were very shy, and blushed a little. I guess that sort of broke the ice.

I was then talking to both of them, but only the one on my right spoke. The other just sat there smiling all the time. I just 'understood' that they did not gang-up on one person in a conversation. When the one speaking to me talked, his voice was heard in my ears and in my head. It was almost like harmony and his voice was so beautiful. It was not like a female or male, but childlike – angelic.

I sat between them, conversing comfortably for what seemed to be about half an hour. There was no physical exam, no paranoia. Just a conversation that seemed business like and important, yet broke up occasionally with shy humour.

I noticed that the room across from me was like a dark bedroom, hard to see the shapes of whatever was there. The interior of this craft was well lit up where I

313

sat, yet there was no visible source of the light. What was interesting was that there were no visible shadows anywhere.

One question that I clearly remember being asked was; "How does it feel to have hair all over your body?" I felt defensive at first, then realised that compared to them, I am almost a primate. We all laughed at that.

Suddenly it was time for me to go. I stood, and the ceiling moved up to accommodate my height. They neither stood, shook hands nor was there any 'goodbye'. I just 'understood' that it was all a waste of energy that was to be used for more productive things. The last thing I remember them saying to me was; "Let your hair grow." I just knew this had something to do with expanding the aura.

I walked up and out the door. The hull tingled my feet again. It seems strange, but I do not remember breathing air, yet it felt like the air out of the craft was very different. The air inside felt like it was full of static electricity – very strange feeling, but not uncomfortable. I walked off the hull, about ten feet, turned and looked back. The door was no longer there.

I walked about seventy-five feet further, and while my back was turned, the entire area exploded into a blinding light, like a flash bulb. I turned and saw the craft was gone. I turned back and began walking. I snapped back into my physical body so fast and hard, I almost flipped completely off the bunk and onto the floor. I was not at all groggy, but completely and fully awake, and fully aware of the experience I just had was real.

Perhaps certain kinds of meditation or spiritual practices are sufficient for certain people to make contact. What interested me about LK's account were the physical sensations he reported during the encounter.

On 12th December 1994, two carloads of people were travelling together north of Marulan in N.S.W. The teenagers were amusing themselves by singing a Tibetan Chant – *'Om Nahmah Shiva'*, which they explained as being a breathing and sound technique.

It was after midnight, and there were no other cars on the highway. They had been chanting for about ten minutes when the driver, one of their fathers, noticed a bright blue light, bigger than the moon, to the right of his windscreen.

It was just above the treetops, and quickly moved in an arc, coming to a halt in front of the vehicle. The youngsters were so astounded they stopped chanting, and the minute this happened, the object quickly moved away and shot back up into the sky.

INSTITUTE PERUANO DE RELATIONES INTERPLANITARIUS

A few years ago, Omar Fowler detailed a fascinating case in his *'OVNI'* magazine.

In 1955 Sixto Paz was born in Lima, Peru - the same year his father, Carlos Paz Garcia, founded the IPRI – a UFO group which, at that time, was composed mainly of his friends from the Peruvian Air Force.

In 1974 they hosted a conference with D. Victor Yanez Aguirre, from Lima's Hospital de Policia, where he advocated the possibility of telepathic communication with interplanetary visitors.

Young Sixto was inspired, and along with his mother and sister, attempted to receive a message by practising yoga and meditation. One night they received a 'psychographic' message, which is a form of telepathic channelling through automatic, but conscious, writing. It didn't involve a trance. Although all three of them received the same message, purportedly from 'Oxale', based on Ganymede, one of the moons of Jupiter, they thought it must be a figment of their imaginations.

The next day they gathered twenty friends together, and to their surprise, another message was received. It told all of them to go to the desert of Chilea, sixty kilometres south of Lima, on the night of the 7th February 1974. Most were very sceptical, but went anyway.

At the appointed time a strange, intense glow appeared behind the hills. A light rose up, illuminating the entire countryside. It travelled above the ridges, and halted on the right side of the horizon. The group's amazement soon turned to fear when it began swinging and descending as it approached, and transformed into a metallic disc-shaped object that rotated upon itself. It had lateral coloured lights and six small windows.

Once it was over the group, it projected a light, which was brighter than daytime. It lasted for quite some time, and the next communication indicated that perhaps the 'visitors' were scanning the witnesses.

A telepathic message was received that they were not coming down because 'the group didn't know how to control its emotions.' After indicating that there would be 'another time and place', the object left at great speed, leaving many visibly shaken witnesses.

Within a month at least eight, mostly young people, channelled messages from Oxale and other entities. A few days later Sixto's father and some of his sceptical research team accompanied him on a field excursion to investigate the matter. They were surprised and impressed when they witnessed a cylindrical object about a thousand metres above in the sky. It was very large, being about one hundred and fifty metres in diameter.

Over the next few months there were more sightings, both day and night, in the Chilca area. The group of interested persons, participating in the field work, had grown to more than fifty. In June, they received a message that seven individuals, who were well tuned, and in 'affinity' with each other, were to go back to the desert for a 'Xendra' experience.

Sixto was walking a little ahead of the others, when inexplicably he found himself behind a hill, confronting a glowing 'half dome' which was about ten metres in diameter. A human silhouette appeared from the interior, and invited him in. He was afraid, and hesitated, only following the being when he saw it was about to go back inside.

Once inside he experienced several different physical symptoms. It was as if his body was burning, and he felt nausea and dizziness until he could distinguish a human looking person in front of him. He was about six feet tall, with a wide, oriental looking face, and very little hair. He wore a loose, shiny garment that reminded Sixto of 'sport attire'. Although he gestured with his hands, the communication was telepathic.

Sixto perceived that the being called this phenomenon a 'Xendra', and it must be a dimensional door, or threshold in Space-Time. The being told him that they are capable of concentrating energy in such a way as to dematerialise an individual, cancelling both his molecular cohesion and atomic weight, and project him to another place. He told Sixto that he would be travelling to one of the moons of Jupiter, and the time that would pass there would not correspond to the time on Earth.

When he got there, he saw a 'Crystal City', full of domes and spherical buildings. There were men, women and children in the streets, and he was told the basis of their society was 'the couple', with sexual division and contact. Their telepathy and clairvoyance were very developed, and that was why there was no divorce or infidelity.

They didn't hold elections like our democracies. They could see and feel who were most suitable to lead them, politically and spiritually. They had originated elsewhere in the galaxy. Most of their cities were below the surface, and they had created an artificial climate and atmosphere.

Oxale showed Sixto images of what the future of Earth would be like if we did not change our ways, and he felt it started with each individual, especially the younger generation. He said that the human mind is powerful, and if many of us agree with the same intention and faith, we can make it. From that time on Sixto has considered himself to be a 'messenger'.

Sixto thought he must have been there for about five days, but only fifteen minutes of Earth time had passed when his group saw him exit the interior of the light.

Two weeks later, six other companions accompanied Sixto on a new 'Xendra' experience, and later, many others repeated them in an individual or collective manner.

Journalist Juan Benitez went to Peru to cover the strange story of the group of young people who claimed to be in contact with extraterrestrials. He claimed, after he saw an apparition of two UFOs, it changed his life, and led him to write two books – *'OVNIS S.O.S. a la Humanidad'* and *'Cien Mil Kilometros Tras los Extraterrestres'*.

PETER GREGORY

In my book *'The Alien Gene'* I mention the strange artefacts and mysterious structures which are known to have existed in, Yakutsk, a remote part of Siberia, since 1853. Large 'domes' or 'cauldrons' made of bronze or copper, are known to the native people as *'olguis'*.

An acquaintance of mine, a highly intelligent and educated, 'no nonsense' woman, was born in Siberia, and often visits family there. She spoke of sightings, and some having contact with aliens through a "Friendship Club', similar to those in Northern Italy and other parts of Europe. Other respected researchers have also investigated the possibility of a secret alien base being present in the area.

Philip Creighton, in a *'Flying Saucer Review'* article *'More on the Siberian Meteorite of September 2002'* said that Valery Uvarov of the Russian National Security Academy, told Graham Birdsall that on September 24/25 2002, 'a meteorite was shot down over Siberia by an unknown installation'. He went on to say that the Russian government was treating the matter very seriously, and was planning an expedition later in the year.

British colleague and fellow researcher, Omar Fowler, wrote an extraordinary article in his *'OVNI'* publication which delves into the 'paranormal' aspect of ufology, and if correct, throws more light on the situation.

Omar had known Peter Gregory, a paranormal investigator, for many years, and could attest to his bone-fides and abilities. On many occasions he had assisted others, including police, with his accurate insights. He also practised 'remote viewing' and became quite skilled in this field.

During the 1990's he saw images of an area of high mountains and dark grey terrain, with red desert which stretched into the distance. He also saw the strange domed structures in Siberia. His description matched those which were only known to relatively few people.

Peter first made telepathic contact with 'Oona' in July 1994. *"She said she had chosen to communicate with me because my abductions since childhood had given me a certain empathy with the Greys, and this could be helpful if understanding between the two races were to materialise."*

Over time, Peter had many telepathic conversations with Oona. She was twenty-three, and an alien hybrid whom had lived at the 'biological unit' her entire life. She admitted that they sometimes implant humans, but usually only to locate them, or to monitor toxins and bacteria in the atmosphere. Her main function was to retrieve embryos and foetuses from their human mothers. Peter remonstrated that children need love and affection, but Oona assured him that they are given all that was required for healthy physical, emotional and spiritual growth, and usually adapt well to the automatic conditioning in their programs.

She explained that producing hybrids was not unusual in their culture. They believed that crossbreeding with other races was the most effective way to control the evolution of other species, and ensure the survival of their own. They only wanted to help us realise our cosmic heritage with the enlightenment, knowledge and wisdom to raise our civilisation to full spiritual awareness.

In June, Peter had found a message, left on his notepad one night. It read; *'In our universe there are infinite perceptions of reality, yet man is capable of understanding only one. If he is to endure, he must learn to expand his acceptance of this simple cosmic truth. Only then will he be able to fully understand our purpose in his creation and join us as equals.'*

Peter asked if it was from her, and what did it mean. She explained; *"It means that the natural laws of time and space are infinitely variable, and do not conform to man's scientific belief. He must rethink his whole conception of physics if he is ever to visit distant planets."*

He also asked about secret bases on Earth. She admitted to many, all over the world. They are deep underground, in most countries. Most, except those under the sea, were known to authorities, and they had their co-operation. She was not allowed to tell Peter any locations, except for the one in Russia, where she was living.

Peter later wrote a booklet, *'Alien Contact; The Oona Story'*.

ANGELS OR ALIENS

My colleague, Rosemary Decker also detailed some more recent episodes of 'divine' or maybe alien intervention when normal humans are in danger.

'Academic, Barbara Sacic, wrote in her thesis about the rescue of a young Tim Anderson. There was a record-breaking cold wave in the US mid-west, and one Christmas Eve, Tim was driving home with his friend Jim. They heard a warning, on the car radio, not to venture out as the wind-chill was eighty below zero. It was too late. The car stalled and gave out.

'Prayer was their only hope: "Well God, you are the only one who can help us now!"

'Suddenly, as if in a dream, headlights appeared. Only a few seconds before they had both looked up and down the highway, and there was nothing in sight! The driver towed their car back home, and Tim went into the house to borrow some money to pay their rescuer. His father looked out of the window and said that he couldn't see any tow-truck!

'Tim and his friend turned around. All they could see was Tim's car parked by the kerb. They hadn't heard the sound of the chains being released from the car. Neither had they heard any doors slam or the sound of an engine pulling away. There was no bill – no receipt – farewell –'thank you' or "Merry Christmas". No anything!

'Tim ran down the driveway and looked both ways - nothing! Only one set of tyre tracks were visible in the driveway – Tim's!

'The rescue of my daughter Melody and myself was also involved with snow, cold and ice. We were driving through the Siskiyou Mountains of Oregon, just following a major January storm in 1963.

'The sun was setting, and the snow that had melted on the highway began to refreeze, forming 'black ice'. As we came over a rise and started downhill, Melody shifted to slow the car – too rapidly as she told me later. The Chevy fish-tailed and began to go into a spin.

'Just to our right, the land dropped off abruptly into a canyon below. In order to avoid a collision with an oncoming vehicle, Melody swung the wheel of the car, expecting that we may drop into the canyon. Fortunately, just where we angled off into the snow, there was a small promontory with foot-deep snow. It was wide enough to halt the car just short of the drop. During this emergency, neither of us had said a word.

'Melody spoke first; "We'll get help soon, because we're girls."

'A minute or so later, a pick-up truck arrived from behind, pulled onto the shoulder just ahead, and the driver got out. From the bed of the truck he picked up a chain, the only thing there, and attached it to the front of our car. He re-entered his truck and pulled us back out onto the highway.

'He then got out, replaced the chain in his truck, climbed back in and drove away. He hadn't spoken a single word – we would have heard because there was no other traffic. As he drove off we were shouting our thanks, but he disappeared around a curve, and we never saw him again.'

Rosemary also told of another couple of events that had an inter-dimensional aspect and bordered on the paranormal, but the witnesses were convinced they were UFO related.

"Two friends I became acquainted with in California, had their experiences during World War II, when both Navy men, (who had not yet met), were serving as Petty Officers in the US Pacific Fleet.

"Harold, a 'spotter' aboard a battleship, had begun to see unidentifiable craft, usually saucer-shaped, as well as US and Japanese war-planes. He became extremely curious about the 'unknowns', and from the end of the war onward was an avid researcher.

"Late in the war, the battleship he served on was bombed and sank. Like many others he was thrown into the water, and stayed afloat in his life-jacket. About the time he thought he was going to die, he perceived a fine looking man hovering just above him. He was told not to fear; he would be rescued and go home safe. The man disappeared, and soon after Harold was picked up.

"Shortly after the end of the war, while working at Ryan Aircraft in San Diego, Harold met Dick, who was also employed there. They learned that they had both been in the Pacific arena at the same time. Dick had also had a strange encounter. He was told that he would go home safe, and given the date the war would end. (It proved accurate within twenty-four hours.)

"In 1952, both fellows, curious about the UFOs they had seen, decided to find out whether Palomar Mountain resident, George Adamski, had actually photographed space-craft. On weekends, they began driving up to Palomar Gardens with their wives.

"One Saturday night, when they were all in one car, starting back towards home, they were approaching the first of three 'switch-backs'. They entered a fog so thick that only one white line was visible at a time. They were very anxious and slowed to a crawl.

"Suddenly they were rescued! A large circle of well lighted 'pavement', as broad as the road, appeared just ahead. There was no sign of the fog in this limited area: Was it dissipated? Was it made invisible? They never knew.

"Dick's wife said, "Listen! Can you hear voices above us?"

"Then they all heard laughter, followed by silence. Just past the 'switchbacks' the fog ended, and their lighted circle disappeared. It was then, off to the right, that a small saucer type craft zipped away and also disappeared."

A similar event occurred to the late singer Jimmy Hendrix. In a biography, Curtis Knight referred to him as a 'Starchild'. He claimed contact with UFOs and 'Space Brothers', with whom he had telepathic contact, and who had only our best interests at heart.

Curtis recalled a cold winter's night in 1965, when Hendrix and the rest of the band were trying to get back to Manhattan, which was over one hundred miles away. They were trying to negotiate one of the worst blizzards they could recall, and the winds were whipping the snow around their van,

They missed the turn-off leading to the State highway, which would have put them in the direction of the city. The next thing they remembered was being stuck in a snow drift that reached the hood of their vehicle. Soon it got so cold that the windows and locks on the door froze up. The heater was on full blast, but they had to make a decision – either leave the van's heater on, risking carbon monoxide poisoning, or turn it off and freeze to death.

Suddenly, on the road in front of them, a bright phosphorescent cone-shaped capsule appeared. It landed on the snow, about one hundred feet ahead, and remained there silently for a few minutes. It had tripod landing gear, and looked just like 'a prop from a science fiction movie'.

They recalled; "At first, we thought it was an apparition caused by the cold and our confused state of mind. We just couldn't believe our eyes. Someone prodded Jimi with their elbow, and asked him out loud if this thing was just part of our imagination, or could he see it too?"

Hendrix only smiled, and kept his gaze on the object. His co-driver tried to wake the others in the back of the van, but they didn't respond, and he was worried that they had succumbed to the carbon monoxide.

Suddenly a door opened on the side of the craft, and an entity emerged. It stood eight feet tall, had yellowish skin and slits instead of eyes. Its forehead came to a point, and the head ran straight into its chest, giving the impression that it had no neck. It floated to the ground and glided towards the van and its trapped occupants. It was then that they noticed that the snow was melting in the wake of the creature. It was as if its body was generating tremendous heat or energy, so much so that as it came across a small rise, the snow disappeared in all directions.

The being went over to the right hand side of the van, and looked right through the window where Hendrix was sitting. They seemed to be communicating telepathically – perhaps he was giving thanks to this being for saving their lives.

The van immediately started to warm up, to the extent everybody felt they were roasting. The heat was enough to evaporate the rest of the snow that had imprisoned the vehicle. They turned the ignition key, 'gunned the motor', and got the hell out of there. Looking in the rear vision mirror they saw the road filling with snow again, and at the same time, the object lifting off 'like a rocket from a launch pad'.

In 1964, Mark Andrews was a radio officer on the Israeli ship, the M.V. Atzmaut (Atid Shipping Company, Haifa). One night, the ship was anchored about half a mile off Jaffa, discharging cargo, when struck by a storm with huge seas. The 'lighters' stopped off-loading the cargo and headed into port.

After a few hours the ship's cable broke, and the vessel was washed to shore. It was hard aground and the hatches filling with water. They were well and truly 'shipwrecked' and Mark was told to send out an SOS message.

Mark said; "I did not waste time writing it out. I did this 'out of my head'. I have the feeling that this was the cause of what followed. I do know that telepathy knows no restraining factor of distances, even to the stars. Otherwise, why pray? When we look at a star, surely our mind is with that star. Mind power is the most powerful force on earth or in the heavens."

It was dawn when he went onto the boat deck, sat down on a bench, and was amazed to see a blue sky, more like a summer's day morning. About a mile away, he could see a 'box-like' object low in the sky. It was silvery, had what looked like criss-cross trellising around the outside, and was reflecting the morning rays of the sun.

He said that as the strange craft hung in the sky, his 'dead-weighted' ship, full of water and half its cargo, suddenly started to slowly 'bump' along the seabed, all the way to the end of a concrete jetty in Jaffa harbour. The whole time, Mark was watching the object in the sky. He turned around while the crew were disembarking, and when he looked back the strange craft was gone.

In the August 2001 *'Mufon UFO Journal'* Walt Andrus wrote about a case in March 1973, when an Arizona woman, Joan George, fell off a ladder whilst pruning a tree. The heavy ladder fell on top of her, breaking her leg, and trapping her underneath. When she regained consciousness, she feared she may bleed to death. Her husband was away, and her neighbours couldn't hear her calls for help.

Suddenly two strange beings came 'floating' over the orchard, lifted the ladder off, and got her onto her feet. Her injuries miraculously healed within four days, leaving only a four inch scar as evidence.

The entities were less than four feet tall, with slim bodies, long arms, a brown-grey complexion, large heads and piercing black eyes. Their skin felt like sandpaper, and their long arms and fingers were intensely cold. One was wearing a tight-fitting one piece blue/grey suit, and the other a suit that looked like rolls of plastic, similar to numerous bicycle 'inner tubes' of various sizes and diameters.

Joan was so grateful that they had rescued her, she invited them into her home for a meal. They communicated telepathically, with unusual voices, saying they did not eat food, and only had juice. When she mentioned having various fruit juices, they advised – 'not that kind of juice'.

The entities advised Joan that they may not see her again as they 'did not travel these trade routes very often.' Before they left, they gave her a small, round metal medallion, with symbols on.

Dudley Robb, one of our INUFOR investigators, attended the Pacific UFO Conference in Hawaii in 1996. During a coffee break he met Dick, a local Hawaiian, who confided his experiences, and when hearing about the conference, decided to accompany Dudley.

Upon his return to Australia, Dudley submitted the following report.

'Dick's UFO experience happened in Hawaii in 1956. He had started to walk down a hill with two friends when a one hundred foot diameter silver disc-shaped craft came over the hill-top at a very low level, moving slowly over them. It was making a humming sound and the three men, intimidated by this machine, and started running down the hill. The craft pursued them, they fell over, and seemed to black out. When they woke up and looked above, the craft was directly overhead. It tilted at a forty-five degree angle, and quickly accelerated away and disappeared.

'Dick said that, looking back over the years, he and his two friends felt a strange compulsion never to talk about the incident to anyone else, or even each other, for many years afterwards. Was a suggestion placed in their memory to forget the incident and the intelligence operating the strange craft?

'He was a Company Commander during the Vietnam War, and he survived, miraculously, on more than one occasion during combat situations when some, or all, of his men around him were killed instantly. The most memorable of these incidents was where an enemy rocket was fired point blank at him. He suffered shrapnel wounds all over, but his comrades around him were killed instantly.

'After all the shrapnel was removed, much later a foreign metal body showed up under x-ray in his skull, behind his ear. There were no entry wound marks in that area of his skull, and medical opinion was against the idea of it being shrapnel. To remove it may kill him, so the object was left in place.

Dick felt that some 'higher power' had saved his life repeatedly during that war. From all the action surrounding him, he felt the odds favoured him being killed along with his buddies who did lose their lives. He firmly believed this to be unexplainable – how he repeatedly survived these 'impossible' situations.'

Dudley went on to say that he believed that Dick and his two buddies were abducted in the 1956 UFO encounter and implanted aboard the craft. He thought that in imminent, dangerous situations maybe a protective force field is triggered by the implant to save the subject for some on-going or later purpose.

'My reason for this thought is generated by a military case I read about some time ago. A sentry confronted an alien who approached him from a landed craft. The sentry aimed his rifle and fired a shot at the creature advancing towards him. The soldier was amazed to see the bullet come slowly out of the gun barrel, and drop on the ground two feet in front of him. The same thing happened with the second shot, and he fled in panic towards the main barracks and reported the incident. When the soldiers came out to investigate, the alien and its landed craft were already gone. Are there some very 'practical guardian angels' around at times?'

EPILOGUE

In order to take our place in a cosmic society, we must evolve into a united, mature, tolerant and peaceful humanity. So far, despite any alien intervention, we have not learned that lesson.

Rather than ending this book with countless theories, I wish to share the beautiful words of two very different people – one a simple contactee and the other a world renowned scientist.

Where did you come from, strangers in the skies?
I see your shining discs, and I can't believe my eyes'
Why do you watch us from far above the Earth?
Was it really you who gave us human birth?
Do you watch with sorrow the wars that rape our land?
Do you see the degradation and cannot understand?
You were here among us, prophets from above,
To show us how to live with compassion and with love,
But we crucified your teachers, burned your gentle saints;
We would not, will not learn, and our evil taints
This planet that is so green and fair,
So you watch, and wait, high in the clean, clear air.
Our scientists tell us you're an illusion,
That we suffer from a strange delusion.
Satellites, balloons or reflections on a mist,
How can we believe that such things exist?
Dreams of flying saucers, of a strange galactic race,
Born of science-fiction writers, of aliens from space.
But I know what I have seen up there,
I feel the sorrow and the love they share.
Perhaps when this world of ours is sane again,
They will land and walk among us without fear or pain.

LYN MALET – Alice Springs – Northern Territory. 1973

REFLECTIONS ON A MOTE OF DUST

My colleague Omar Fowler, from Derby Britain, researcher and president of 'Phenomenon Research Association' sent me this very moving passage written by the late Carl Sagan.

'As the Voyager I Spacecraft headed out of the Solar System in 1990, it looked back and snapped a 'family portrait' of the Sun and planets. From beyond Pluto the Sun looks like a bright star surrounded by a few faint dots. The Earth is one of those dots.

Reprinted below is an excerpt from a presentation made by Carl Sagan in 1996 about the striking image. This eloquent speech reveals how astronomy has given us a unique perspective on humankind and our precious home.

Reflections on a Mote of Dust

By Carl Sagan – Astronomer

We succeeded in taking a picture, and if you look at it, you see a dot.

That's here. That's home. That's us.

On it, everyone you have ever heard of, every human being that ever lived – lived out their lives. The aggregate of all our joys and sufferings, thousands of confident religions, ideologies and economic doctrines, every hunter and forager, every hero and cowards, every creator and destroyer of civilizations, every king and peasant, every young couple in love, every hopeful child, every mother and father, every inventor and explorer, every teacher of morals, every corrupt politician, every superstar, every supreme leader, every saint and sinner in the history of our species, lived there on a mote of dust, suspended in a sunbeam.

The Earth is a very small stage in a vast cosmic arena. Think of the rivers of blood spilled by all those generals and emperors so that in glory and triumph they could become the momentary masters of a fraction of a dot. Think of the endless cruelties visited by the inhabitants of one corner of the dot on scarcely distinguishable inhabitants on some other corner of the dot. How frequent their misunderstandings, how eager they are to kill one another, how fervent their hatreds. Our posturing, our imagined self-importance, the delusion that we have some privileged position in the Universe, are challenged by the point of pale light.

Our planet is a lonely speck in the great enveloping cosmic dark. In our obscurity – in all this vastness – there is no hint that help will come from elsewhere to save us from ourselves.

It is up to us.

It's been said that Astronomy is humbling, and I might add, a character building experience. To my mind there is no better demonstration of the folly of human conceits than this distant image of our tiny world. To me, it underscores our responsibility to deal more kindly and compassionately with one another, and to preserve and cherish that pale blue dot, the only home we've ever known'.

Carl Sagan (1934-1996)

INDEX

CPSIA information can be obtained
at www.ICGtesting.com
Printed in the USA
LVHW010154070520
654941LV00003B/32

9 780958 704588